€35

GW00985595

ARCHAEOLOGICAL INVENTORY OF COUNTY LAOIS

FARDAL SEANDÁLAÍOCHTA CHONTAE LAOIS

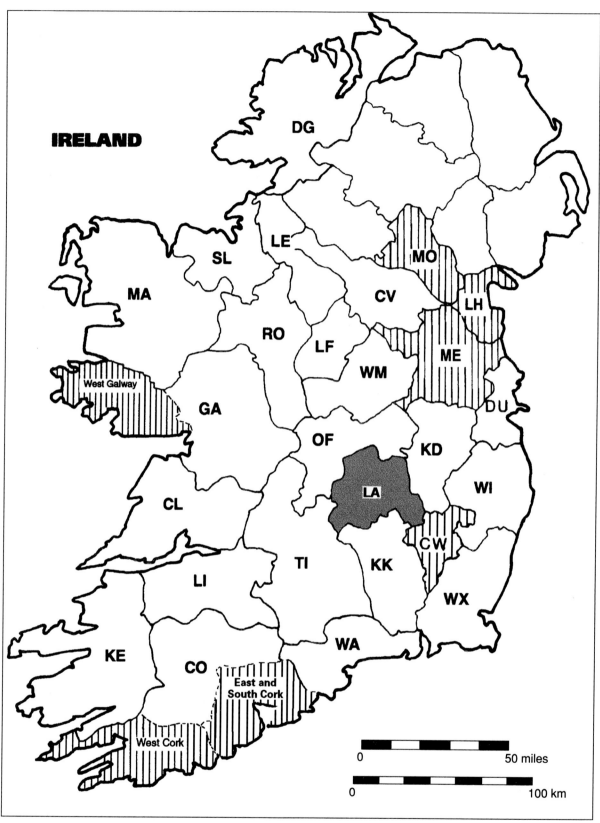

IRELAND

DG

SL
LE

MA
CV
MO
LH

RO
LF
ME

West Galway
WM

GA
DU

OF
KD

CL
LA
WI

TI
KK
CW

LI
WX

WA
KE

CO
East and
South Cork

West Cork

0   50 miles

0   100 km

Inventories and surveys to date

Archaeological Inventory of County Laois

Compiled by
P. David Sweetman
Olive Alcock
Bernie Moran

BAILE ÁTHA CLIATH
ARNA FHOILSIÚ AG OIFIG AN tSOLÁTHAIR
Le ceannach díreach ón
OIFIG DHÍOLTA FOILSEACHÁN RIALTAIS
TEACH SUN ALLIANCE, SRÁID THEACH LAIGHEAN, BAILE ÁTHA CLIATH 2
nó trí aon díoltóir leabhar

DUBLIN
PUBLISHED BY THE STATIONERY OFFICE
To be purchased through any bookseller, or directly from the
GOVERNMENT PUBLICATIONS SALE OFFICE
SUN ALLIANCE HOUSE, MOLESWORTH STREET, DUBLIN 2

Price:£16.00

General Editor
P. David Sweetman

Field Archaeologists
Bernie Moran
P. David Sweetman

Text Editor
Olive Alcock

Chapter on Megalithic Tombs
Eamon Cody

Cover Design
John O'Regan

Photographs
Con Brogan

Location Maps
Annaba Kilfeather
Catherine Martin

ACKNOWLEDGEMENTS

The Commissioners of Public Works gratefully acknowledge the assistance of the Archaeological Division of the Ordnance Survey office; the staff of the Antiquities Division of the National Museum of Ireland; Elizabeth FitzPatrick and Michael Moore (OPW), and Bridget O'Brien, Mary Tunney and Jean Farrelly (OPW) for assistance in the production of this volume. We also wish to thank Redmonds Photographers, Roscrea.

Contents

Black and White Plates

Colour Plates

Introduction

This is the 8th in a series of county archaeological inventories to be produced by the Archaeological Survey, Office of Public Works. It follows the compilation of the Sites and Monuments Record (Stage 2) for County Laois, which was completed together with constraint maps in May 1989. The inventory was produced from the computerised database now being compiled by the Archaeological Survey.

While the Sites and Monuments Record was devised specifically for planning purposes, the Archaeological Inventory of County Laois is directed towards a more general readership. It is based on an examination of available paper sources: the Down Survey (1655), eighteenth- and early nineteenth-century estate maps, Ordnance Survey maps and letters, aerial photographs (in particular the Cambridge University collection and the Geological Survey of Ireland collection), the Irish Tourist Association and An Foras Forbartha surveys, and records in the National Museum of Ireland. In addition to local information and traditions collected in the course of fieldwork, monuments were examined in the field between 1990 and 1991, with some additional work being carried out in 1993 and 1994.

The inventory is essentially a condensed version of this work. It has been prepared both for those interested in the archaeology of their own local area and for those working on more widescale regional or national projects. The maps have been designed to facilitate those seeking monuments within their own locality and as an aid to researchers compiling distribution maps of monuments in the county.

Each chapter is devoted to a particular group of monuments and contains entries for all definite and possible monuments and sites identified. Each entry is preceded by a number for text reference purposes and for use with the accompanying location maps. Entries are arranged alphabetically by townland name in numerical order, except where reclassification has taken place. Where several townlands with the same name occur on the Ordnance Survey 6-inch sheet, the Barony (By.) and the electoral division (ED) are given in brackets after the townland name, and where the monument occurs within an urban area, this is also indicated after the townland name. Where monuments straddle townland boundaries, both townland names are given. Each chapter is preceded by a short introduction, detailing the principal features and functions of the monuments described.

Locational information related to the OS 6-inch sheet follows the townland name including the OS 6-inch Sheet/Plan/Trace division; next, in brackets, the Easting and Northing co-ordinates measured in millimetres; then the designation, if any, of the site on the current OS 6-inch sheets, whether Hachured (shown by hachures), Indicated (shown by solid or broken lines), or the OS name of the site (if any). The Ordnance Datum (OD) is given in feet, bracketed in 100-foot intervals, except where trigonometrical points occur on site. Finally, a ten-figure National Grid Reference follows. Monuments or sites which are not precisely located have only as much location data as is available and are noted 'NPL' (not precisely located).

A classification of the monument follows this information. Use of the word 'site' also indicates whether surface destruction had occurred before the time of the last inspection. It should be noted that total destruction is very rare; for example, where the enclosing banks of a ringfort have been levelled, the archaeology of the fosses and the interior may well remain. The descriptions 'no visible surface traces' or 'not visible on the ground' are used to indicate that archaeological material may still exist below the present ground surface.

A brief condensed description follows this classification with one or two dimensions and with some limited information on the siting and present condition of the monument. References are cited where applicable. The date on which the monument or site was last visited is given at the end of each entry.

The entries can be cross-referenced to the Sites and Monuments Record by means of the SMR number given below the description. Two things should be noted however: firstly; a monument may have a different classification to that which it has in the Sites and Monuments Record; this is usually because additional information has become available, and secondly; a small number of monuments included in the Sites and Monuments Record were not deemed relevant for inclusion in the Archaeological Inventory. This does not mean, however, that the monuments or sites are not worthy of attention in their own right. Monuments and sites are described in a clockwise manner, for example, a bank visible from N–S implies that it survives from N through E to S.

The text is accompanied by a county index map and 19 location maps. Single monuments or sites are shown as dots and multiple monuments are shown as ringed dots. These symbols are for locational purposes only and are not intended to define in any way an area of archaeological significance. Shaded areas around medieval boroughs and towns show the areas of archaeological potential as defined by the Urban Archaeology Survey. The inventory numbers occur alongside. The location maps are based on the Ordnance Survey Index maps (1909), showing townland boundaries, main roads and some towns.

Archaeological Survey of Ireland
Office of Public Works
Dublin 1995

Abbreviations and contractions used in the text are as follows

By.	Barony
C	chord
c.	circa
cm	centimetre
D	depth
DP	detached portion
diam.	diameter
dim.	dimension
dims.	dimensions
E	east
ed.	edition
eds.	editions
ext.	external
f.p.	facing page
ft	feet
H	Height
ibid.	ibidem
int.	internal
L	length
m	metre
max.	maximum
min.	minimum
N	north
n.d.	not dated
NPL	Not precisely located
OD	Ordnance Datum
pers. comm.	personal communication
SMR	Sites and Monuments Record
T	thickness
W	West
Wth	Width

1. Megalithic Tombs

Following the introduction of farming and the establishment of settled communities during the Neolithic period, the practice of building great stone tombs for collective burial became widespread in western Europe. These tombs are walled and roofed with large stones and, in essence, consist of one or more burial chambers set at or towards one end of a cairn through which access was gained to the burial area. Some 1,500 megalithic tombs are known in Ireland and date to the period between about 4000 and 2000 BC. Megalithic tombs are rare in the midlands and no definite examples are known in County Laois. However, a number of sites are referred to in the literature or are named on the various editions of the Ordnance Survey 6-inch to one mile maps of the county as 'Giant's Grave', 'Druid's Altar' etc., terms commonly applied to megalithic tombs but none has proved to be definitely such. These are described below. Among them is the destroyed site at Cuffsborough (No. 1). This is one of a number of generally small sealed chambers found under round mounds in the southern half of the country, the majority of them in Leinster (Ryan, 1981). All share similarities in structural detail to a greater or lesser degree. Some can be identified as Neolithic in date by the presence of diagnostic pottery, while a smaller number are apparently of Early Bronze Age date (Brindley, Lanting and Mook, 1983). Others, like Cuffsborough, remain undated.

Fig. 1—*Manger, megalithic tomb (possible)* (**6**)

1 CUFFSBOROUGH
OS 22 NPL

Megalithic tomb (possible, site) Graves (1852, 358) has recorded the discovery of a 'beehive-shaped chamber' under an earthen mound. The chamber measured five feet (*c.* 1.50m) in diameter and was built with large stones rising about three and a half feet (*c.* 1.05m) above the ground. These orthostats supported tiers of corbelling on which rested a single large roofstone. The bones of two skeletons were found on the floor of the chamber. The monument was removed at the time and its precise location is not known. (Ryan 1981, 143)

22:61/28:82*/29:55*   14-5-1992

1

2 KILLINAPARSON
OS 6:1:2 (106,536) *'Giants Grave'* OD 800–900
22585,20809

Megalithic tomb (possible) The site, in a clear-felled area of forest, lies just uphill from a stream on the W slope of Barradoos Mountain which is on the N side of the Slieve Bloom range. A stone, 2.30m long, 70cm thick and 70cm high, aligned N–S, seems to be set. Alongside to the W are four prostrate stones measuring 1.50m to 2.10m in maximum dimension and a fifth is partly buried. There may have been some form of megalithic structure here but its nature is not known. According to a local story, the stones were dislodged by the soldiery in 1798 (de Valera and Ó Nualláin 1972, 97, No. 1).
6:1   14-5-1992

3 KNOCKBAUN
OS 24:16:6 (855,28) *'Druid's Altar'* OD 800–900
25351,18378

Megalithic structure Marked only on the 1909 ed. OS 6" map. Situated on a rock-strewn SW-facing slope, this feature consists of a stone, 1.40m by 1.30m by 60cm thick, resting horizontally above a slight hollow in the ground. On its upper surface are portions of a circular groove which seems to have been about 1m in diameter. The groove is 1cm wide and 0.05cm deep (de Valera and Ó Nualláin 1972, 97, No. 2).
24:52   19-7-1991

4 KNOCKBAUN
OS 24:16:6 (898,39) *'Druid's Altar* (Site of)'
OD 900–1000 25397,18390

Megalithic structure (site) Marked only on the 1909 ed. OS 6" map. There is no trace of this feature nor does there appear to be any information about it (de Valera and Ó Nualláin 1972, 97, No. 3).
24:55   19-7-1991

5 KYLE (Clandonagh By.)
OS 34:9:5 (85,179) OD 600–700 22598,17231

Megalithic structure (site) Not marked on the 1840 or 1906 eds. OS 6" maps. Ledwich (1803, 321) has recorded what he termed an ancient judgement seat on the hill of Kyle and reproduced a sketch of same (*ibid.*). The sketch shows what appears to be a large section of rock, apparently outcrop, in the shape of a chair. This is not now readily identifiable on the partly furze-grown hill. It may have been largely, if not wholly, natural in origin. Whether it ever served the purpose mentioned by Ledwich is not known.
34:25   4-7-1991

6 MANGER
OS 25:7:4 (522,346) *'Ass's Manger'* OD 700–800
25972,18721

Megalithic tomb (possible) The site, a small stone-built structure incorporated in a road-side fence at the rim of an old quarry which has been infilled in recent years, is located on elevated arable land. It consists of a cover-slab, 2.50m by 2.20m by 30cm thick, supported by a number of upright stones. Under this slab there is a cavity some 80cm deep, open to the NE. The slab has slipped from the top of two stones at its NE end but still rests on an upright stone and drystone-walling alongside at about its mid-line. Just E of the structure there was a line, some 2.50m long, of three upright stones (de Valera and Ó Nualláin 1972, 97–8) only two of which are now visible. An early account (O'Byrne 1849–51, 131) would suggest that this is the remnant of a larger and substantially buried structure, and that it was surrounded by a circle of stones. Cists (No. 32) containing bones were said to have been uncovered close by. The whole may have been some form of burial monument but its nature is uncertain.
25:18   15-5-1992

7 MONAMANRY
OS 25:6:5 (312,314) *'Druids Altar'* OD 900–1000
25750,18685

Megalithic structure This site stands on elevated arable land. It is a circular mound, 9m to 10m in diameter and 75cm in maximum height. A kerb of small stones survives around much of the circumference but is absent or concealed at the W. Two set stones, about 1m inside the kerb in the NE quadrant, may indicate an inner kerb. There is a hollow measuring some 3.50m by 2m at the centre of the mound where a slab, 1.20m by 80cm, lies partly embedded in the ground (de Valera and Ó Nualláin 1972, 97, No. 4).
25:13   16-7-1990

8 NEWTOWN or SKIRK
OS 21:16:1 NPL

Megalithic structure Within the large henge (No. 15) there is a standing stone (No. 16) and a motte and bailey (No. 915). In addition, according to Ledwich (1803, 73), the remains of a 'cromleach' were to be seen towards the eastern side of the enclosure. It is not clear to what feature Ledwich applied this term unless it was to a block of stone which, along with the standing stone and motte already mentioned, are shown within the enclosure on a sketch of the site reproduced by him (*ibid.* Plate III). There is no trace of this stone now. (O'Byrne 1856, 19; O'Hanlon and O'Leary 1907, vol. 1, 316)
21:21(03)   24-6-1991

2. Standing Stones, Stone Circle, Henge-type Monument

S tanding stones: Isolated single standing stones, often located in prominant positions, are common throughout the Irish countryside. Known variously as dallán, gallán or long stones, they simply consist of a large stone set upright in the ground, sometimes with packing stones placed around the base for additional support. They are generally dated to the Bronze Age (2500–500 BC) and they were used for a variety of purposes. Some have been found to mark the position of burials, others may have been boundary or route markers, while others still may have had a commemorative or ritual function.

Stone circles: These consist of circles of stones arranged symmetrically so that one stone, the axial stone lying horizontally in the south-western quadrant of the circle, is directly opposite the entrance which is marked by the two tallest stones. These sites are regarded as ritual sites dating to the Bronze Age. It is thought that the main axis of the circle may be orientated on significant solar or lunar events such as an equinox or solstice. In Ireland, stone circles are concentrated in south Kerry/west Cork and mid-Ulster. They appear to be totally absent from inland counties such as Carlow and Kilkenny. The Laois example (No. 18) is unusual in that the stones barely project above the ground surface.

Henges: These are large earthen enclosures, generally circular in plan, defined by a single bank with or without a fosse. The enclosing bank was built up by scooping out earth from the interior of the site and/or from a fosse, and as a result they often appear dished in profile. The large size (diameters generally in excess of 100m) and non defensive nature (no external fosse) of these sites suggest that they were used by a community for ritual or ceremonial purposes as well as for burial. Henges date to the Late Neolithic/Early Bronze Age period.

9 BALLAGHMORE LOWER
OS 21:2:3 (428,584)   OD 300–400   21968,18933
Standing stone (possible, site)   Marked 'stone' on the 1841 ed. OS 6" map. Reference to a standing stone here (Feehan 1983, 236–7). No visible surface traces.
21:2   24-6-1991

10 CLEANAGH
OS 24:16:3 (854,77)   *'Standing Stone'*   OD 800–900
25349,18430
Standing stone (site)   Reference to a standing stone here (Roe *c*. 1940). Not marked on the 1841 ed. OS 6" map. No visible surface traces.
24:48   19-7-1991

11 GORTNAGLOGH
OS 10:16:5 (824,19)   OD 700–800   22380,19620
Standing stone (site)   Not marked on the 1841 or 1962 eds. OS 6" maps. A sandstone conglomerate (max. base L 1.08m, Wth 1.13m, H 1.38m) roughly rectangular in plan, narrowing towards top and tilting slightly to W. Two small pieces of sandstone protrude from the soil around its base. The ground around it has been eroded, probably by cattle using the stone as a scratching post. Known locally as the 'Mass Rock' and believed to have been used in Penal times as a mass site. (Feehan 1979, 237)
10:4   23-5-1994

12 KNOCKBAUN
OS 24:16:6 (897,75)   *'Standing Stone'*   OD 900–1000
25395,18429
Standing stone   Marked only on the 1909 ed. OS 6" map. An irregularly shaped stone, tapering towards the top (H *c*. 1.3m, max. Wth *c*. 1.25m, min. Wth *c*. 0.65m, T *c*. 0.38m).
24:50   19-7-1991

13 KNOCKBAUN
OS 24:16:6 (873,26)   *'Standing Stone'*   OD 800–900
25370,18376
Standing stone   Marked only on the 1909 ed. OS 6" map. An irregularly shaped stone (H *c*. 1.05m, Wth *c*. 0.75m, T *c*. 0.3m) lying horizontally.
24:53   19-7-1991

14 KYLE (Clandonagh By.)
OS 15:6:4 (758,55)   OD 300–400   22316,19017
Standing stone   Situated in a marshy field immediately W of St Molua's church (No. 773). This standing stone, aligned N–S, is roughly D-shaped in plan (H 1.1m, Wth at base 1.6m, T 0.35m) and tapers towards the top. The area around the base of the stone is hollowed out, probably the result of cattle using it as a scratching post (pers. comm. E. FitzPatrick).
15:34   23-10-1993

15 NEWTOWN or SKIRK
OS 21:16:1 (731,150)   *'Moat of Skirke'*
OD 500–600   22293,18477
Henge   An almost circular enclosure (dims. 96m E–W, *c*. 90m N–S) defined by bank (Wth 8–9m, int. H *c*. 1m, ext. H 2.5–3m) and external fosse (Wth *c*. 7m) except at N. This site appears to have been a henge-type monument before it was adapted as a motte and bailey (No. 915). The banks were originally formed by

scooping out the clay from inside the line of the bank, leaving the central area higher than the extremities of the enclosure. This is a typical feature of the henge-type sites in Ireland. (Cunningham 1987, 163–4)
21:21(01)   24-6-1990

16   NEWTOWN or SKIRK
OS 21:16:1 (731,146) *'Stone'* OD 500–600
22293,18474
Standing stone   A limestone slab (H *c.* 2.4m, Wth *c.* 1.1m, T *c.* 0.5m) situated within a henge-type enclosure (No. 15).
21:21(04)   24-6-1991

17   NEWTOWN or SKIRK
OS 21:16:2 (781,104) *'Stone'* OD 400–500
22346,18430
Standing stone   A large irregularly shaped boulder (H *c.* 2m, Wth at base 1.3m, Wth at top 0.7m) tapering towards the top. Orientated NW–SE.
21:23   25-6-1991

18   SLATT LOWER
OS 31:2:4 (250,529)   OD 669   25688,18271

Stone circle   Not marked on the 1841 or 1906 eds. OS 6" maps. A circular area (diam. *c.* 14m) defined by a low bank with twenty-two stones protruding slightly above the ground, except at E. From N–E the stones touch each other. There is a slight rise in the centre of enclosure. Large erratic boulder to S, possible outlier.
31:19   12-8-1991

19   SLATT LOWER
OS 31:2:1 (288,559)   OD 700–800   25728,18303
Standing stone   Not marked on the 1841 or 1906 eds. OS 6" maps. Irregular greenstone slab (H *c.* 1.2m, Wth *c.* 0.63m, T *c.* 0.4–0.11m), orientated N–S. Another stone (H *c.* 1.1m, Wth *c.* 0.22–0.55m), immediatly to the SW, may have broken off the standing stone.
31:27   12-8-1991

20   TULLOMOY
OS 19:15:1 (483,84) *'Standing stone'* OD 500–600
25927,19084
Standing stone   Known as 'Clogh Leachdain' (Comerford 1886, vol. 3, 129); a large standing stone tapering towards the top (H *c.* 2.5m, Wth *c.* 1.1–1.35m). Orientated NW–SE.
19:25(01)   10-9-1990

3. Cist and Urn Burials

During the Early Bronze Age (c. 1800–1300 BC) common burial practices involved placing inhumed or cremated remains in cists (box-like, slab-built compartments) or pits, with or without surface indications marking their location. For example, cists and pits have been found within custom-built mounds of earth or cairns of stone, within pre-existing mounds or incorporated in natural features. Others have been found, purely by chance, as a result of ploughing or gravel-quarrying operations. The graves were generally only used once but could contain either single or multiple internments. Cemeteries of the period are classified as either flat or raised cemeteries, depending again on their surface indications.

Inhumations were placed in a crouched position within the cists, while cremated remains were placed in a heap on the cist or pit floor. The burials were accompanied by a range of distinctive pottery vessels, either food vessels or urns, and sometimes by grave goods such as bracelets.

21 AGHNAHILY
OS 13:16:2 (828,134)   OD 500–600   25309,19770
Cist (site)   Discovered in 1845 in a 'Danish Rath' (No. 129) was a cist containing an inhumed burial and two food vessels which are now in the National Museum (Bradley *et al.* 1986, 22).
13:62(02)   6-6-1990

22 AGHONEY
OS 24 NPL
Urn burial (site)   An urn containing 'small broken bones' was found underneath a flat slab (*JRSAI* 1850, 139).
24:56/25:35*

23 BALLINACLOGH LOWER
OS 24:4:2 (793,580)   OD 400–500   25280,18961
Cist (site)   A rectangular short cist, containing cremated bones, was discovered during the removal of sand from a quarry (*JRSAI* 1858, 106).
24:16

24 COOLNAMONA
OS 12 NPL
Cist (site)   In 1734 a cist of rough flags covered by earth and stones was discovered (O'Byrne 1856, 18). Exact location unknown.
12:12

25 CUFFSBOROUGH
OS 22 NPL
Cist (site)   Reference to a crouched skeleton and a pottery vessel discovered within a short cist (*JRSAI* 1867, 7).
22:38/28:83*/29:71*

26 near DUNAMASE
OS 13:16:0 NPL
Cist (site)   An urn and unburnt bones were discovered in a small stone chamber in a rath or tumulus (No. 49) (Waddell 1990, 104).
13:106

27 FOSSY UPPER
OS 25 NPL
Cist (site)   An urn containing small human bones was discovered in a triangular cist, formed by three upright flags with a flag at the top and bottom, on a high hill called the Commons of Fossy, near Timahoe (*JRSAI* 1990, 105).
25:42

28 HAYWOOD DEMESNE
OS 30 NPL
Cist (site)   Cremated bones were found within a short rectangular cist (L *c.* 0.9m, Wth *c.* 0.6m, D *c.* 0.45m) (*JRSAI* 1970, 122).
30:37

29 IRONMILLS or KILRUSH
OS 30:11:2 (602,228)   OD 900–1000   25088,17946
Cist (site)   A segmented cist with cremated bone and some small unclassifiable pot sherds was discovered during ploughing (*JRSAI* 1937, 295).
30:29   20-6-1991

30 KNOCKARDAGUR
OS 30 NPL
Cist (site)   Reference to a cist (L *c.* 1.5m, Wth *c.* 0.6m) with a paved floor and capstone, and containing a small decorated vessel; the vessel was not preserved and no bones were noted (*JRSAI* 1970, 122).
30:42

31 LUGGACURREN
OS 25 NPL
Cists (sites)   Two short cists, 3m apart and parallel to each other, were found in 1881 during ploughing operations. One was a rectangular slab-built cist (L *c.* 1–1m, Wth *c.* 0.48m, D *c.* 0.48m) containing a bowl and unburnt skeletal remains. The second was a double cist, the larger compartment (L *c.* 0.96m, Wth *c.* 0.56m, D *c.* 0.53m) of which was separated from the smaller (L *c.* 0.53m, Wth *c.* 0.56m, D *c.* 0.53m) by an endstone. It was covered by two capstones, one placed above the other. The larger cist contained a bowl and

both may have contained unburnt bones. Grave goods found in the bowls included two possible faiance beads; two bronze bracelets were also found (Waddell 1990, 104–5).
25:51

32 MANGER
OS 25 NPL
Cists (site) O'Byrne (1856, 6–7) refers to 'many small rectangular cists formed of six flags and containing burned bones', to the SE of the 'Ass's Manger' (No. 6).
25:52

33 MOYNE
OS 29:11:1 (485,244) OD 200–300 23989,17954
Urn burial (site) A quantity of human bones including fragments of a skull, parts of ribs and long bones, and sherds of an encrusted urn were discovered in 1952 in the grounds of Moyne House (*PRIA* 1973, 551).
29:32   14-8-1990

34 NEWTOWN or SKIRK
OS 21:16:1 (731,150) OD 500–600 22293,18477
Urn burials Urns and traces of burials were found

beside Skirk standing stone (No. 16). (Feehan 1983, 236)
21:21(07)   24-6-1991

35 SHANAHOE
OS 23:10:3 (459,284) OD 300–400 23954,18636
Urn burial (site) An unprotected cremation, found in a gravel ridge in 1936, was set on a flat stone and covered with an elaborately decorated encrusted urn (*JRSAI* 1946, 210–12).
23:21   15-9-1990

36 TIMAHOE
OS 18:16:6 (868,27) OD 300–400 25359,19018
Urn burial (site) Discovered under a flag near Timahoe castle (No. 967) was a vessel containing small human bones (*JRSAI* 1850, 139).
18:62

37 TIMOGUE
OS 19 NPL
Cist (site) A cist containing a skeleton, below which may have been a second cist, was found during ploughing operations in the vicinity of Timogue (*JRSAI* 1858–9, 106).
19:65

4. Barrows, Cairns, Tumuli

The practice of constructing mounds of earth and stone over burials has a long tradition in Irish prehistory. Included in this chapter are various types of mounds generally associated with burial, though some cairns may have functioned as boundary markers. Barrows are earthen mounds; the term bowl-barrow refers to those with central dome-shaped mounds; where the mound is enclosed by a fosse and outer bank the term ring-barrow is applied. Nine ring-barrows have been noted on the Heath indicating its importance in prehistoric times as a place for burial. Cairns are composed primarily of stone and are usually associated with hilltop locations where outcropping bedrock is readily available. Tumuli are mainly made up of earth.

To date none of these monument types have been excavated in County Laois and, therefore, it is difficult to determine their date and cultural context. However, excavations elsewhere in Ireland have revealed that barrows range in date from the Neolithic to the Early Iron Age (4000 BC–AD 300); hilltop cairns from the Neolithic to the Early Bronze Age (4000–2000 BC); and tumuli from the Early Neolithic to the Early Iron Age.

Fig. 2— *Carrowreagh, ring-barrow* (**46**)

38 AGHABOE
OS 22 NPL

Cairn Reference to a cairn, possibly a leacht, within the Aghaboe area (O'Hanlon and O'Leary 1907, vol. 1, 159). Not located.
22:19(15)   12-8-1991

39 BALLYCOOLAN
OS 19:10:6 (446,157) 'Castlepierce' OD 800
25887,19160

Cairn An almost circular grass-covered cairn (max. diam. 30.7m N–S, H 3m). Two depressions at NE may represent possible cists. No kerb visible.
19:11(02)   9-8-1990

40 BALLYHORAHAN
OS 16:3:5 (559,477)   Hachured   OD 500–600
23077,19470

Ring-barrow A circular mound (diam. *c.* 22.4m), with a central depression, surrounded by a fosse (Wth *c.* 3.2m, D *c.* 1.3m) and external bank (Wth *c.* 2.7m, ext. H *c.* 0.6m) except at N and NE.
16:8   23-7-1991

41 BALLYMADDOCK (Stradbally By.)
OS 14 NPL

Cairn (possible) Reference to a possible cairn around the base of which a regular circle, indicated by a darker colour in the grass, was visible (O'Hanlon and O'Leary 1907, vol. 1, 276).
14:49

Fig. 3—*Cummer, barrow* (**47**)

42 BARRADOOS
OS 6:6:1 (241,429)   Hachured   OD 1000–1100
22729,20697

Barrow (possible, site)   Situated close to mountain top
in previously afforested area. Not marked on the 1841
ed. OS 6" map but depicted on subsequent eds. as a
circular enclosure (diam. *c.* 30m), and appears to have
been a barrow. Not located and presumed levelled.
6:7   14-6-1991

43 BARRADOOS
OS 6:6:1 (261,437)   Hachured   OD 1000–1100
22750,20705

Barrow (possible, site)   Situated close to mountain top
in afforested area now felled and replanted. Not
marked on the 1841 ed. OS 6" map but shown as a
mound (diam. *c.* 30m) surrounded by a fosse on 1910
ed. and was possibly a barrow. Site not located and
appears to have been levelled by a forest roadway.
6:8   14-6-1991

44 CARROWREAGH (Upperwoods By.)
OS 10:16:5 (790, 3)   OD 800–900   22344,19602
Barrow (possible, site)   Situated on a precipitous E-
facing slope in an area of dense coniferous forest. Site
not located.
10:11   12-9-1991

45 CARROWREAGH (Upperwoods By.)
OS 15:4:2 (806,594) Hachured OD 700–800
22361,19587

Bowl-barrow   Situated on high ground. Impressive
bowl-shaped mound (summit dims. 6.5m E–W, 5.3m
N–S, H 3m) surrounded by a broad deep fosse (Wth
3.5m, D 1.6m) which is enclosed by a denuded
counterscarp bank (max. ext. H 0.6m). Summit of
mound slightly hollow and overgrown with rowan and
crab-apple trees.
15:2   12-9-1991

46 CARROWREAGH (Upperwoods By.)
OS 15:4:2 (810,604)   OD 700–800   22365,19598
Ring-barrow   Marked on the 1841 ed. OS 6" map. Situated on marshy ground midway down a NE-facing slope.
A flat-topped circular mound (diam. *c.* 10m, max. H
1.35m) surrounded by a waterlogged and partially
infilled fosse (average Wth 2.1m, D 0.7m) which
broadens out from SE–SW (max. Wth 3.7m) and is
enclosed by a low counterscarp bank (Wth 2.6m, max.
ext. H 0.6m). A field boundary skirts the counterscarp
at S. Site overgrown with hawthorn and brambles.
15:3   12-9-1991

47 CUMMER
OS 11:9:6 (214,198) Hachured   OD 600–700
22709,19812

Barrow   A flat-topped circular mound (diam. *c.* 22m,

H *c.* 1.75m) with slight dome in the centre.
11:8   25-7-1991

48 DERRYCARROW
OS 16:1:3 (166,585) Hachured OD 500 22660,19580
Ring-barrow A circular platform (diam. *c.* 15.6m, H *c.* 1.2m) surrounded by a shallow fosse (Wth *c.* 3.6m) from SW–E. No other visible surface traces.
16:2   23-7-1991

49 near DUNAMASE
OS 13:16:0 NPL
Tumulus (possible) A cist (No. 26) was discovered in a 'rath' — possibly a tumulus (Waddell 1990, 104).
13:106(02)

50 GARRANBAUN
OS 10:15:1 (494,114) 'Farbreague or Hardyman'
OD 1410 22030,19717
Cairn (site) Located on the mountains above Ballaghmore is a cairn called 'Fear Breige' or 'The Hardy Man' (Roe *c.* 1940). The area is now forested; not located.
10:1   12-9-1991

51 GREATHEATH (Maryborough East By.)
OS 13:4:4 (756,509) OD 300–400 25229,20165
Ring-barrow On level ground beside an ESB pylon. A ring-barrow (max. diam. 15.5m) defined by a low circular mound (diam. 7m, H 0.3–0.4m) surrounded by a flat-bottomed fosse (Wth 1m, D 0.5–0.7m) which is infilled with cleared vegetation from SSW–NNE. No outer bank.
13:9   18-5-1994

52 GREATHEATH (Maryborough East By.)
OS 13:4:4 (757,502) OD 300–400 25230,20157
Ring-barrow Situated S of an E–W trackway leading W from sixth fairway of golf course. A ring-barrow (max. ext. diam. 21m N–S), completely overgrown with furze, defined by a domed central mound (diam. 12m, H 0.5–0.7m), a flat-bottomed fosse (Wth 0.7–1m), and an outer bank (Wth 3.5m, int. H 0.6m, ext. H 0.3m). The trackway abuts the outer bank at N.
13:10   21-5-1994

53 GREATHEATH (Maryborough East By.)
OS 13:4:4 (751,493) OD 300–400 25224,20149
Ring-barrow On a local prominance, N of sixth fairway of golf course. A ring-barrow (max. ext. diam. 15.7m), most of which is overgrown with furze and briars, defined by a circular platform (diam. 11m, H 0.2–0.6m) and a shallow V-shaped fosse (Wth 2–2.4m, D 0.2m at SE, 0.7m at NE).
13:11   18-5-1994

54 GREATHEATH (Maryborough East By.)
OS 13:4:4 (730,486) Hachured OD 300–400 25202,20141
Ring-barrow On flat ground on edge of Heath. A large circular ring-barrow (max. ext. diam. 33.8m) defined by a platform (diam. 16m, H 1.2–1.4m) except from NW–NNE, a flat-bottomed fosse (base Wth 0.8–1.5m) and an outer bank (Wth 4.5m at E, max. int. H 1.8m, max. ext. H 0.8m). The fosse has been infilled with bank material and rubbish from WNW–NNE. Cattle gaps at S and W.
13:12   18-5-1994

55 GREATHEATH (Maryborough East By.)
OS 13:4:4 (728,474) OD 300–400 25200,20128
Ring-barrow At W edge of Heath, in a garden. A subcircular ring-barrow (max. ext. diam. 25m) defined by a slightly dished platform (diam. 10m E–W, H 0.4–0.8m), a flat-bottomed fosse (base Wth 0.8–1.2m) and an outer bank (Wth 0.5–0.6m, ext. H *c.* 0.4m) which is planted with pine trees and clipped by a wire fence from NNW–NNE. Cattle gap at SW. A drain from a sewage tank at SE runs into fosse at N.
13:13   18-5-1994

56 GREATHEATH (Maryborough East By.)
OS 13:4:4 (740,462) OD 300–400 25212,20116
Ring-barrow On a local prominance at W edge of Heath. A subcircular ring-barrow (max. ext. diam. 10.7m N–S) defined by a central mound (diam. 4–4.5m, max. H 0.5m) and a flat-bottomed fosse (Wth 1–1.5m, D 0.8m) which is shallowest at S (D 0.4m).
13:14   18-5-1994

57 GREATHEATH (Maryborough East By.)
OS 13:4:5 (772,499) Hachured OD 371 25246,20155
Ring-barrow Situated just NW of seventh tee on golf course; a platform associated with the tee-off occupies the SE quadrant of the monument. A circular ring-barrow (max. ext. diam. 18m) defined by a central mound (base diam. 15m, H 0.3m) and a fosse. Traces of an outer bank at W appear to be modern and associated with the golf course trackway here.
13:15   18-5-1994

58 GREATHEATH (Maryborough East By.)
OS 13:8:1 (740,450) OD 300–400 25213,20102
Ring-barrow At W edge of Heath. A ring-barrow (max. ext. diam. *c.* 14m N–S), overgrown with briars and furze, defined by a D-shaped platform (dims. 7.2m N–S, 5.9m E–W, H 0.5m), with the straight side at W where part of the monument has been removed, a flat-bottomed fosse (Wth 0.6–1m) and an outer bank (Wth 2–2.5m, max. int. H 0.8m, ext. H 0.2–3m) except from S–WNW. Small quarry in interior at S. An earthwork (No. 636) lay immediately to SW.
13:30(01)   18-5-1994

9

59 GREATHEATH (Maryborough East By.)
OS 13:8:1 (746,436)   OD 300–400   25219,20088
Ring-barrow   On a local prominance at S edge of
Heath. A subcircular ring-barrow (max. ext. diam.
15.7m N–SE) defined by a flat-topped central mound
(max. diam. 5.6m, H 0.5m) the interior of which has
been quarried out, a round-bottomed fosse (max. Wth
4.7m), and an outer bank (Wth 3–4m, max. int. H
0.7m, ext. H 0.2m) which is incorporated into a field
boundary at W. A stone is visible on outer edge of
mound at SSW.
13:31   18-5-1994

60 KILLINAPARSON
OS 6:1:3 (196,564)   OD 900–1000   22680,20838
Barrow (possible, site)   In upland afforested area.
Depicted on the 1910 ed. OS 6" map as a mound with
an enclosing feature (max. diam. *c.* 35m E–W);
possibly a barrow. Not located.
6:2   14-6-1991

61 MAYO
OS 36:4:1 (705,549)   OD 700–800   26175,17656
Cairn (possible, site)   Possible cairn visible on aerial
photographs (GSI, S 25–6). Not visible on ground. A
possible enclosure (No. 478) lay to SW.
36:1(02)   5-9-1990

62 MONDREHID
OS 16:13:1 (45,88) Hachured   OD 300–400
22538,19054
Ring-barrow   Low circular flat-topped mound (diam.
c. 14m, H *c.* 1m) surrounded by a fosse (Wth *c.* 3m, D
c. 0.4m).
16:20   16-9-1990

63 PARK or DUNAMASE
OS 13:12:4 (741,157)   OD 300–400   25216,19794
Barrow   Low subcircular mound of earth (max. basal
diam. *c.* 9m N–S, H 0.75–1m) situated 120m SSW of
ringfort (No. 245) on W-facing slope of hill. Not
marked on any ed. of OS map.
13:109   3-3-1994

64 RAHANAVANNAGH
OS 24:10:2 (354,288)   Hachured   OD 400–500
24819,18648
Tumulus   A circular earthen mound (diam. *c.* 18.5m, H
c. 2.5m).
24:35   28-8-1990

65 RATHBRENNAN
OS 13:11:2 (603,303)   OD 300–400   25070,19946
Barrow   Low earthen mound (diam. *c.* 15m, H 0.5m)

located in flat wet land. Not marked on any ed. of OS
6" map and discovered during work on Portlaoise by-
pass in 1992. (See also No. 66). (Information from V.
Keely)
13:107   6-5-1992

66 RATHBRENNAN
OS 13:11:2 (603,297)   OD 300–400   25070,19940
Barrow   Low earthen mound (diam. *c.* 15m, H 0.5m)
located in wet flat land. Not marked on any ed. of OS
6" map and discovered during work on Portlaoise by-
pass in 1992. (See also No. 65). (Information from V.
Keeley)
13:108   6-5-1992

67 SLATT LOWER
OS 31:2:1 (260,536)   OD 600–700   25699,18278
Ring-barrow   A subcircular area (dims. *c.* 15.9m N–S,
c. 14.2m E–W) with dome-shaped rise in the centre.
Slight evidence of internal fosse and external bank.
31:20   12-8-1991

68 SLEATY/KNOCKBEG
OS 32 NPL
Tumulus   Reference to a tumulus which contained a
number of earthen vessels or urns (Comerford 1886,
vol. 3, 265).
32:33

69 TOORTAUN
OS 15:16:3 (882,110)   Hachured   OD 300–400
22447,19077
Tumulus   A flat-topped circular mound (diam. *c.* 14m,
H *c.* 2m) with a circular depression (Wth *c.* 4.7m, D *c.*
0.5m) at the top.
15:24   8-5-1991

70 TOWNPARKS (Clandonagh By.)
OS 22:1:4 (38,475)   Hachured   OD 300–400
22533,18823
Barrow (possible)   Described in report (OPW file) as
a low oval platform (dims. *c.* 22.5m N–S, 18m E–W)
with an external fosse (Wth *c.* 2.1m, D *c.* 0.15m)
visible at NW and faint traces elsewhere. Now appears
as a low flat-topped mound (diam. 21m, H *c.* 1m). No
visible surface traces of fosse.
22:2   9-5-1991

71 TULLORE
OS 24 NPL
Tumulus   O'Byrne (1856, 54) refers to a 'beautiful
tumulus' situated in a field known as the 'Battle Field'.
24:84

10

5. Mounds

The term 'mound' is used here to denote unclassifiable mounds, monuments whose precise identification is uncertain. Included are features marked on aerial photographs and OS maps which were levelled prior to inspection, and mounds which cannot be definitely identified as tumuli, cairns, or mottes, or assigned to any other particular category. See the chapter on earthworks for other possible mounds.

72 BALLYLEHANE LOWER
OS 25:12:6 (868,217)   OD 300–400   26338,18587
Mound (site)   Mound visible on aerial photograph (BKS, 75964–5). No visible surface traces.
25:30   23-8-1990

73 BALLYMEELISH
OS 21:16:3 (901,78) Hachured   OD 400–500 22473,18403
Mound   A circular low earthen mound (diam. *c.* 11m, H *c.* 1.8m).
21:26   26-6-1991

74 BALLYMEELISH
OS 21:16:3 (922,79) Hachured   OD 400–500 22495,18404
Mound   A circular earthen mound (diam. *c.* 16m, H *c.* 1.4m).
21:27   26-6-1991

75 BARNABOY
OS 15:11:1 (497,246) Hachured   OD 800 22038,19216
Mound   A circular earthen mound (diam. *c.* 15.7m, H *c.* 6.8m).
15:14   13-9-1991

76 EMO PARK/LOUGH
OS 9:1:4 (33,470) Hachured   OD 200–300 25435,20766
Mound (site)   Not marked on the 1841 ed. OS 6" map but hachured as an oval area (dim. *c.* 30m NNW–SSE) on 1909 ed. Site levelled *c.* 1984 and owner stated it consisted of a low earthen mound. Nothing noted during course of levelling. No visible surface traces.
9:1   24-7-1990

77 FARRANEGLISH GLEBE
OS 23:13:2 (102,97)   OD 300–400   23580,18434
Mound   On lower N-facing slope of low hill overlooking marsh to NW. A large tree-covered elongated earth and stone mound (dim. 17.5m E–W, H 1.8m) with last traces of upper cairn material, composed of small stones, in situ at W end. Middle of mound hollowed by tread of cattle.
23:49   27-5-1994

78 GORTNACLEA
OS 23:9:6 (188,160)   Hachured   OD 300–400 23669,18501
Mound   Not marked on the 1841 ed. OS 6" map but on subsequent eds. A low circular mound (diam. *c.* 18m) defined by a scarp (H *c.* 1m).
23:18   17-8-1990

79 INCHACOOLY
OS 5:8:5 (777,377)   OD 200–300   26215,21316
Mound   A low flat-topped almost circular mound (max. diam. 13.5m N–S), in low-lying area, defined by a scarp (H 0.5–1m). Possibly the remains of a barrow.
5:2   29-5-1990

80 INCHACOOLY
OS 5:8:5 (824,370) Hachured   OD 200–300 26265,21309
Mound   Roughly oval flat-topped mound (max. dims. *c.* 42m N–S, *c.* 28m E–W, max. H *c.* 3.5m) situated in a low-lying area on W bank of the Black River. Parts of W and N sides have been quarried away. Surrounded by shallow fosse (Wth *c.* 2.5m, D 0.5m) on all but the river side, and a slight external bank from SE–SSW.
5:3   29-5-1990

81 KILCORAN
OS 28 (NPL)
Mound (site)   Carrigan (1905, vol. 2, 341) refers to a mound, to S of ringfort (No. 221), which was circular, '40 ft. in diameter (*c.* 12m) and 9 ft. high (*c.* 2.7m)'. It was levelled around 1850, and was found to contain a large quantity of human bones.
28:96   24-6-1991

82 NEWTOWN or SKIRK
OS 21:16:1 (730,145)   OD 500–600   22292,18472
Mound   Immediately to NW of standing stone (No. 16) is a low artificial mound (diam. 7m, H. 0.5m); possibly a barrow (OPW file).
21:21(05).   24-6-1991

6. Fulachta Fiadh

Fulachta fiadh are Bronze Age cooking places. They appear as low, grass-covered mounds of burnt stone, usually crescent-shaped. Cooking took place in an associated water-filled pit or wooden trough which was heated by adding hot stones from a nearby fire. The stones shattered after repeated contact with the water and were discarded, forming the crescent-shaped mound. Fulachta fiadh are usually found in low-lying marshy areas near water. They are often discovered by farmers after ploughing or soil-stripping and are evident as black spreads. Unfortunately the majority of the examples known from County Laois are levelled.

83 ARCHERSTOWN
OS 35:11:5 (584,192)   OD 400–500   24100,17260
Fulacht fiadh   Not marked on the 1841 or 1908 eds. OS 6" maps. Reference to a fulacht fiadh (Candon 1987, 24). A subcircular area (dims. *c.* 13.1m E–W, *c.* 12.5m N–S, H *c.* 0.3m) containing burnt stone.
35:50   23-9-1990

84 BALLYGEEHIN LOWER
OS 29:2:2 (318,584)   OD 200–300   23809,18311
Fulacht fiadh (site)   Reference to fulacht fiadh here (Candon 1987, 23). No visible surface traces. According to local information, it was levelled *c.* 1979.
29:8   12-9-1990

85 CARROWREAGH (Upperwoods By.)
OS 15:4:2 (797,582)   OD 700–800   22352,19574
Fulacht fiadh (possible)   In a low-lying marshy area, stream to E, deserted house and associated outbuildings immediately to W. Possible fulacht fiadh indicated by a small oval-shaped mound (dims. 11m N–S, 7m E–W).
15:1   23-5-1994

86 FEARAGH
OS 29:2:4 (244,483)   OD 200–300   23732,18203
Fulacht fiadh (site)   Reference to a fulacht fiadh here (Candon 1987, 23). No visible surface traces. According to local information, it was levelled *c.* 1955.
29:6   13-9-1990

87 KILMINFOYLE
OS 29:1:5 (120,492)   OD 300–400   23601,18212
Fulacht fiadh (site)   Reference to a fulacht fiadh here (Candon 1987, 23). No visible surface traces.
29:3   13-9-1990

88 MONAMANRY
OS 25:6:5 (329,304)   OD 900–1000   25768,18673
Fulacht fiadh (site)   According to local information, a fulacht fiadh here was levelled during land reclamation *c.* 1966. No visible surface traces.
25:14   12-9-1990

89 MONAMANRY
OS 25:10:2 (338,282)   OD 900–1000   25777,18650
Fulacht fiadh (site)   According to local information, a fulacht fiadh was levelled here *c.* 1976. No visible surface traces.
25:24   19-7-1990

90 MONAMANRY
OS 25 NPL
Fulacht fiadh   A horseshoe-shaped area (dims. *c.* 9.6m N–S, 8.6m E–W) defined by an earthen bank (Wth *c.* 2.6m, max. H *c.* 0.55m) from NW–NE. Depression in the centre.
25:62   15-7-1990

91 MOYADD
OS 31 NPL
Fulacht fiadh   Oval mound of burnt stone (dims. *c.* 8m N–S, 5m E–W) discovered during ploughing.
31:22   12-8-1991

92 NEWTOWN or SKIRK
OS 21:11:6 (646,190)   OD 400–500   22203,18519
Fulacht fiadh (site)   Reference to a fulacht fiadh here (Candon 1986, 20). No visible surface traces.
21:8   24-6-1991

93 NEWTOWN or SKIRK
OS 21:11:6 (656,195)   OD 400–500   22214,18524
Fulacht fiadh (site)   Reference to a fulacht fiadh here (Candon 1986, 20). No visible surface traces.
21:9   24-6-1991

94 NEWTOWN or SKIRK
OS 21:16:1 (698,108)   OD 500–600   22258,18432
Fulacht fiadh (site)   Reference to a fulacht fiadh here (Candon 1986, 20). No visible surface traces.
21:19   27-12-1990

95 NEWTOWN or SKIRK
OS 21:16:1 (701,108)   OD 500–600   22261,18433
Fulacht fiadh (site)   Reference to a fulacht fiadh here (Candon 1986, 20). No visible surface traces.
21:20   27-2-1991

96 SLATT LOWER
OS 31:2:4 (254,473)   OD 600–700   25694,18212
Fulacht fiadh (site)   Traces of a fulacht fiadh evident in

1956 (NMI file). No visible surface traces.
31:2   17-7-1990

97   SLATT LOWER
OS 31:2:4 (273,464)   OD 600–700   25713,18203
Fulacht fiadh (site)   Discovered while excavating for fire-clay in 1956. An oblong pit, orientated N–S, with the remains of a wooden trough dating to 3500 ± 35 BP (OPW file; *JIA* 1989–90, 27).
31:3   17-7-1990

98   SLATT LOWER
OS 31:2:1 (262,583)   OD 600–700   25701,18328
Fulacht fiadh (site)   A ploughed out fulacht fiadh noted during fieldwork
31:23   12-8-1991

99   SLATT LOWER
OS 31:2:1 (263,581)   OD 700–800   25701,18326

Fulacht fiadh (site)   A low mound with burnt stone, now destroyed (Local information).
31:24   12-8-1991

100   SLATT LOWER
OS 31:2:1 (267,582)   OD 600–700   25706,18327
Fulacht fiadh   A slightly raised subcircular area (dims. *c.* 9.3m N–S, *c.* 7m E–W) containing burnt stone. Site noted during fieldwork.
31:25   12-8-1991

101   SLATT LOWER
OS 31:2:1 (305,534)   OD 700–800   25747,18277
Fulacht fiadh (site)   According to local information, burnt stone was discovered here. No visible surface traces.
31:26   12-8-1991

7. Crannóg

The term crannóg is used to describe an artificially constructed island which has been used for the purposes of habitation. They are usually situated on lake shores or on small islands and can date from Neolithic to late Medieval times. Crannógs are made up of layers of brushwood, peat and stones with a wooden palisade of closely set wooden stakes around the perimeter to consolidate the structure, and act as a defensive barrier. The interior contained either one large circular hut or several smaller ones. Access to the crannóg was gained by means of a dug-out canoe or a causeway. Irish sites appear to be defended, single unit homesteads, unlike some in parts of England which are more like villages. There is only one known example in County Laois.

102 GRANTSTOWN
OS 28 NPL

Crannóg Not marked on the 1841 or 1908 eds. OS 6" maps. Revealed in 1860 when lowering the water-level of Grantstown Lough. It was defined by pointed stakes. Further stakes, grooved and nailed together, were laid horizontally across the centre. Finds included an iron clasp, two nails with large heads, an arrow or spear of charred wood, a polished piece of bone, a large amount of animal bones and charred timber, a lump of gypsum and a rude box containing two small bones (Wood-Martin 1886, 208).
28:90

8. Field Systems

Most of the field boundaries in Ireland are probably seventeenth to nineteenth century in date. However, the practice of enclosing fields for agricultural and farming purposes dates back to Neolithic times. With the exception of the field bank (No. 103), none of the sites included here are marked on the OS maps. Most were located from aerial photographs; while they are of unknown date, some may be pre-Norman in origin.

103 BALLYCOOLAN/GUILEEN (Stradbally By.) Luggacurren ED
OS 19:10:4 (282,179) Indicated   OD 600–700
25714,19182
Field bank   Field bank following the townland boundary. Unknown date.
19:11(05)   9-8-1990

104 BUNLACKEN
OS 35:9:3 (187,270)   OD 600–700   23680,17338
Field banks (site)   Field banks and enclosures (No. 343) are visible on aerial photographs (GSI, S 35–6; S 101–2). Not visible on the ground.
35:40(02)   22-9-1990

105 GARRANMACONLY
OS 21:15:5 (572,66)   OD 500–600   22125,18387
Field bank (site)   Not marked on the 1841 or 1909 eds. OS 6" maps. A field bank, extending to the E and NW of ringfort (No. 198), is visible on aerial photographs (GSI, S 79–80). Not visible on the ground.
21:15(02)   24-6-1991

106 GORTEENNAMEALE
OS 11:2:1 (263,549)   OD 800–1000   22757,20184
Field system (possible)   Possible early field system visible on aerial photographs (ACAP, V 300, 780–1). The area is now forested.
11:1   25-7-1991

107 GRANGE UPPER
OS 13:16:6 (848,48)   OD 500–700   25331,19680
Field system   Not marked on the 1841 or 1909 eds. OS 6" maps. Visible on aerial photographs (GSI, S 223–4). A series of low earthen banks (H *c.* 0.9m). Date unknown.
13:64   6-6-1990

108 GUILEEN (Stradbally By.) Luggacurren ED
OS 19:10:5 (334,167)   OD 700–800   25768,19169
Field systems   A series of low banks, visible on aerial photographs (GSI, S 168–9), survive in a poor condition on the ground. Date unknown.
19:11(04)   9-8-1990

109 KILPURCEL
OS 28:1:3 (200,550)   OD 300–400   22710,18264
Field system   Cropmarks of field boundaries visible on aerial photographs (GSI, S 77–8). Date unknown.
28:1(01)   22-8-1991

110 MOHER WEST
OS 11:6:5 (364,341)   OD 700–900   22866,19965
Field system (site)   Field system visible on aerial photographs (GSI, S 232–3). No visible surface traces.
11:3   25-7-1991

111 MONDREHID
OS 16:13:4 (66,17)   OD 300–400   22561,18980
Field system (site)   Reference to a field system here (O'Hanlon and O'Leary 1907, vol. 1, 297). Not marked on the 1841 or 1909 eds. OS 6" maps. No visible surface traces.
16:22(03)   16-9-1991

112 OLDTOWN (Maryborough West By.)
OS 17:8:1 (764,409)   OD 300–400   24269,19410
Field system (site)   Field system visible on aerial photographs (GSI, S 226–7). Not visible on the ground. Enclosure (No. 492) lies to S.
17:8(02)   28-8-1990

113 RATHNALEUGH
OS 27:4:4 (728,477)   OD 300–400   22292,18183
Field system (possible)   A possible field system is visible on aerial photographs (GSI, S 78–9). Low ill-defined banks are visible on the ground. Date unknown.
27:4(05)   7-11-1990

9. Toghers and Roadways

A togher, from the Irish *tochar*, is a trackway or causeway across a tract of bog. They are common in the midlands where there are large areas of raised bog and are often uncovered during turf-cutting operations. They are usually constructed of lengths of timber set crossways on beams and held in place by wooden pegs. They may date to Neolithic or late medieval times (*PRIA* 1985, 37–60). Modern roads run along the line of some of them.

According to early Irish historic sources, five great roads lead from Tara to the five kingdoms of Ireland. The road to the SW, which ran through Laois, was known as the *Slighe Dhála*. Two sections of it are recorded on the OS 6-inch maps, in Ballaghmore Lower (No. 115) and Cashel (No. 117), where it is known as the *Bealach Mor Moy Dala*. Details of its date and construction are unknown.

114 AGHABOE
OS 22 NPL

Roads (site) Reference to remains of old roads around the motte and bailey (No. 900) (Carrigan 1905, vol. 2, 47). No definite remains visible.
22:19(12)   12-8-1991

115 BALLAGHMORE LOWER
OS 15:15:4 (466,14) 'Bealach Mor Moy Dala' OD 400–500 22008,18971

Road (site) Marked on the 1909 ed. OS 6" map. Known as 'the great road of the plain of meeting', this road extended southwards from the Hill of Tara through Ballaghmore (O'Hanlon and O'Leary 1907, vol. 1, 65; O'Hanlon *et al.* 1914, vol. 2, 461–2). No visible surface traces.
15:18   15-9-1991

116 BAUNAGHRA
OS 33:15:3 (633,104) OD 400–500 22202,17147
Togher A togher (L *c.* 495m), running E–W, was discovered in 1958 during turf-cutting and excavated by Rynne (NMI file). It was constructed of roughly parallel, heavy longitudinal timbers (diam. 0.1–0.15m), 2m apart. Transverse planks were laid over them and held in place by pegs or stakes. There was a layer of stones and sandy gravel in the centre.
33:15

117 CASHEL (Upperwoods By.)
OS 22:2:4 (286,530) 'Bealach Mor Moy Dala' OD 400–500 22794,18883

Road (site) Remains of part of the old road from Castletown to Borris-in-Ossory passed midway between the 'caiseal' (No. 706) and 'Brandybush fort' (No. 172) (Carrigan 1905, vol. 2, 180). Laneway here now.
22:5(05)   5-8-1991

118 CLONENAGH
OS 17:2:6 (412,514) OD 300–400 23897,19517
Road A low flat ridge (H *c.* 1m, Wth *c.* 8m) running NW–SE, in direction of Clonenagh church (No. 713), with possible drain and outer bank on either side may

represent an old road.
17:5   31-8-1990

119 DRUMMOND
OS 3:6:3 (457,442) 'Derringawan Togher, Ardmadrim Togher' OD 200–300 23926,21362
Toghers (site) Two toghers, running virtually at right angles to each other, are marked on the 1841 and 1910 eds. OS 6" maps. Modern roads have been built on top of them. No visible surface traces.
3:5   13-8-1990

120 EMO PARK
OS 9:5:5 (131,355) 'Togher' OD 200–300 25539,20646

Togher (site) Site has been levelled and forested. No visible surface traces.
9:8   20-7-1990

121 KILPURCEL
OS 28:1:3 (195,556) OD 300–400 22704,18270
Trackway (site) Cropmark of trackway visible on aerial photographs (GSI, S 77–8). No visible surface traces.
28:1(02)   22-8-1991

122 KILVAHAN
OS 18 NPL

Road Reference to an old road in Kilvahan townland (O'Hanlon and O'Leary 1907, vol. 1, 188–9). Unlocated.
18:17(04)   12-6-1990

123 MORETT
OS 8:16:6 (851,35) 'Ancient Road' OD 300–400 25328,20305

Road (site) Over a mile long section of ancient road, running E–W, is marked on all eds. of OS 6" maps. The E section is marked 'Site of' on the 1909 ed. No visible surface traces. The W section is covered by a modern road. (O'Flanagan 1933, vol. 1, 219)
8:19   21-6-1990

10. Hillforts

Hillforts, as their name implies, are prominently located enclosures encompassing hills, thus making maximum use of naturally defended positions. They may consist of a single bank and fosse or a series of widely spaced banks and fosses, and the ramparts generally tend to follow the contour of the hill. The size of the enclosed area, which can vary greatly from one site to another, suggests that these monuments were tribal centres rather than single family units. They appear to have fulfilled a number of functions, including habitation, defended refuges and cattle-corralling. Evidence from the excavations at Rathgall, County Wicklow, Dún Ailinne, County Kildare and Freestone Hill, County Kilkenny, indicate that hillforts were constructed from the Late Bronze Age into the Iron age, and may have continued to be used into post-medieval times.

124 BOLEY (Ballyadams By.)
OS 25:11:3 (686,255) *'Boley Fort'* OD 733 26146,18626
Hillfort Prominently located at the end of a N–S ridge. A circular area (diam. *c.* 112m) defined by a massive bank (Wth *c.* 10.6m, int. H *c.* 3.5m, ext. H *c.* 1m) and external fosse, except at NE. Possible entrance at ESE. Well in fosse at E.
25:27(01)   22-8-1990

125 BOLEY UPPER
OS 23:10:6 (414,190)   Hachured   OD 300–400 23908,18535
Hillfort A circular enclosure (diam. *c.* 70m), on high ground overlooking surrounding area, defined by a bank of earth and stone (Wth *c.* 5.3m, ext. H *c.* 1.9m), and external fosse (Wth *c.* 7.7m, ext. D *c.* 0.9m). Now very degraded at S. No evidence of original entrance.
23:24   17-8-1990

126 CAPARD
OS 7:2:5 (332,517)   OD 800–900   23799,20800
Hillfort (possible) An enclosure (max. dims. *c.* 100m N–S, *c.* 90m E–W), surrounding the top of a hill, defined by a bank with an entrance at NNW is visible on aerial photographs (ACAP, V 300, 731–2). The area is now covered with forestry but the remains of an earthen bank (Wth 1.5m, H *c.* 2m), much interfered with, may be in part original. No evidence of fosse. This site might be classified as a hilltop enclosure.
7:2   12-9-1990

127 CLOPOOK
OS 19:14:6 (406,73) *'Dun of Clopook'* OD 500–600 25845,19070
Hillfort A circular area (diam. *c.* 200m) defined by a bank (Wth *c.* 7m, int. H *c.* 1.75m) constructed of earth and stone, except at E where it is defined by a stone wall (Wth *c.* 6m, H *c.* 1m). Modern ramp at E. No evidence of fosse. Reference to a hut site here (Walsh 1972, 17), and a possible castle site (No. 988) O'Hanlon and O'Leary 1907, vol. 1, 243).
19:21(01)   16-8-1990

11. Cliff-edge Fort

Cliff-edge forts are more usually associated with coastal locations, on naturally formed sea cliffs and promontories where artifical defences are required along the landward side only. They are occassionally, though not commonly, found inland where a sheer drop occurs naturally, for example, at river ravines and exposed inland cliff faces. Here penannular enclosures are built at the cliff edge, incorporating it as part of a natural defensive mechanism. The defences are usually not carried along the cliff edge itself. Only one example of this monument-type is known in County Laois. Like other prehistoric defensive sites, such as hillforts or coastal forts, it may date to the Iron Age. However, its small size may indicate that it is related to ringforts; a number of ringfort-type enclosures built against the edges of steep streams and river ravines have been found in County Cork.

128 BALLYPRIOR
OS 19:10:5 (355,215)   Hachured   OD 600–700
25790,19220
Cliff-edge fort   A subcircular area (dims. 34m SSE–NNW, *c.* 28m ESE–WNW) defined by an earth and stone bank (Wth *c.* 2.4m, int. H *c.* 0.5m, ext. H *c.* 1.2m) except at W and N where it is delimited by a scarp. A sheer cliff face forms the enclosing element from S–W. An external shallow fosse (Wth *c.* 2m) is evident. Entrance via causeway (Wth *c.* 6.5m) at NE.
19:11(03)   9-8-1990

12. Ringforts

Ringforts, the most numerous and widely distributed field monuments in Ireland, are defended homesteads dating mainly to the Early Christian period (500–1100 AD). They consist of an area, usually circular but occasionally oval or D-shaped, enclosed by one or more earthen (or earth and stone) banks and fosses or by a rampart of stone. Earthen forts are commonly known as raths, while stone examples are called cashels. Cashels are rare in Laois and only one definite example is known at Baunaghra (No. 163). Ringforts vary greatly in size, ranging from less than 20m at Park or Dunmase (No. 245) to over 70m at Raheenahoran (No. 250). However, the majority in the county are between 25–55m in diameter. Entrances with causeways across the fosse are generally located in the eastern half of the site. It is believed that ringforts were occupied by single extended families. The interior would have contained circular or rectangular houses and farm buildings. The enclosing bank/wall and fosse acted as a protective barrier against marauding cattle-raiders and wild animals such as wolves.

The internal diameter measurement is given for upstanding monuments, while the maximum external diameter is given for monuments measured from the maps. It is likely that many of the entries listed in the enclosures and earthworks chapters are badly defaced or levelled ringforts.

Fig. 4—*Baunaghra, cashel* (**163**)

129 AGHNAHILY
OS 13:16:2 (827,138)   OD 500–600   25307,19774
Ringfort (possible, site)   A rath, within which a cist (No. 21) was found, was situated 135m from the Rock of Dunamase (Comerford 1886, vol. 3, 288). Not marked on the 1841 or 1909 eds. OS 6" maps. No visible surface traces.
13:62(01)   6-6-1990

130 AGHNAHILY
OS 13:16:3 (851,115)   Hachured   OD 500–600
25333,19750
Ringfort (site)   Marked on the 1841 and 1909 eds. OS

6" map. A circular area (diam. *c.* 40m) defined by a bank and external fosse. Entrance possibly at NE (OPW file). No visible surface traces.
13:63   5-6-1990

131 AHARNEY
OS 35:10:6 (446,211)   Hachured   OD 500–600
23955,17278
Ringfort   Only S portion of bank remaining. Described as a circular area (diam. *c.* 40m) defined by a bank (Wth *c.* 3m, int. H *c.* 0.5–0.8m) with a fosse (Wth *c.* 4m, ext. D *c.* 0.6m) at E. Entrance at E (OPW file). Known as 'Rathpatrick' (Carrigan 1905, vol. 2, 309).
35:46   27-9-1990

19

132 AKIP
OS 28:6:2 (378,391)   Hachured   OD 300–400
22899,18098
Ringfort A circular area (max. diam. *c.* 50m) defined by an earthen bank (Wth *c.* 3.4m, int. H *c.* 0.8m, ext. H *c.* 1.7m) and external fosse (Wth *c.* 3.9m, ext. D *c.* 1.1m). No visible evidence of original entrance.
28:28   16-9-1991

133 ARCHERSTOWN
OS 35:11:5 (579,186)   Hachured   OD 400–500
24095,17252
Ringfort A circular area (diam. 45.3m) defined by a low bank (Wth *c.* 2m, int. H *c.* 0.2m, ext. H *c.* 1.1m) with an external fosse (Wth *c.* 6.2m) visible at E, SE–W, NW and N. No evidence of original entrance.
35:51   12-11-1990

134 BALLAGHARAHIN
OS 27:15:6 (642,19)   Hachured   OD 400–500
22207,17698
Ringfort A circular area (diam. *c.* 25.8m) defined by an earthen bank (Wth *c.* 2.1m, int. H *c.* 0.9m, ext. H *c.* 1.3m) with slight evidence of fosse at N and E.
27:27   8-10-1990

135 BALLAGHARAHIN
OS 27:15:6 (682,3)   Hachured   OD 400–500
22248,17682
Ringfort A raised circular area (max. diam. *c.* 38m) defined by a low inner bank (Wth *c.* 7.1m, int. H *c.* 0.35m, ext. H *c.* 0.2m), intervening fosse (Wth *c.* 3.5m) and possible outer bank (Wth *c.* 9.2m, int. D *c.* 0.2m). Original entrance not identifiable. A linear feature (No. 676) lies to SSW.
27:28(01)   8-11-1990

136 BALLINACLOGH LOWER
OS 24:4:2 (782,570)   Hachured   OD 552
25268,18950
Ringfort (possible, site) Possible ringfort reused as a motte and bailey (No. 901) (OPW file).
24:15(01)   26-8-1990

137 BALLINFRASE
OS 34:11:1 (494,243)   Hachured   OD 300–400
23030,17302
Ringfort A circular area (diam. *c.* 34m) defined by an earthen bank (Wth *c.* 3.7m, int. H *c.* 0.8m, ext. H *c.* 1.2m) and barely discernible fosse (Wth *c.* 4.2m). No evidence of original entrance.
34:26   3-7-1991

138 BALLINTUBBERT
OS 19:11:2 (603,253)   Hachured   OD 400–500
26052,19263
Ringfort A subcircular area (diam. *c.* 35.6m E–W) defined by an earthen bank (Wth *c.* 2.7m, int. H 0.4m, ext. H *c.* 1.2m) at E, S and W, and by an external fosse at S and W. Northern section destroyed. No evidence of original entrance.
19:13   16-8-1990

139 BALLYBRITTAS
OS 9:6:1 (294,415)   *'Ashgrove Rath'*   OD 200–300
25711,20711
Ringfort Situated in a low-lying area. An almost circular levelled enclosure (int. diam. *c.* 56m E–W). Slight traces of the bank and external fosse survive at W and N. The fosse (max. Wth 8m, max. D 2.5m) is best preserved at E and SE where it is wide and deep.
9:9   24-7-1990

140 BALLYBUGGY
OS 34:1:2 (149,585)   Hachured   OD 400–500
22661,17660
Ringfort A circular area (diam. 40m) defined by a bank (Wth *c.* 4.5m, int. H *c.* 0.5m, ext. H *c.* 1.75m) at W and N, and an external shallow fosse at SE and S. Church site and graveyard (No. 698) lie in S half of interior.
34:4(03)   27-9-1990

141 BALLYCARROLL (Maryborough East By.)
OS 13:12:1 (766,257)   Hachured   OD 400–500
25242,19899
Ringfort A circular area (diam. *c.* 27.1m) defined by a low bank (Wth 1.1m, int. H 0.3m, ext. H 0.5m) from SE–NE, and elsewhere by a scarp. Fosse (Wth *c.* 1.3m) visible from N–S. No evidence of original entrance.
13:48   31-5-1990

142 BALLYCARROLL (Maryborough East By.)
OS 13:12:6 (918,170)   Hachured   OD 600–700
25403,19810
Ringfort A subcircular area (dims. *c.* 39m N–S, *c.* 36m E–W) defined by a bank (Wth *c.* 3.4m, ext. H *c.* 1m) and external fosse (Wth *c.* 3m). Entrance at S.
13:55   8-7-1990

143 BALLYCOLLA
OS 29:5:3 (161,441)   OD 300–400   23645,18158
Ringfort Marked on the 1841 ed. OS 6" map. A subcircular area (dims. *c.* 37m N–S, 32.7m E–W) defined by an inner bank (Wth *c.* 2.1m, int. H *c.* 0.2m, ext. H *c.* 0.9m) from SE–W; elsewhere a scarp forms the enclosing element. An intervening fosse (Wth *c.* 2.7m) and outer bank are visible at W. Possible souterrain (No. 283) in interior at SE.
29:18(01)   28-9-1990

144 BALLYCOOLAN
OS 19:10:6 (386,211)   Hachured   OD 700
25823,19216
Ringfort A circular area (diam. *c*. 45.3m) defined by
an earthen bank (Wth *c*. 4.7m, int. H *c*. 0.6m, ext. H *c*.
1.2m), and external fosse (Wth at base 1.8m) from
S–NNW. Possible original entrance at NW.
19:11(07)   9-8-1990

145 BALLYDAVIS
OS 13:8:4 (723,348) Hachured OD 300–400
25196,19996
Ringfort A circular area (diam. *c*. 41m) defined by a
bank (Wth *c*. 1.4m, int. H *c*. 0.3m, ext. H *c*. 1.1m) at
SSW, and elsewhere by a scarp. Possible original
entrance at NNW. No evidence of fosse.
13:33   23-5-1990

146 BALLYGAUGE BEG
OS 29:10:5 (332,183)   Hachured   OD 200–300
23828,17887
Ringfort A circular area (diam. *c*. 42.5m) defined by a
bank (Wth *c*. 2.3m, int. H *c*. 0.7m, ext. H *c*. 1.4m) and
external fosse (Wth *c*. 3.8m) at E and S. Possible
original entrance at NE.
29:30   14-8-1990

147 BALLYGAUGE MORE
OS 29:6:4 (258,352)   Hachured   OD 300–400
23748,18065
Ringfort An oval area (dim. 28m NE–SW) defined by
an earthen bank (Wth 1.5m, int. H *c*. 0.5m, ext. H *c*.
1–2m), except from NW–N. An external fosse (Wth *c*.
3m) survives from SE–SW. Original entrance not
visible.
29:20   22-8-1990

148 BALLYHORAHAN
OS 16:3:5 (546,478)   Hachured   OD 500–600
23063,19471
Ringfort Not marked on the 1841 ed. OS 6" map. A
circular area (diam. *c*. 34.7m) defined by an earthen
bank (Wth *c*. 3.2m, int. H *c*. 0.4m, ext. H *c*. 1.5m) and
a fosse (Wth *c*. 4.3m). Possible original entrance at E.
16:7   23-7-1991

149 BALLYKEALY
OS 35:14:1 (284,144)   Hachured   OD 600–700
23784,17206
Ringfort A circular area (max. diam. *c*. 56m) defined
by a low bank (Wth *c*. 3.5m) except at SW where a
scarp forms the enclosing element. Evidence of an
external fosse survives from N–E and from S–SW. No
evidence of original entrance.
35:58   3-10-1990

150 BALLYMOONEY
OS 13:11:1 (535,253)   Hachured   OD 400–500
24998,19893
Ringfort A subcircular area (dims. *c*. 61m N–S, 48m
E–W) defined by a bank (Wth *c*. 3.8m, int. H *c*. 0.4m,
ext. H *c*. 1.3m) from E–S. Evidence of fosse at NE.
Several gaps in bank but the original entrance is not
identifiable.
13:46   22-5-1990

151 BALLYMULLEN
OS 30:1:4 (29,499)   Hachured   OD 400–500
24480,18228
Ringfort A circular area (diam. *c*. 32.5m) defined by
an earthen bank (Wth *c*. 2.2m, int. H *c*. 0.8m, ext. H *c*.
1.5m) from NE–NW, and an external fosse (Wth *c*.
4.3m) from NE–SE. No other visible surface traces.
30:4   17-6-1991

152 BALLYPRIOR
OS 19:10:2 (364,243)   Hachured   OD 700–800
25799,19250
Ringfort A circular area (diam. *c*. 47.5m) defined by
an earthen stone-faced bank (Wth *c*. 2.9m, int. H 0.5m,
ext. H *c*. 1.2m). Original entrance at NNE. Traces of a
circular hut site (diam. *c*. 11m) in NE quadrant.
Entrance at N.
19:11(01)   9-8-1990

153 BALLYPRIOR
OS 19:6:5 (353,307)   Hachured   OD 700–800
25787,19318
Ringfort A raised circular area (diam. *c*. 25m) defined
by a bank (Wth *c*. 4.1m, int. H *c*. 0.5m, ext. H *c*. 1m)
from NE–SSW, and elsewhere by a scarp. External
fosse most pronounced at S and from S–SW. No
evidence of original entrance.
19:11(06)   9-8-1990

154 BALLYROAN (Cullenagh By.)
OS 24:1:5 (98,472)   Hachured   OD 300–400
24548,18839
Ringfort A subcircular area (diam. *c*. 29m SE–NW)
defined by a scarp (ext. H *c*. 1.3m), and by a fosse (Wth
c. 4.4m) at ESE. Gap at SW may be original entrance.
24:5   27-8-1990

155 BALLYTARSNA (Cullenagh By.)
OS 23:12:1 (698,291)   Hachured   OD 300–400
24207,18645
Ringfort A subcircular area (max. diam. *c*. 35m
NW–SE) defined by a bank (Wth *c*. 3.6m, int. H *c*.
0.1m, ext. H *c*. 1m) from NW–SW, and by a scarp at
W. External fosse (Wth *c*. 2.9m) present from SSE–N.
Original entrance at SE.
23:27   17-8-1990

156 BALLYTHOMAS
OS 14:5:3 (190,411)   Indicated   OD 300–400
25607,20066

Ringfort Marked on the 1841 ed. OS 6" map and
indicated by a curving field fence on the 1909 ed.
Reference to a rath here (Comerford 1886, vol. 3, 282).
Now defined by a scarp (max. H 1.6m) from SSW–E.
No evidence of fosse or original entrance.
14:10   22-5-1990

157 BALLYTHOMAS
OS 14:5:6 (193,353)   Hachured   OD 362
25612,20004

Ringfort Reference to a rath here (Comerford 1886,
vol. 3, 282). A circular area (diam. *c.* 50m) defined by
a bank (Wth *c.* 1.9m, int. H *c.* 1.6m, ext. H *c.* 1.9m)
from SW–NE. No evidence of fosse or original
entrance.
14:11   15-6-1990

158 BARNABOY
OS 15:11:1 (482,295)   Hachured   OD 900–1000
22022,19268

Ringfort A circular area (diam. *c.* 26.3m) defined by a
low earthen bank (Wth *c.* 2.4m, int. H *c.* 0.4m, ext. H
c. 1.2m), and a shallow fosse (Wth *c.* 3.2m) at N and
E. No evidence of original entrance.
15:13   13-9-1991

159 BARRADOOS
OS 6:6:1 (234,450)   Hachured   OD 1000–1100
22722,20718

Ringfort Situated close to mountain top in afforested
land now felled. A circular area (diam. *c.* 25m)
delimited by an earthen bank (Wth *c.* 2m, max. ext. H
1m) and an external fosse (Wth 1m).
6:6   14-6-1991

160 BARRAWINGA
OS 33:4:4 (725,474)   Hachured   OD 300–400
22296,17539

Ringfort A circular area (diam. *c.* 38m) defined by an
earthen bank (Wth *c.* 3.2m, int. H *c.* 0.3m, ext. H *c.*
1.8m) from S–NE; elsewhere a scarp forms the
enclosing element. Remains of an external fosse (Wth
c. 3.8m) are visible.
33:4   14-8-1991

161 BARROWHOUSE
OS 20:15:4 (477,48)   Hachured   OD 100–200
26896,19054

Ringfort (site) Marked on the 1888 and 1909 eds. OS
6" maps. A circular area (diam. *c.* 28m) defined by a
bank and shallow fosse, with a slightly raised interior
(OPW file). No visible surface traces.
20:7   15-7-1990

162 BAUNAGHRA
OS 33:12:5 (791,153)   Hachured   OD 400–500
22368,17201

Ringfort A circular area (max. diam. *c.* 50m) defined
by a bank (Wth *c.* 3.2m, int. H *c.* 0.3m, ext. H *c.* 1.5m)
and external fosse (Wth *c.* 4m) from N–SW. No other
visible surface traces.
33:13   16-8-1991

163 BAUNAGHRA
OS 33:16:1 (697,138)   'The Bawn'   OD 400–500
22269,17184

Cashel A subcircular cashel (dims. *c.* 60m E–W, 51m
N–S) defined by a roughly coursed limestone wall (T
c. 1.1m, max. H *c.* 5m). Only the lower courses of the
wall remain from SW–ENE. Described as being 19ft
high (*c.* 5.7m) with walls 4–4.5 ft (*c.* 1.2m) in
thickness, with a residence or castle (No. 980) in the
interior (Carrigan 1905, vol. 2, 283).
33:16(01)   25-10-1990

164 BAUNOGE
OS 28:15:2 (567,138)   Hachured   OD 300
23101,17833

Ringfort A circular area (diam. *c.* 26.4m) defined by
an earthen bank (Wth *c.* 2.7m, int. H *c.* 0.3m, ext. H *c.*
1.2m) and fosse (Wth *c.* 3.5m), now barely discernible.
28:63   4-9-1991

165 BECKFIELD
OS 28:3:4 (491,524)   Hachured   OD 400
23017,18240

Ringfort (possible, site) Marked on the 1841 and 1908
eds. OS 6" maps; an almost circular area (max. diam.
c. 80m NW–SE). Reference to a partly square rath
with a double rampart on W and N sides and the site of
a building in the interior (Carrigan 1905, vol. 2, 354).
No visible surface traces.
28:12(01)   12-9-1991

166 BELADD
OS 13:10:5 (378,195)   Hachured   OD 300–400
24833,19830

Ringfort Marked on the 1841 and 1909 eds. OS 6"
maps; a subcircular area (max. dims. *c.* 70m NE–SW,
50m NW–SE). Only slight traces of the bank survive at
NE. No other visible surface traces.
13:45   23-5-1990

167 BOLEY (Ballyadams By.)
OS 25:8:5 (783,310)   Hachured   OD 300–400
26247,18685

Ringfort A circular area (diam. *c.* 36m) defined by a
bank (Wth *c.* 4m, int. H *c.* 0.35m, ext. H *c.* 1.5m) from
SE–N and a shallow external fosse (Wth *c.* 7m).
Known as 'Rath Easpuic' or 'the Bishop's Rath'

Fig. 5—*Carrowreagh, ringfort* (**171**)

(O'Hanlon and O'Leary 1907, vol. 1, 301).
25:22   22-8-1990

168 BOLEYBEG
OS 24:14:3 (453,188) Hachured   OD 500–600
24925,18437
Ringfort A subcircular area (max. dims. *c*. 34m E–W,
30m N–S) defined by a bank (Wth 2.5m, int. H 0.5m),
and a shallow external fosse (Wth *c*. 2m). Possible
original entrance at NE.
24:45   21-10-1991

169 CAPPANAFEACLE
OS   20:13:1   (14,85)   Hachured   OD 200
26396,19088
Ringfort A circular area (diam. *c*. 41.7m) defined by a
scarp, intervening fosse (Wth *c*. 7.2m, int. H *c*. 1.2m),
and outer bank (Wth *c*. 1.4m, int. H *c*. 2.3m, ext. H *c*.
0.95m). Gap at S may be original.
20:3   4-5-1990

170 CARROWREAGH (Upperwoods By.)
OS   10:16:5   (801,3)   Hachured   OD 800
22356,19603

Ringfort On elevated ground surrounded by marsh at
S. A circular ringfort (diam. 31m) defined by a low
much-denuded bank (Wth 2m, int. H 0.45m), a deep
fosse (Wth 1.8m, D 1.05m) and an external bank (Wth
2.2m, int. H 1.5m, ext. H 0.6m). Inner face of inner
bank appears to be stone-revetted. Causewayed
entrance (Wth 2m) at NNE. Interior very marshy,
banks and fosse overgrown with trees and shrubs.
10:3   23-5-1994

171 CARROWREAGH (Upperwoods By.)
OS 15:4:2 (828,560)   Hachured   OD 600–700
22385,19551
Ringfort A circular area (diam. *c*. 24.5m) defined by a
low bank (Wth *c*. 2m, int. H *c*. 0.2m, ext. H *c*. 1.4m)
and external fosse (Wth *c*. 5m). Possible entrance at E.
15:4   12-9-1991

172 CASHEL (Upperwoods By.)
OS 22:2:4 (287,517) *'Brandy Bush Fort'*   OD 465
22795,18870
Ringfort An oval-shaped area (dims. *c*. 86m N–S,
64m E–W) defined by a very low bank at E and W, and
by a scarp at N. Traces of the fosse and outer bank are
visible at E, as well as the possible original entrance.
No other visible surface traces. Originally known as

'the Fort of the Brake', it was ploughed in 1855 (Carrigan 1905, vol. 2, 179–80).

22:6   9-5-1991

173 CLOGHOGE
OS 30:6:5 (362,334)   Hachured   OD 500–600
24834,18057
Ringfort A circular area (diam. *c.* 41m) defined by a low earthen bank (Wth *c.* 2.2m, int. H *c.* 0.5m, ext. H *c.* 1.7m) and a barely discernible external fosse (Wth *c.* 3.8m). Possible original entrance at NE.
30:23   21-6-1991

174 CLOGRENAN
OS 37:10:3 (417,267)   Hachured   OD 300–400
26849,17365
Ringfort Not marked on the 1841 ed. OS 6" map. A circular area (diam. *c.* 47.3m) defined by an earthen bank (Wth *c.* 2.3m, int. H *c.* 0.5m, ext. H *c.* 1.8m) and external fosse (Wth *c.* 3.4m) from SE–NE. Possible original entrance at E.
37:7   15-11-1990

175 CLONADDADORAN
OS 18:9:5 (101,222)   Hachured   OD 402
24546,19215
Ringfort An oval-shaped area (dim. 61m N–S) defined by a low bank (Wth *c.* 3.2m, int. H 0.2m, ext. H 1.5m) and an external fosse (Wth *c.* 4.6m, ext. D *c.* 0.9m), except at W. Entrance with causeway at NW.
18:15   15-5-1990

176 CLONENAGH
OS 17:2:3 (395,551)   Hachured   OD 400–500
23878,19556
Ringfort A circular platform (diam. *c.* 23m, H *c.* 2.5m) with evidence of a surrounding fosse. No other visible surface traces.
17:3(09)   31-8-1990

177 COLT
OS 18:13:4 (37,24)   Hachured   OD 300–400
24481,19006
Ringfort A circular area (diam. *c.* 46m) defined by a low bank (Wth *c.* 2.8m, int. H *c.* 0.5m, ext. H *c.* 1.5m) at S and W, and an external fosse except at S. No evidence of original entrance.
18:23   9-5-1990

178 COOLAGH (Tinnahinch By.)
OS 2:9:6 (202,200)   *'Raheen'*   OD 500
22683,21095
Ringfort A large raised circular platform (diam. *c.* 50m, max. H *c.* 3m), situated on high ridge, enclosed by a shallow fosse with a possible outer bank. The outer bank consists mainly of stone, and in places is incorporated in the surrounding field fence. Remains of stone wall (Wth 1.7m), one course high, on perimeter of the platform.
2:5   6-9-1990

179 COOLBANAGHER
OS 13:4:1 (704,588)   Hachured   OD 300–400
25173,20248
Ringfort A subcircular area (max. dims. *c.* 50m N–S, 38m E–W) defined by a low earthen bank (Wth *c.* 2.2m, int. H *c.* 0.1m, ext. H *c.* 0.4m) at S, W and N, and by a scarp at E. The site is destroyed at SE. A shallow fosse (Wth *c.* 2.1m) is visible from S–E. No evidence of original entrance.
13:7   9-10-1990

180 COOLKERRY
OS 28:14:3 (452,125)   Hachured   OD 300–400
22980,17818
Ringfort A circular area (diam. *c.* 33.8m) defined by an earthen bank (Wth *c.* 3.2m, int. H *c.* 0.7m, ext. H *c.* 1.8m) and external fosse (Wth *c.* 4.5m). Possible original entrance at NE.
28:56   30-9-1991

181 COORLAGHAN
OS 37:2:1 (250,559)   Hachured   OD 900–1000
26670,17672
Ringfort A circular area (diam. *c.* 45.7m) defined by a bank (Wth *c.* 3m, int. H *c.* 0.7m, ext. H *c.* 1.9m) and external fosse (Wth *c.* 3.8m) from SE–N.
37:2   15-11-1990

182 CORBALLY (Ballyadams By.)
OS 25:3:5 (559,492)   Hachured   OD 500–600
26009,18874
Ringfort An oval-shaped area (dims. *c.* 46m N–S, *c.* 40.7m E–W) defined by a low bank and an external fosse. Entrance (Wth *c.* 3m) at ESE.
25:9   28-8-1990

183 CORBALLY (Ballyadams By.)
OS 25:7:3 (672,412)   OD 400–500   26129,18792
Ringfort Not marked on the 1841 or 1909 eds. OS 6" maps. A subcircular area (dims. *c.* 38m SW–NE, *c.* 31m SE–NW) defined by a scarp (H *c.* 2.3m) at NW, and elsewhere by a bank (Wth *c.* 3m) with a deep U-shaped fosse (Wth *c.* 7.6m) from W–SE. Outer bank (Wth *c.* 4.6m) present except at SSE, where the site is enclosed by a ravine. Possible original entrance at SW (OPW file).
25:17   19-7-1990

184 CRANNAGH (Upperwoods By.)
OS 16:7:5 (578,312)   *'Moat'*   OD 300–400
23098,19296
Ringfort Situated on a natural hill, NW of the River
Nore. A circular area (diam. *c.* 51m) with an almost
flat-topped raised interior, surrounded by a fosse (Wth
c. 6.3m) and external bank (Wth *c.* 8m, int. H *c.* 1.4m).
Possible original entrance with causeway at E.
16:14(02)   8-5-1991

185 CROSSNEEN
OS 37:3:6 (662,469)   *'Crossneen Fort'*   OD 197
27106,17581
Ringfort A subcircular area (dims. *c.* 54.8m N–S, *c.*
38m E–W) defined by an earthen bank (Wth *c.* 2.8m,
int. H *c.* 0.3m, ext. H *c.* 1.8m), and external fosse (Wth
c. 3.5m) from SE–NE. Possible original entrance at E.
37:3   15-11-1990

186 CULLAHILL MOUNTAIN
OS 35:13:2 (103,149)   Hachured   OD 800
23593,17209
Ringfort A raised circular area (diam. 20.7m) defined
by a low bank (Wth 1.9m, int. H *c.* 0.2m, ext. H *c.*
2.5m), except from NW–NNE where a scarp forms the
enclosing element. An external fosse (Wth 2.9m) is
visible from NW–SE. Possible original entrance at SE.
35:54   12-11-1990

187 CURRAGH (Slievemargy By.)
OS 32:14:3 (428,132)   OD 100–200   26856,17863
Ringfort (site) Not marked on the 1841 or 1908 eds.
OS 6" maps. A subcircular area (dims. 79.2m N–S,
67.5m E–W) defined by a low bank (Wth *c.* 5.4–6.3m)
and a shallow fosse (Wth *c.* 2.7m) (OPW file). No
visible surface traces.
32:19   14-8-1990

188 DERREEN and CARROWREAGH
OS 35:2:1 (257,545)   Hachured   OD 300–400
23751,17629
Ringfort A circular area (diam. *c.* 24.8m) defined by
an earthen bank (Wth *c.* 3.4m, int. H *c.* 0.3m, ext. H *c.*
1.2m) and traces of an external fosse.
35:5   22-9-1990

189 DERRYKEARN
OS 23:3:5 (571,458)   Hachured   OD 300–400
24071,18819
Ringfort A large roughly circular ringfort (diam.
50m), the height of which has been greatly accentuated
from W–NE by the lowering of the surrounding field
level as a result of quarrying. Remains of the bank
(Wth 1.5m, int. H 1.1m) are distinguishable from S–W
where its outer face has been heavily scarped.
Elsewhere it is heavily overgrown with hawthorn and

bushes. The interior is rough and uneven and
overgrown with briars and nettles.
23:5   27-5-1994

190 ANNAGH
See under enclosures.

191 DONAGHMORE
OS 28:9:3 (190,240)   Hachured   OD 300–400
22702,17936
Ringfort A circular area (diam. *c.* 32.3m) defined by
an inner bank (Wth *c.* 3.1m, int. H *c.* 0.7m, ext. H *c.*
1.3m), intervening fosse (Wth *c.* 4.2m) and outer bank
(Wth *c.* 2.7m, int. H *c.* 1.1m, ext. H *c.* 0.5m) at N.
Possible original entrance with causeway at E.
28:38   17-9-1991

192 DOOARY
OS 24:2:5 (385,468)   Hachured   OD 600–700
24850,18838
Ringfort A circular area (diam. *c.* 35m) defined by a
bank (Wth *c.* 3m, ext. H *c.* 1.3m), and external fosse
(Wth *c.* 4m) from NE–SE. Possible entrance at SW.
24:13   31-7-1990

193 DOOARY
OS 24:6:3 (414,440)   Hachured   OD 600–700
24881,18809
Ringfort A circular area (diam. *c.* 43m) defined by a
bank (Wth *c.* 4.8m) and fosse (Wth *c.* 5.2m). Possible
original entrance at SW.
24:22   31-7-1990

194 DRIMATERRIL
OS 30:5:3 (157,440)   Hachured   OD 500–600
24616,18167
Ringfort A subcircular area (dims. *c.* 47m NE–SW, *c.*
33m NW–SE) defined by an earthen bank (Wth *c.*
3.7m, int. H *c.* 0.5m, ext. H *c.* 1.3m), and external
fosse (Wth *c.* 4.2m) from SE–NE. No evidence of
original entrance.
30:17   17-6-1991

195 DUNBRIN UPPER
OS 20:10:6 (390,188)   Hachured   OD 200
26802,19202
Ringfort (possible, site) Marked on the 1841 and
1909 eds. OS 6" maps; a roughly D-shaped enclosure
(max. dim. *c.* 40m NNW–SSE). Reference to a rath
here (O'Hanlon and O'Leary 1907, vol. 1, 184). No
visible surface traces.
20:1   8-8-1990

196 EGLISH
OS 27:16:3 (868,120)   Hachured   OD 300–400
22444,17807
Ringfort (site) A partially destroyed low mound (diam. 58m) defined by a scarp (max. H *c.* 1.75m). Probably the natural platform on which the site was built. Described as a rath (Carrigan 1905, vol. 2, 66, 352).
27:29   8-11-1990

197 FALLOWBEG LOWER
OS 25:2:1 (243,568)   Hachured   OD 300–400
25674,18952
Ringfort An oval-shaped area (dim. 30m N–S) defined by a bank (Wth *c.* 4m, int. H *c.* 0.35m, ext. H *c.* 1.5m), except from NE–E, and a shallow external fosse (Wth *c.* 7m, ext. D *c.* 1m). No evidence of original entrance.
25:2   22-8-1990

198 GARRANMACONLY
OS 21:15:5 (574,69)   Hachured   OD 500–600
22128,18390
Ringfort A circular area (diam. *c.* 29m) defined by a low bank of earth and stone (Wth *c.* 3m, max. H *c.* 0.6m). Entrance at NE. Field bank (No. 105) lies to E and NW.
21:15(01)   27-2-1991

199 GARRANMACONLY
OS 21:15:6 (630,38)   Hachured   OD 500
22187,18357
Ringfort (possible) A raised circular area (diam. *c.* 30m) defined by a scarp (H *c.* 1m) from SW–NE, and a shallow external fosse from W–NW. No evidence of original entrance.
21:16   27-2-1991

200 GARRANMACONLY
OS 21:15:6 (665,20)   Indicated   OD 500–600
22224,18339
Ringfort A circular area (diam. *c.* 37m) defined by a bank of earth and stone (Wth *c.* 3m, ext. H *c.* 0.6m). Possible entrance at NW.
21:18   27-2-1991

201 GARRANMACONLY
OS 21:16:4 (726,15)   Hachured   OD 500–600
22289,18335
Ringfort A subcircular area (diam. *c.* 44.7m N–S) defined by an earthen bank (Wth *c.* 3.4m, int. H *c.* 1.2m, ext. H *c.* 0.7m), and by an external fosse (Wth *c.* 2.8m) at SE. No evidence of original entrance.
21:28   26-6-1991

202 GARRYNISKA
OS 28:4:4 (725,475)   Hachured   OD 400–500
23264,18190
Ringfort A subcircular area (dims. *c.* 48.4m NW–SE, *c.* 42.7m NE–SW) defined by an inner bank (Wth *c.* 3.2m, int. H *c.* 0.8m, ext. H *c.* 1.7m), intervening fosse (Wth *c.* 3.8m), except at S, and an outer bank (Wth *c.* 2.7m, int. H *c.* 1.6m, ext. H *c.* 0.5m) from SW–E. Possible original entrance at SE.
28:16   13-9-1991

203 GLENBOWER
OS 16:3:2 (613,564)   Hachured   OD 600
23133,19563
Ringfort Not marked on the 1841 ed. OS 6" map. A circular area (diam. *c.* 28.4m) defined by a scarp (H *c.* 1.4m) and external fosse (Wth *c.* 2.5m) at N. No evidence of original entrance.
16:9   23-7-1991

204 GORTNALEE
OS 27:8:2 (846,400)   Hachured   OD 300–400
22418,18103
Ringfort A subcircular area (diam. *c.* 38.7m N–S) defined by a low bank from NE–SSE, and elsewhere by a scarp (H *c.* 0.5–2m). Possible evidence of fosse from NE–SSE. Original entrance not identifiable.
27:11   6-10-1990

205 GORTNALEE
OS 28:5:1 (3,453)   Hachured   OD 400   22503,18159
Ringfort A circular area (diam. *c.* 27.5m) defined by an earthen bank (Wth *c.* 2.8m, int. H *c.* 0.7m, ext. H *c.* 1.3m) with some evidence of a fosse. Possible original entrance at S. Castle (No. 957) lies to SE.
28:18(02)   14-9-1991

206 GRAIGUEADRISLY
OS 33:12:5 (823,163)   Hachured   OD 400–500
22402,17212
Ringfort A circular area (diam. c. 28.5m) defined by an earthen bank (Wth c. 2.3m, int. H c. 0.8m, ext. H c. 1.5m) except at SE. Traces of an external fosse visible.
33:14   16-8-1991

207 GRAIGUEADRISLY
OS 33:16:2 (835,111)   Hachured   OD 400–500
22416,17157
Ringfort A circular area (diam. *c.* 35m) defined by an earthen bank (Wth *c.* 2.5m, int. H *c.* 0.8m, ext. H *c.* 1.3m) and fosse (Wth *c.* 3.2m) at S. Possible original entrance at NE.
33:19   17-8-1991

208 GRAIGUEADRISLY
OS 33:16:3 (866,138)   Hachured   OD 500–600
22448,17186
Ringfort A circular area (diam. *c.* 39.2m) defined by
an earthen bank (Wth *c.* 2.8m, int. H *c.* 0.6m, ext. H *c.*
0.9m) from E–SW, and from NW–NNE. Original
entrance at NE.
33:20   17-8-1991

209 GRAIGUEADRISLY
OS 33:16:3 (882,148)   Hachured   OD 500–600
22464,17196
Ringfort A circular area (diam. *c.* 55m) defined by an
inner bank (Wth *c.* 3.2m, int. H *c.* 0.8m, ext. H *c.*
2.1m), an intervening fosse (Wth *c.* 4.3m) and an outer
bank (Wth *c.* 2.4m, int. H *c.* 1.8m, ext. H *c.* 0.6m) from
W–E. Possible original entrance at SE. A rectangular
house site (L. *c.* 16.2m, Wth *c.* 5m) defined by a low
earthen bank is visible in interior at E.
33:21(01)   17-8-1991

210 GRAIGUEADRISLY
OS 33:16:3 (913,128)   Hachured   OD 500–600
22498,17176
Ringfort A circular area (diam. *c.* 25.4m) defined by a
barely discernible earth and stone bank (Wth *c.* 2.3m,
int. H *c.* 0.3m, ext. H *c.* 0.5m) and a shallow fosse
(Wth *c.* 4.2m). Carrigan (1905, vol. 2, 282) refers to
the site as a 'caiseal'.
33:22   17-8-1991

211 GRAIGUEANOSSY
OS 34:3:1 (481,546)   Indicated   OD 400–500
23013,17622
Ringfort A circular area (diam. *c.* 34m) defined by a
scarp (H *c.* 1.1m), intervening fosse (Wth *c.* 3m) and
outer bank (Wth *c.* 2m, int. H *c.* 1m, ext. H *c.* 0.7m)
from NW–SE. No evidence of original entrance.
34:9   30-6-1991

212 GRAIGUEARD
OS 34:2:6 (408,500)   Indicated   OD 400–500
22936,17573
Ringfort Hachured on the 1841 ed. OS 6" map. A
circular area (diam. *c.* 33m) defined by an earthen
bank (Wth *c.* 2.3m, int. H *c.* 0.3m, ext. H *c.* 0.9m) from
NW–N, and elsewhere by a scarp. Traces of an
external fosse (Wth *c.* 3m) survive from E–S and from
NW–N. No evidence of original entrance.
34:7   30-6-1991

213 GRAIGUEAVOICE
OS 35:5:6 (177,353)   'Raheennagorta'   OD 300–400
23669,17425
Ringfort An oval area (dims. *c.* 30m SW–NE, 24m
SE–NW) defined by an inner bank (Wth *c.* 3.2m, int. H

c. 0.5m, ext. H *c.* 0.5–1m) and traces of an external
fosse. Outer bank at NNE. Causewayed entrance at N.
35:23   27-9-1990

314 GRAIGUEAVOICE
OS 35:9:3 (212,294)   Hachured   OD 500–600
23707,17363
Ringfort A circular area (diam. *c.* 27.4m) defined by a
bank (Wth *c.* 2.3m, int. H 0.5m, ext. H *c.* 0.5m) with
evidence of a fosse at N and SW. A field boundary cuts
the site at E and W. No obvious evidence of original
entrance.
35:41   28-9-1990

215 GREATHEATH (Maryborough East By.)/
GREATHEATH (Portnahinch By.)
OS 13:4:5 (798,525)   'Rathshane'   OD 300–400
25273,20183
Ringfort Situated on the highest point of the Heath,
the surrounding land slopes dramatically to NE and
SW. A subcircular ringfort (dims. 40.5m NW–SE, 37m
NE–SW) defined by an earthen bank (Wth 6m, max.
int. H 1m, max. ext. H 1.6m), except from NE–E and
from S–WSW where it has been scarped in connection
with the approaching golf course fairway, and a flat-
bottomed fosse (Wth 1.5–2m, max. D 0.6m). A
gravelled entrance and causeway at NE appear modern.
The interior of the ringfort, which also slopes steeply
to NE and SW, is now used as the thirteenth hole of the
golf course, and, according to local information, bones
were found when the green was made.
13:16   18-5-1994

216 HARRISTOWN (Clandonagh By.)
OS 34:1:1 (18,533)   Hachured   OD 387
22524,17604
Ringfort (site) A circular area (diam. 27m) defined by
a bank (Wth *c.* 2.4–2.7m, int. H *c.* 1.8m, ext. H *c.*
2.4–2.7m), external fosse and possible outer bank
(OPW file). The site was levelled and no visible
surface traces survive.
34:2(01)   1-7-1991

217 HARRISTOWN (Slievemargy By.)
OS 32:11:5 (556,155)   Hachured   OD 100–200
26991,17888
Ringfort (possible, site) Marked on the 1908 ed. OS
6" map as a circular enclosure (max. diam. *c.* 30m).
Reference to a rath here (Comerford 1886, vol. 3, 265).
No visible surface traces but the site appears as a
cropmark on aerial photographs (GSI, S 61–2).
32:17   15-8-1990

218 JOHNSTOWN GLEBE
OS 28:9:5 (110,166)   Hachured   OD 300–400
22619,17857

Ringfort A circular area (max. diam. *c.* 40m) defined by an earthen bank (Wth *c.* 2.8m, int. H *c.* 0.8m, ext. H *c.* 1.9m). Possible original entrance at NE. No evidence of fosse.
28:40   17-9-1991

219 JOHNSTOWN GLEBE
OS 28:13:2 (104,92)   Hachured   OD 300–400
22613,17779
Ringfort A circular area (max. diam. *c.* 46m) defined by a bank (Wth *c.* 2.4m, H *c.* 1.5m) and slight evidence of an external fosse. No visible traces of original entrance.
28:53   30-9-1991

220 KILCOKE
OS 22:14:4 (282,58)   Hachured   OD 400–500
22795,18385
Ringfort (possible, site) Marked on the 1841 and 1909 eds. OS 6" map; a subcircular area (max. dims. *c.* 30m E–W, 25m N–S). The site was levelled in 1968 (OPW file). No visible surface traces but the site is clearly visible as a cropmark on aerial photographs (GSI, S 76–7).
22:20   8-8-1991

221 KILCORAN
OS 28:14:5 (337,46)   Hachured   OD 300–400
22860,17733
Ringfort A circular area (diam. *c.* 43m) defined by a scarp from SW–E and elsewhere by an earthen bank (Wth *c.* 2.8m, int. H *c.* 0.3m, ext. H *c.* 1.4m). Remains of an external fosse (Wth *c.* 3.5m) are visible. Tradition of church site (No. 754) in interior.
28:57(03)   6-9-1991

222 KILDELLIG
OS 22:15:5 (552,31)   Hachured   OD 400–500
23080,18359
Ringfort A circular area (diam. *c.* 46m) defined by an inner bank (Wth *c.* 2m, int. H *c.* 0.5m, ext. H *c.* 3–4m), intervening fosse (Wth *c.* 7.9m) and the remains of an outer bank (Wth *c.* 2m, H *c.* 0.5m) at S and W. No evidence of original entrance.
22:24   10-8-1991

223 KILDELLIG
OS 28:2:3 (412,576)   Hachured   OD 400–500
22933,18293
Ringfort A circular area (diam. *c.* 30m) defined by a low earthen bank (Wth *c.* 2.7m, int. H *c.* 0.4m, ext. H *c.* 0.8m) and faint traces of an external fosse. No evidence of original entrance.
28:7   11-9-1991

224 KILDRINAGH
OS 16:14:2 (375,102)   OD 300–400   22886,19072
Ringfort (possible, site) Marked on the 1841 ed. OS 6" map. Carrigan (1905, vol. 2, 180) refers to the site of a church and graveyard (No. 757) here. Cropmark of circular enclosure visible on aerial photographs (GSI, S 158–9). No surface traces survive.
16:23(05)   16-9-1991

225 KILFEACLE
OS 25:15:5 (552,73)   Hachured   OD 600–700
26005,18432
Ringfort A subcircular area (max. diam. *c.* 70m N–S) defined by a low bank, except at ESE and S where it is defined by a scarp, and an external fosse (Wth *c.* 4.3m, int. D *c.* 1m). No evidence of original entrance. A burial (No. 897) may have been found here.
25:33(01)   22-8-1990

226 KILLASMEESTIA
OS 21:16:6 (855,48)   Hachured   OD 400–500
22425,18371
Ringfort A subcircular area (dims. *c.* 38m N–S, *c.* 26m E–W) defined by an earthen bank (Wth *c.* 3.4m, int. H *c.* 0.8m, ext. H *c.* 1.4m) and external fosse (Wth *c.* 2.7m) at N and E. No evidence of original entrance.
21:29   26-6-1991

227 KILLASMEESTIA
OS 21:16:6 (850,11)   Hachured   OD 400–500
22420,18332
Ringfort A circular area (diam. *c.* 38.5m) defined by an earthen bank (Wth *c.* 3.1m, int. H *c.* 0.5m, ext. H *c.* 1.2m), and external fosse (Wth *c.* 2.7m) from SW–NW. Possible original entrance at E. Carrigan (1905, vol. 2, 141) refers to a chamber here and suggests that the ringfort may be the site of a castle (No. 998).
21:30(01)   26-6-1991

228 KILLEANY
OS 23:10:2 (311,256)   Hachured   OD 300–400
23799,18604
Ringfort A circular area (diam. *c.* 49m) defined by a bank (Wth *c.* 6m, ext. H *c.* 3.5–4m) and external fosse (Wth *c.* 7m). Possible original entrance (Wth *c.* 3.75m) at E. Cropmark of an enclosure (No. 446) lies immediately to SE.
23:19(01)   21-10-1991

229 KILLERMOGH
OS 29:10:3 (415,294)   Hachured   OD 200–300
23914,18005
Ringfort (possible, site) Marked on the 1909 ed. OS 6" map as a circular area (max. diam. *c.* 25m). Carrigan (1905, vol. 2, 220) refers to the site as the 'lis

or rath of Liscomyn'. No visible surface traces.
29:31   13-8-1990

230 KNOCKFIN
OS 28:15:5 (592,62)   Hachured   OD 300–400
23129,17752
Ringfort A circular area (max. diam. *c.* 44m) defined
by a scarp (H *c.* 1.5m). Slight evidence of fosse at E
and SE. No evidence of original entrance.
28:68   4-9-1991

231 KYLEBEG (Clarmallagh By.)
OS 19:3:1 (503,558)   Hachured   OD 200–300
25942,19583
Ringfort A circular area (diam. *c.* 40m) defined by a
bank (Wth *c.* 4.5m, int. H *c.* 1m, ext. H *c.* 1m) and an
external fosse (Wth *c.* 6.5m) from S–NW. No evidence
of original entrance.
19:4   2-5-1990

232 LAMBERTON DEMESNE
OS 18:7:3 (641,452)   Indicated   OD 500–600
25114,19463
Ringfort On N-facing slope in pastureland. A circular
earthen ringfort (diam. 40.5m) defined by a well-
preserved tree-planted bank (max. Wth 6m, int. H
0.6m, max. ext. H 1.8m), except from NNW–N where
it is flattened, and a fosse (Wth 2.5m), most
pronounced from NNW–SE; from SSW–NW it is
infilled. The interior is rough and uneven, and the S
half is obscured by bushes and briars (pers. comm. E.
FitzPatrick).
18:11   15-3-1994

233 LAMBERTON DEMESNE
OS 18:7:5 (574,366)   Hachured   OD 400–500
25044,19373
Ringfort An oval-shaped area (dim. *c.* 40m E–W)
defined by an inner bank (Wth *c.* 4m, int. H *c.* 1.1m),
intervening fosse (Wth *c.* 8m), except at SW, and outer
bank (Wth *c.* 3.3m, int. H *c.* 1.1m, ext. H *c.* 0.5m) from
W–N. No evidence of original entrance.
18:12   4-5-1990

234 LONGFORD
OS 16:2:1 (268,546)   Hachured   OD 400–500
22769,19540
Ringfort A circular area (diam. *c.* 32.6m) defined by
an earthen bank (Wth *c.* 3.5m) and external fosse (Wth
c. 3.2m). No evidence of original entrance.
16:4   23-7-1991

235 LUGGACURREN
OS 25:2:5 (363,501)   Hachured   OD 400–500
25802,18882

Ringfort Marked on the 1906 ed. OS 6" map as a
subcircular enclosure (max. diam. *c.* 55m NW–SE).
The site, which was divided by a field wall, has been
partly levelled. A slight rise in field level indicates the
E section with evidence of the fosse at N and SE. No
surface traces of W section. Reference to rath here
(O'Hanlon and O'Leary 1907, vol. 1, 184).
25:6   28-8-1990

236 MANNIN
OS 22:6:3 (437,434)   Hachured   OD 400–500
22955,18784
Ringfort (site) Marked on the 1841 and 1909 eds. OS
6" maps. Remains of an oval ringfort (dims. 48m E–W,
42m N–S) with slight evidence of bank at S. Shallow
fosse (Wth *c.* 6m) largely filled in (OPW file). No
visible surface traces.
22:7   6-8-1991

237 MOAT
OS 30:2:2   (348,564)   Hachured   OD 600
24816,18299
Ringfort A subcircular raised area (max. diam. *c.* 64m
E–W) defined by a bank (Wth *c.* 1.9m, int. H *c.* 0.9m,
ext. H *c.* 1.5m) at SW and W, and elsewhere by a
scarp. External fosse at NE, E and S.
30:10   13-8-1990

238 MONAFERRICK
OS 14:15:3 (632,136)   Hachured   OD 200–300
26077,19780
Ringfort A circular area (diam. *c.* 42m) defined by a
bank (Wth *c.* 2.6m, int. H *c.* 2.65m, ext. H *c.* 3.3m),
and external fosse (Wth *c.* 6.2m) from NE–NW.
Possible entrance with causeway at N.
14:43   12-6-1990

239 MORETT
OS 8:16:2 (841,83)   'Doon Fort'   OD 300–400
25317,20357
Ringfort Situated in slightly elevated position. A
circular area (diam. *c.* 52m) defined by a large earthen
bank (max. Wth *c.* 7m, int. H 2.6m, ext. H 3.5m). A
large gap (Wth 4m) at NNE probably indicates the
position of the original entrance, now widened. No
evidence of fosse, the outer face of which has been cut
back by earth-moving machinery. (*JKAS* 1904, 236–7)
8:17   20-6-1990

240 MOYADD
OS 31:1:5 (141,525)   Hachured   OD 500–600
25573,18265
Ringfort A circular area (C *c.* 40m N–SE) defined by
a bank from NW–NNW, and a scarp (H *c.* 0.4m) from
NNW–E. An intervening fosse (Wth *c.* 3.5m) and
outer bank (Wth *c.* 4.1m, int. H *c.* 0.35m, ext. H *c.*

0.25m) are visible from N–E. Possible entrance at E. Spoil, probably resulting from the construction of a nearby silage tank, has been piled in the SW quadrant of the interior.

31:1   17-7-1990

241 NEWTOWN or SKIRK
OS 21:16:2 (788,108)   Hachured   OD 400–500
22354,18434

Ringfort A circular area (diam. *c*. 41m) defined by an earthen bank (Wth *c*. 2.3m, int. H *c*. 1.1m, ext. H *c*. 1.7m) and fosse (Wth *c*. 2.8m). Possible original entrance at SE.

21:24   25-6-1991

242 OLDGLASS
OS 29:13:1 (10,143) Hachured OD 300
23488,17841

Ringfort (site) Hachured on the 1890 and 1906 eds. OS 6" maps; a circular area (max. diam. *c*. 40m). The site was levelled approximately ten years ago and only a slight indication of the bank survives at NW and E. No other visible surface traces.

29:39   13-9-1990

243 OLDTOWN (Clarmallagh By.)
OS 34:12:4 (754,183) Hachured OD 400–500
23304,17242

Ringfort A circular area (diam. *c*. 46m) defined by a stone-faced inner bank (Wth *c*. 5.9m, int. H *c*. 0.8m, ext. H *c*. 1.9m), intervening fosse (max. Wth *c*. 11m) and outer bank (Wth *c*. 5m, int. H *c*. 0.9m, ext. H *c*. 1.4m) from SW–NW. Entrance with causeway (Wth *c*. 2.1m) at E.

34:34   27-9-1990

244 PALMERSHILL
OS 22:15:3 (637,87) Hachured OD 400–500
23170,18420

Ringfort A circular area (diam. *c*. 42m) defined by an earthen bank (Wth *c*. 2.5m, int. H *c*. 0.4m, ext. H *c*. 1.8m), traces of an intervening fosse (Wth *c*. 3.8m) and outer bank (Wth *c*. 2.9m, int. H *c*. 1.6m, ext. H 0.7m) from NE–SE. Possible original entrance at SE.

22:25   19-6-1991

245 PARK or DUNAMASE
OS 13:12:4 (750,173)   'Sally's Bower'
OD 300–400   25226,19810

Ringfort Situated on S-facing slope on high ground. Slightly dished circular area (diam. *c*. 17m) defined by an earth and stone bank (H *c*. 1m) and external fosse. Fosse (Wth *c*. 3m) best defined at N, elsewhere barely discernible. Entrance at NE. Deserted settlement (No. 934) to SE.

13:51(02)   3-3-1994

246 PARKNAHOWN
OS 34:12:2 (832,277) 'Rathkilmurry' OD 300–400
23385,17342

Ringfort A circular area (diam. *c*. 50m) defined by an inner bank (Wth *c*. 6.6m, ext. H *c*. 2.2m), intervening fosse (Wth *c*. 10m) and an outer bank (Wth *c*. 6.4m, int. H *c*. 2.2m, ext. H *c*. 2m) from N–SE. Entrance (Wth *c*. 3m) with causeway at W. The site is over-grown with trees. Based on the name 'Rathkilmurry', Carrigan (1905, vol. 2, 240) suggested that there was once a church (No. 786) within the ringfort.

34:28(01)   26-9-1990

247 PARKNAHOWN
OS 34:12:3 (879,267)   OD 300–400   23436,17332

Ringfort A subcircular area marked on the 1841 ed. OS 6" map. Remains of bank (Wth *c*. 4m, ext. H *c*. 0.7m) are visible from SW–NW. No other surface traces survive.

34:29   3-7-1991

248 RAHANDRICK UPPER
OS 28:7:2 (561,411)   Hachured   OD 400–500
23092,18120

Ringfort A circular area (diam. *c*. 33m) defined by an earthen bank (Wth *c*. 3.4m, int. H *c*. 0.3m, ext. H *c*. 1.7m), best preserved at N, and an external fosse (Wth *c*. 4.2m). Possible original entrance with causeway at SE.

28:32   18-9-1991

249 RAHANDRICK UPPER
OS 28:7:2 (590,449)   Hachured   OD 400–500
23122,18161

Ringfort A circular area (diam. *c*. 38.6m) defined by an earthen bank (Wth *c*. 3.2m, int. H *c*. 0.7m, ext. H *c*. 1.4m), and external fosse (Wth *c*. 4m) from NE–W. No evidence of original entrance.

28:33   18-9-1991

250 RAHEENAHORAN
OS 13:8:4 (751,355)   Hachured   OD 300–400
25226,20003

Ringfort A subcircular area (diam. *c*. 75m NE–SW) defined by a bank at NE (Wth *c*. 1.5m, int. H *c*. 0.35m, ext. H *c*. 1.4m), and elsewhere by a scarp. Fosse (Wth *c*. 4.4m) present from W–NE and from E–S. No evidence of original entrance.

13:35   23-5-1990

251 RAHEENANISKY
OS 18:4:5 (827,521)   Hachured   OD 400–500
25310,19539

Ringfort (site) Described as a ringfort (OPW file), the site is now levelled. It is indicated by a slight rise in the ground level (max. diam. 47m E–W) and on aerial photograph (CUCAP, AYN 35) as a subcircular

cropmark. No other visible surface traces.
18:8   4-5-1990

252 RAHEENSHEARA (Clandonagh By.)
Ballybrophy ED
OS 27:4:5 (804,529)   Hachured   OD 300–400
22372,18238
Ringfort   A subcircular area (diam. *c.* 32.2m
SSE–NNW) defined by a low bank (Wth *c.* 1.2m, int.
H *c.* 0.2m, ext. H *c.* 0.3m). No visible trace of fosse.
Gap at E may be original entrance.
27:5   6-10-1990

253 RALISH
OS 30:1:2 (117,595)   OD 400–500   24572,18330
Ringfort (possible)   Marked on the 1841 ed. OS 6"
map. An oval area defined by a slight scarp at N. No
other visible surface traces. Reference to rath here
(O'Hanlon and O'Leary 1907, vol. 1, 289).
30:2   7-8-1990

254 RATHBRENNAN
OS 13:7:5 (572,334)   Hachured   OD 400–500
25037,19979
Ringfort   A circular raised area (diam. *c.* 33m) defined
by an inner bank (ext. H *c.* 1.8m), an intervening fosse
(Wth *c.* 2.5m) and an external bank (int. H *c.* 1.8m,
ext. H *c.* 1.5m) except at N.
13:28   23-7-1990

255 RATHGILBERT
OS 19:16:6 (885,6)   Hachured   OD 300–400
26351,19005
Ringfort   A circular area (diam. 26.4m) defined by an
earthen bank (Wth *c.* 1.3m, int. H 0.7m, ext. H *c.*
1.8m). External fosse (Wth *c.* 6m) visible at S.
Possible original entrance at S.
19:32   16-8-1990

256 RATHMILES
OS 5:14:4 (236,4)   '*Rathmiles*'   OD 300–400
25647,20916
Ringfort   Large subcircular ringfort (int. diam. *c.* 61m
N–S), situated on level ground above valley, defined by
a single bank (max. base Wth *c.* 2.6m, int. H *c.* 2.5m, ext.
H *c.* 2.75m) except at N where it is represented by a field
fence. The fosse (base Wth *c.* 2m, max. Wth *c.* 5.5m) is
visible from N–SW. Possible entrances at NE and SE.
5:16   12-6-1990

257 RATHMORE (Ballyadams By.)
OS 19:11:6 (672,157)   Hachured   OD 400
26125,19163
Ringfort   A circular area (max. diam. *c.* 60m) defined
by a low earthen bank (Wth 1.7m, int. H 0.15m, ext. H

4.8m) with external fosse (Wth 5.3m, ext. D *c.* 1.2m)
from N–E. No evidence of original entrance.
19:15   10-8-1990

258 RATHMORE (Clandonagh By.)
OS 28:1:5 (94,516)   '*Rath More*'   OD 400
22598,18226
Ringfort   A circular area (diam. *c.* 48m) defined by an
earthen bank (Wth *c.* 3.4m, int. H *c.* 0.7m, ext. H *c.*
1.4m) at E and S, and by a scarp at W. Remains of
fosse (Wth *c.* 2.9m) at E and S. No other visible
surface traces.
28:2   11-9-1991

259 RATHMORE (Clandonagh By.)
OS 28:1:6 (156,503)   Hachured   OD 300–400
22664,18214
Ringfort   A circular area (diam. *c.* 43m) defined by an
inner bank (Wth *c.* 2.7m, int. H *c.* 0.5m, ext. H *c.*
1.1m), intervening fosse (Wth *c.* 3.8m) and outer bank
(Wth *c.* 3m, int. H *c.* 1m, ext. H *c.* 0.4m). Possible
original entrance (Wth *c.* 4m) with causeway at W.
28:3   11-9-1991

260 RATHMORE (Stradbally By.)
OS 14:10:4 (243,182)   Hachured   OD 300–400
25666,19825
Ringfort   A circular area (diam. *c.* 45m) defined by a
bank (Wth *c.* 1.4m, int. H *c.* 1.5m, ext. H *c.* 1.9m), and
external fosse (Wth *c.* 2.8m) from NE–W. No evidence
of original entrance.
14:34   16-6-1990

261 RATHMOYLE
OS 24:9:1 (15,230)   Hachured   OD 400–500
24462,18582
Ringfort   Marked as an oval enclosure (max. dim. *c.*
44m NW–SE) on the 1906 ed. OS 6" map. Remains of
a flat-topped bank (H *c.* 1.7m) are visible at W and
NW. No evidence of fosse or original entrance. The N
section of the site has been destroyed as a result of the
construction of a golf clubhouse on it.
24:28   7-8-1990

262 RATHMOYLE
OS 24:9:2 (101,246)   Hachured   OD 400–500
24552,18601
Ringfort (possible, site)   Marked on the 1906 ed. OS
6" map as a trivallate enclosure, and as a univallate
circular enclosure (max. diam. 60m) on the current 25"
map. Apart from differential growth indicating the line
of the fosse (Wth *c.* 5.5m), no other surface traces
survive. Reference to a rath (O'Hanlon and O'Leary
1907, vol. 1, 156).
24:29   7-8-1990

263 RATHMOYLE
OS 24:9:5 (86,179) Hachured OD 500–600
24538,18530
Ringfort A circular area (diam. *c.* 27m) defined by an
earthen bank (Wth *c.* 2.6m, int. H *c.* 0.5m, ext. H *c.*
1.8m) and fosse (Wth *c.* 3.8m) at W. No evidence of
original entrance.
24:32   28-8-1990

264 RATHNAMANAGH
OS 13:2:5 (373, 474) *'Rathnamanagh'*
OD 300–400 24825,20125
Ringfort A large subcircular enclosure (diam. c. 90m
NW–SE) marked on the 1909 ed. OS 6" map.
Reference to a fort with deep fosses and level interior
(O'Hanlon and O'Leary 1907, vol. 1, 193). The site
has been reused and adapted as a motte and bailey (No.
916).
13:4(01)   25-7-1990

265 RATHSARAN GLEBE
OS 28:13:4 (7,58) Hachured OD 300–400
22511,17742
Ringfort A circular area (diam. *c.* 38.5m) defined by
an earthen bank (Wth *c.* 3.2m, int. H *c.* 0.9m, ext. H *c.*
2.1m) and external fosse (Wth *c.* 4.7m). No visible
evidence of original entrance.
28:54   30-9-1991

266 REDCASTLE
OS 17:2:1 (253,586) *'Red Castle Fort'*
OD 400–500 23728,19592
Ringfort A massive subcircular bivallate earthen
ringfort (max. ext. diam. *c.* 120m) defined by an inner
bank (Wth *c.* 3.7m), best preserved at S, an intervening
fosse (Wth *c.* 7.5m), an outer bank (Wth *c.* 9m) and an
outer fosse (Wth *c.* 4–5m, int. D *c.* 2.7m, ext. D *c.* 1m)
except at S. Site of possible tower house (No. 1005)
lies in the interior.
17:2(02)   31-8-1990

267 ROSSBAUN
OS 15:11:2 (557,268) Hachured OD 700–800
22101,19240
Ringfort The remains of a circular ringfort (C *c.* 50m
NW–NE) defined by an inner bank (Wth *c.* 2.9m, int.
H *c.* 0.3m, ext. H *c.* 1.4m), intervening fosse (Wth *c.*
3.4m) and outer bank (Wth *c.* 1.2m, ext. H *c.* 0.2m)
from NW–SE. Levelled from SE–NW.
15:15   13-9-1991

268 ROSSMORE (Clandonagh By.)
OS 27:12:3 (854,242) Hachured OD 300–400
22428,17936
Ringfort A circular area (diam. *c.* 45.7m) defined by
an earthen bank (Wth *c.* 2.4m, int. H *c.* 1.2m, ext. H *c.*

0.9m) and slight remains of an external fosse. Possible
original entrance at E.
27:17   7-10-1990

269 SHANAHOE
OS 23:7:4 (476,317) Hachured OD 300–400
23973,18670
Ringfort A circular area (diam. *c.* 30.5m) defined by a
bank (Wth *c.* 7m, int. H *c.* 1m, ext. H *c.* 2m) and
external fosse (Wth *c.* 6m). Possible original ramp
entrance at SSW.
23:13   21-10-1991

270 SRAH
OS 34:3:4 (484,511) Hachured OD 400–500
23016,17585
Ringfort A subcircular area (diam. *c.* 35m
SSW–NNE) defined by a low bank (Wth *c.* 2.8m)
except at NE. Evidence of fosse at W.
34:10(01)   8-10-1990

271 SRAH
OS 34:3:1 (514,546) Hachured OD 400–500
23047,17622
Ringfort A circular area (diam. *c.* 45m) defined by a
bank (Wth *c.* 3m, int. H *c.* 1.1m). No evidence of fosse
or original entrance.
34:12   30-6-1991

272 STOOAGH
OS 15:6:3 (432,450) Hachured OD 900–1000
21968,19431
Ringfort A circular area (diam. *c.* 33.4m) defined by
an earthen bank (Wth *c.* 3.1m, int. H *c.* 0.7m, ext. H *c.*
1.2m) with traces of an external fosse. Possible
original entrance at E.
15:7   13-9-1991

273 STOOAGH
OS 15:7:1 (472,407) Hachured OD 900–1000
22010,19386
Ringfort Visible on aerial photographs (GSI, S
530–1). A circular area (diam. *c.* 31m) defined by an
earthen bank (Wth *c.* 2.5m, int. H *c.* 0.7m, ext. H *c.*
1.3m) and external fosse (Wth *c.* 3.1m). Possible
original entrance at NE. A possible souterrain (No.
284) lies in NE quadrant of interior.
15:8(01)   13-9-1991

274 TIMOGUE
OS 19:5:5 (143,334) Hachured OD 300–400
25565,19344
Ringfort A circular area (diam. *c.* 17.4m) defined by
an inner bank (Wth *c.* 2.6m, int. H *c.* 0.5m, ext. H *c.*
0.35m) from S–N, with intervening fosse (Wth *c.* 5m)

Fig. 6—*Vickerstown (Dodd), ringfort* (**281**)

and outer bank (Wth *c.* 5.5m, int. H *c.* 0.35m, ext. H *c.* 0.65m) at NW and N. No evidence of original entrance.

19:8   20-5-1990

275 TINNACLOHY
OS 28:2:3 (394,537)   Hachured   OD 400–500
22915,18252
Ringfort   A subcircular area (dims. *c.* 37m N–S, *c.* 31.8m E–W) defined by an earthen bank (Wth *c.* 2.3m, int. H *c.* 0.7m, ext. H *c.* 1.5m), now very degraded. No other visible surface traces. Known as 'Skayhawn' or the 'rath of the bushes' (Carrigan 1905, vol. 2, 354).
28:8   11-9-1991

276 TINNACLOHY
OS 28:2:5 (356,499)   Hachured   OD 300–400
22875,18212
Ringfort   A circular area (diam. *c.* 39.4m) defined by an inner bank (Wth *c.* 3.1m, int. H *c.* 0.7m, ext. H *c.* 1.5m), intervening fosse (Wth *c.* 3.4m) and an outer bank (Wth *c.* 2.4m, int. H *c.* 1.3m, ext. H 0.9m) from NW–N.
28:9   12-9-1991

277 TINNAHINCH
OS 3:13:6 (156,3)   Hachured   OD 500   23613,20896
Ringfort   Situated on S face of E–W valley; a circular area (max. diam. *c.* 28m) defined by a bank (H 2–2.5m); no evidence of a fosse. Possible entrance at NE.
3:14   8-8-1990

278 TINNARAGH
OS 28:4:4 (756,509)   Hachured   OD 400–500
23297,18226
Ringfort   A circular area (diam. *c.* 27.3m) defined by an earthen bank (Wth *c.* 2.8m, int. H *c.* 0.6m, ext. H *c.* 1.3m) and slight evidence of an external fosse. Reference to a rath with a whitethorn bush known as 'the monument' or the 'Priest's Bush' here (O'Hanlon *et al.* 1914, vol. 2, 572–3).
28:17(01)   14-9-1991

279 TINTORE
OS 29:9:1 (8,302)   Hachured   OD 300–400
23484,18009
Ringfort   A circular area (diam. *c.* 28.5m) defined by an inner bank (Wth *c.* 2.8m, int. H *c.* 0.4m, ext. H *c.*

33

1.1m), an intervening fosse (Wth *c.* 3.4m) from NE–SE, and an outer bank (Wth *c.* 2.3m, int. H *c.* 0.9m, ext. H *c.* 0.3m) from NE–E.

29:15   14-8-1990

280 TULLACOMMON
OS 27:8:2 (840,452) Hachured OD 383
22410,18157
Ringfort A subcircular area (dims. *c.* 25.5m E–W, 20.7m N–S) defined by a bank (Wth *c.* 4.9m, ext. H *c.* 1.15m) from ESE–W, and by a scarp from W–NW. A wide external fosse (Wth *c.* 3.3m) survives from ESE–NW. No visible entrance.

27:10   7-11-1990

281 VICARSTOWN (DODD)
OS 14:4:3 (876,561) *'Dunrally'* OD 100–200
26330,20231
Ringfort A circular area (diam. *c.* 42m) defined by an inner bank (Wth *c.* 6.2m, int. H *c.* 1.65m, ext. H *c.*

1.5m) best preserved at W, an intervening deep flat-bottomed fosse (Wth *c.* 7m) and an outer bank (Wth *c.* 5.5m, int. H *c.* 1.1m, ext. H *c.* 4.5m). Entrance visible at E. Remains of modern house in E section of the interior. In the Annals of the Four Masters, the site is referred to under the date 'AD 860 (Comerford 1886, vol. 3, 376). In 1782 Henry Grattan purchased Moyanna estate and built a residence within the ringfort and planted gardens (O'Hanlon and O'Leary 1907, vol. 1, 291–3).

14:6(01)   12-5-1990

282 WATERCASTLE
OS 29:12:2 (784,271) Hachured OD 352
24304,17984
Ringfort A subcircular area (dims. *c.* 44.7m NW–SE, 37m NE–SW) defined by a bank (Wth *c.* 2.7m, int. H *c.* 0.8m, ext. H *c.* 1.4m) and external fosse (Wth *c.* 3.5m). Possible original entrance at NE.

29:37   13-8-1990

13. Souterrains

The term souterrain, derived from the French 'sous' (under) and 'terre' (ground), refers to a man-made cave. In its simplest form, it consists of a passage, sometimes of considerable length. More usually, the passage is divided into a series of chambers which are connected by tunnels or creepways barely large enough to allow a person through them. Two basic methods of construction were employed: the souterrain was either tunnelled into the rock or clay or, more commonly, the sides of an excavated trench were lined with stone and roofed with slabs.

Souterrains are mainly associated with ringforts and like them are dated to the Early Christian period. Generally, there is no surface evidence to indicate their presence and many come to light as a result of ploughing or subsidence. Some are indicated on the OS maps by the term 'cave'. From their design, it would appear that their primary function was that of refuge for people in times of trouble. The more simple forms may have just been used for storage of foodstuffs. No definite souterrains have been found to date in County Laois; included below are two possible sites.

283 BALLYCOLLA
OS 29:5:3 (161,441)   OD 300–400   23645,18158
Souterrain (possible)   Not marked on the 1841 or 1909 eds. OS 6" maps. A slight depression, in SE quadrant of ringfort (No. 143), may indicate the line of a souterrain.
19:18(02)   28-9-1990

284 STOOAGH
OS 15:7:1 (472,407)   OD 900–1000   22010,19386
Souterrain (possible)   Not marked on the 1841 or 1909 eds. OS 6" maps. A slight depression, visible in NE quadrant of ringfort (No. 273), may indicate the line of a souterrain.
15:8(02)   13-9-1991

14. Enclosures

It is often difficult to classify some archaeological earthworks because of their present condition. With the passing of time, monuments are altered and modified, trampled by cattle or simply denuded naturally, and without archaeological excavation it may be impossible to accurately categorize them. For the purposes of the inventory, such monuments are generally classified as enclosures, rectilinear enclosures and earthworks

The term 'enclosure' is used here to denote any earthwork enclosing a circular, oval or D-shaped space which cannot be more precisely identified. 'Enclosure (site)' refers to levelled sites and includes enclosures marked on the current OS 6-inch maps, as well as, cropmarks and monuments visible on aerial photographs. It is possible that a number of the enclosures may be badly defaced ringforts, while some of the cropmarks may be the remains of ring-barrows, henges or ringforts.

The internal diameter is given for upstanding monuments; monuments measured from the maps are given an external maximum diameter.

285 ACRAGAR
OS 8:10:1 (238,271)   Hachured   OD 200–300
24678,20549
Enclosure (site)   Hachured as a subcircular area (max. diam. *c.* 60m NNW–SSE) on the 1910 ed. OS 6" map with an extra element indicated at NW side, possibly a berm, and clipped by road at SW. The site has been levelled and no surface traces survive. Visible on aerial photographs (ACAP, V 300, 704–5) as tree-covered enclosure.
8:7   11-6-1990

286 AGHADREEN
OS   25:13:3   (163,83)   Hachured   OD 800
25595,18439
Enclosure (site)   Marked on the 1841 and 1909 eds. OS 6" map; a subcircular area (max. diam. *c.* 45m NE–SW). No visible surface traces.
25:31   23-8-1990

287 AGHNACROSS
OS 30:3:4 (484,516)   Indicated   OD 600–700
24960,18249
Enclosure   Indicated on the 1841 and 1908 eds. OS 6" maps. A circular area (diam. *c.* 39.2m) defined by an earthen bank (Wth *c.* 2.8m, int. H *c.* 1.2m, ext. H *c.* 1.6m) from SW–NE, and elsewhere by a scarp. No other visible surface traces.
30:15   18-6-1991

190 ANNAGH
OS 16:6:5 (329,377)   Hachured   OD 400–500
22835,19362
Enclosure   A circular area (diam. *c.* 18m) defined by a low earthen bank (Wth 2.3m, int. H *c.* 0.3m, ext. H *c.* 0.8m) at N and E, and elsewhere by a scarp.
16:12   22-7-1991

288 ARCHERSTOWN
OS 35:11:5 (593,222)   Indicated   OD 400–500
24109,17291
Enclosure   Part of a subcircular enclosure (C *c.* 100m SW–NNW) indicated on the 1908 ed. OS 6" map, and visible on aerial photographs (GSI, S 33–4; S 103–4).

It is defined by a scarp from S–SW, and by a bank (Wth *c.* 2.5m, ext. H *c.* 1m) from SW–NNW. An external fosse (Wth *c.* 3.8m) is present from SE–NNW. No other visible surface traces.
35:49   3-10-1990

289 ASHFIELD
OS 32:1:4 (8,462)   Indicated   OD 400–500
26408,18207
Enclosure   A subcircular area (diam. *c.* 27m SE–NW) defined by a low bank at W, and elsewhere by a scarp. Possible entrance at E. No evidence of fosse.
32:2   15-8-1990

290 BALLAGHMORE LOWER
OS 21:2:3 (428,600)   Indicated   OD 300–400
21968,18949
Enclosure   Marked on the 1841 ed. OS 6" map. A circular area (diam. *c.* 21.5m) defined by a bank (Wth *c.* 4.7m, int. H *c.* 0.8m, ext. H *c.* 0.8m). Possible original entrance (Wth *c.* 3.5m) at W. No evidence of fosse.
21:1   24-6-1991

291 BALLAGHMORE UPPER
OS 15:14:2 (319,88)   Indicated   OD 500–600
21852,19047
Enclosure   Marked on the 1841 and 1909 eds. OS 6" maps. A circular area (diam. *c.* 16m) defined by a bank (Wth *c.* 3m, int. H *c.* 0.3m, ext. H *c.* 1.5m) at S and W, and elsewhere by a scarp.
15:16   15-9-1991

292 BALLINLOUGH (Maryborough East By.)/
BALLYMADDOCK (Stradbally By.)
OS 13:8:6 (912,314)   OD 400–500   25396,19961
Enclosure (site)   Marked on the 1841 ed. OS 6" map as a subcircular enclosure (max. diam. *c.* 85m NW–SE). Cropmark of enclosure visible on aerial photographs (CUCAP, ATA 24; AYN 24). No visible surface traces.
13:39   31-5-1990

293 BALLINTLEA UPPER
OS 24:8:2 (794,436)   Hachured   OD 600–700
25282,18808
Enclosure (site) A roughly oval enclosure (max. dim. *c.* 70m NNW–SSE) marked on the 1841 and 1909 eds. 6" OS map. No visible surface traces.
24:27   21-10-1991

294 BALLYADAMS
OS 19:16:3 (852,118)   OD 200–300   26316,19123
Enclosure (site) Hachured on the 1841 ed. OS 6" map. Cropmark of subcircular enclosure and linear features (No. 677) visible on aerial photograph (CUCAP, BGN 69). Not visible on the ground.
19:29(01)   3-5-1990

295 BALLYBEG
OS 26:6:6 (409,316)   OD 200–300   26828,18697
Enclosure (site) Cropmark of oval enclosure visible on aerial photographs (GSI, S 137–8). Not visible on the ground.
26:8   5-7-1990

296 BALLYCARROLL (Maryborough East By.)
OS 13:8:5 (792,304)   OD 300–400   25269,19949
Enclosure (site) Cropmark of E half of subcircular enclosure visible on aerial photograph (CUCAP, AYN 26). Not visible on the ground.
13:36   31-5-1990

297 BALLYCARROLL (Maryborough East By.)
OS 13:12:2 (829,298)   OD 400–500   25308,19943
Enclosures (sites) Cropmark of subcircular enclosures visible on aerial photograph (CUCAP, AYN 29). Not visible on the ground.
13:49   31-5-1990

298 BALLYCARROLL (Maryborough East By.)
OS 13:12:6 (882,159)   Hachured   *'Cromwell's Lines'*
OD 600–700   25365,19797
Enclosure (site) Marked on the 1841 and 1909 eds. OS 6" maps as a circular trivallate enclosure (int. diam. *c.* 25m, max. diam. *c.* 80m). Now ploughed out. Vague outline visible in the grass colouring; possibly a ringfort.
13:54   8-7-1990

299 BALLYCARROLL (Portnahinch By.)
OS 9:2:2 (330,588)   OD 300–400   25748,20894
Enclosure (site) A subcircular enclosure with a possible mound is visible on aerial photographs (ACAP, V 300, 665–6). No visible surface traces.
9:3   24-7-1990

300 BALLYCLIDER
OS 13:11:2 (555,277)   Hachured   OD 300–400
25019,19919
Enclosure A circular raised area (diam. *c.* 18m) defined by a scarp (ext. H *c.* 0.8m). No evidence of fosse or original entrance.
13:47   22-5-1990

301 BALLYCOLLA
OS 29:5:2 (116,454)   Hachured   OD 300–400
23597,18171
Enclosure (site) Marked on the 1841 and 1906 eds. OS 6" maps as a circular enclosure (max. diam. *c.* 30m). Differential growth indicates the outline of the enclosure at N and NE. No other surface traces survive. Described as a platform-type enclosure (H 0.9m above surrounding ground level) (OPW file).
29:4   15-8-1990

302 BALLYCOOLAN
OS 19:15:1 (462,146)   Hachured   OD 700–800
25904,19148
Enclosure A raised circular area (max. diam. *c.* 30m) defined by a scarp. No indication of fosse or entrance.
19:11(08)   9-8-1990

303 BALLYCOOLID
OS 28:6:6 (419,345)   OD 300–400   22943,18050
Enclosure Marked as a subcircular enclosure (max. diam. *c.* 40m NW–SE) on the 1841 ed. OS 6" map. Remains of an earthen bank (Wth *c.* 2.4m, int. H *c.* 0.8m, ext. H *c.* 1.3m) survive from NW–NE. No other visible surface traces.
28:30   18-9-1991

304 BALLYCOOLID
OS 28:10:3 (386,260)   Hachured   OD 300–400
22909,17959
Enclosure (site) Marked on the 1841 and 1908 eds. OS 6" maps as a circular enclosure (max. diam. *c.* 30m). No visible surface traces.
28:44   29-9-1991

305 BALLYCOOLID
OS 28:10:3 (414,232)   Hachured   OD 200–300
22939,17930
Enclosure (site) Marked on the 1841 and 1908 eds. OS 6" maps as a subcircular enclosure (max. diam. *c.* 40m NNW–SSE). No visible surface traces.
28:45   27-9-1991

306 BALLYFOYLE
OS 26:11:5 (609,203)   OD 200–300   27040,18580
Enclosures (sites) Cropmarks of circular enclosures

visible on aerial photographs (CUCAP, BGN 56–7).
No visible surface traces.
26:14(01)   1-8-1990

307 BALLYHORAHAN
OS 16:3:4 (508,484)   Indicated   OD 500–600
23023,19477
Enclosure (possible)   Poorly preserved remains of a
possible circular enclosure (diam. *c.* 14m) defined by a
scarp (H *c.* 0.7m) from NE–SW. No other visible
surface traces.
16:6(01)   23-7-1991

308 BALLYKEALY
OS 35:10:1 (287,249)   Indicated   OD 500–600
23786,17316
Enclosure (site)   Indicated on the 1841 and 1908 eds.
OS 6" map; a subcircular enclosure (max. diam. *c.*
45m NE–SW). No visible surface traces.
35:44   22-9-1990

309 BALLYKEALY
OS 35:13:3 (218,140)   Indicated   OD 800–900
23715,17200
Enclosure   A circular area (diam. *c.* 48m) defined by a
scarp (H *c.* 1.2m). No other visible surface traces.
35:55   23-9-1990

310 BALLYKENNEEN LOWER
OS 2:14:2 (349,95)   OD 700–800   22840,20985
Enclosure (possible, site)   A subcircular enclosure is
visible on aerial photographs (ACAP, V 300, 724–5).
The area is now densely covered by forestry. Not
located.
2:16   29-5-1991

311 BALLYLUSK
OS 12:6:5 (367,350)   *'Kylealiss'*   OD 400–500
23844,19983
Enclosure   A subcircular area (dims. *c.* 70m E–W, *c.*
67m N–S) defined by a low bank at N, and elsewhere
by a scarp. The fosse (Wth *c.* 4m) is present at W. A
children's burial ground (No. 876) is visible in SW
quadrant of interior. No evidence of original entrance.
12:5 (01)   9-8-1990

312 BALLYLYNAN
OS 26:1:4 (48,528)   OD 200–300   26444,18917
Enclosure (site)   Cropmark of a large subcircular
enclosure visible on aerial photographs (CUCAP, BGN
65–6). Not visible on the ground.
26:1   4-8-1990

313 BALLYLYNAN
OS 26:1:4 (48,504)   OD 200–300   26445,18892
Enclosure (site)   Cropmark of circular enclosure
visible on aerial photograph (CUCAP, BGN 65). Not
visible on the ground.
26:2   4-8-1990

314 BALLYLYNAN
OS 26:1:5 (91,511)   OD 200–300   26489,18900
Enclosure (site)   Cropmark of subcircular enclosure
visible on aerial photograph (CUCAP, BGN 64). Not
visible on the ground.
26:4   4-8-1990

315 BALLYLYNAN
OS 26:1:6 (164,466)   OD 200–300   26567,18853
Enclosure (site)   Cropmark of subcircular enclosure
visible on aerial photograph (CUCAP, BGN 63). Not
visible on the ground.
26:5   4-8-1990

316 BALLYMADDOCK (Stradbally By.)
OS 14:9:2 (102,276)   Hachured   OD 300–400
25516,19922
Enclosure (site)   The N portion of an enclosure is
marked on the 1841 ed. OS 6" map; on the 1909 ed.
hachures indicate the line of a bank (C *c.* 40m) from
W–NW. No visible surface traces.
14:25   1-6-1990

317 BALLYMULLEN
OS 24:13:4 (52,26)   Hachured   OD 400–500
24503,18368
Enclosure (site)   Marked on the 1841 and 1909 eds.
OS 6" map; a semicircular enclosure (max. diam. *c.*
30m NW–SE). Described as a small C-shaped
enclosure with gap on E side (OPW file). No visible
surface traces.
24:39   7-8-1990

318 BALLYNOWLAN
OS 14:10:1 (280,234)   OD 200–300   25704,19880
Enclosure (site)   Marked on the 1841 ed. OS 6" map
as a subcircular enclosure (max. diam. *c.* 55m E–W).
Traces of bank visible at NNE and NE as differential
growth.
14:29   16-6-1990

319 BALLYRIDER
OS 14:6:5 (371,322)   Indicated   OD 200–300
25800,19974
Enclosure   Part of a circular enclosure (diam. *c.* 65m)
defined by an earthen bank (Wth *c.* 3.4m, int. H *c.* 1.4m,
ext. H *c.* 1.6m) from S–N. No other visible surface traces.
14:18   12-7-1990

320 BALLYROAN (Cullenagh By.)
OS 18:13:6 (170,10)   Hachured   OD 300–400
24622,18993
Enclosure   A circular enclosure visible on the aerial photographs (GSI, S 145–6; 164–5). Slight remains of bank (H *c.* 0.2m) visible.
18:24   14-6-1990

321 BALLYROAN (Cullenagh By.)
OS 24:1:2 (136,590)   OD 300–400   24586,18964
Enclosure (site)   Cropmark of subcircular enclosure with annexe and linear features (No. 679) visible on aerial photographs (CUCAP, AJQ 55–6). Not visible on the ground.
24:1(01)   27-8-1990

322 BALLYROAN (Cullenagh By.)
OS 24:2:1 (287,550)   Hachured   OD 500–600
24745,18924
Enclosure   Marked on the 1841 and 1909 eds. OS 6" maps; a circular enclosure (max. diam. *c.* 40m). No visible surface traces.
24:8(03)   31-7-1990

323 BALLYROAN (Maryborough East By.)
OS 13:10:2 (380,274)   Hachured   OD 300–400
24834,19913
Enclosure (site)   Marked on the 1841 and 1909 eds. OS 6" maps; a subcircular enclosure (max. diam. *c.* 60m NE–SW). No visible surface traces.
13:44   11-6-1990

324 BALLYRUIN
OS 18:14:1 (259,91)   OD 400–500   24715,19079
Enclosure   A subcircular enclosure (diam. *c.* 19.7m N–S) visible on aerial photographs (GSI, S 164–5). Faint traces of bank present at NE, SE, S and W. No other visible surface traces.
18:25   8-5-1990

325 BARNABOY
OS 15:11:1 (470,252)   Hachured   OD 800–900
22010,19222
Enclosure   Remains of a circular enclosure (C *c.* 31m) defined by a low bank (Wth *c.* 2.9m, int. H *c.* 0.7m, ext. H *c.* 1.2m) from S–NW. No other visible surface traces.
15:11   13-9-1991

326 BARNABOY
OS 15:11:1 (474,269)   OD 800–900   22014,19240
Enclosure   Marked on the 1841 ed. OS 6" map. Depicted on 25" map as a subcircular enclosure (diam. *c.* 21m N–S). Remains of a low bank (Wth *c.* 3m, H *c.* 0.2m) survive at W and N. No other visible surface traces.
15:12   13-9-1991

327 BARRACKQUARTER or ROSS
OS 35:9:2 (107,269)   Hachured   OD 400–500
23596,17335
Enclosure   A subcircular area (diam. *c.* 48m) defined by a low bank (Wth *c.* 2m, int. H *c.* 0.1m, ext. H *c.* 0.7m). Several small cattle gaps visible in bank but the original entrance is not identifiable. No evidence of fosse.
35:39   4-10-1990

328 BARRADOOS
OS 6:2:4 (260,465)   Indicated   OD 900–1000
22749,20735
Enclosure (possible, site)   In upland area where forest has been felled. Not marked on the 1841 ed. OS 6" map but appears on 1888 and 1910 eds. as a subcircular enclosure (max. diam. *c.* 30m N–S). Not located; it appears to have been destroyed by afforestation.
6:4   14-6-1991

329 BARROWHOUSE
OS 20:14:6 (417,31)   OD 200–300   26832,19037
Enclosure (site)   Cropmark of subcircular enclosure visible on aerial photographs (CUCAP, BDH 62–3). Not visible on the ground.
20:4   10-7-1990

330 BARROWHOUSE
OS 20:15:4 (504,10)   Hachured   OD 100–200
26924,19014
Enclosure (possible, site)   Marked on the 1888 and 1909 eds. OS 6" maps; S portion of possible enclosure (C *c.* 20m SE–SW). No visible surface traces.
20:8   15-7-1990

331 BAUNOGEMEELY
OS 24:12:6 (872,227)   OD 700–800   25367,18589
Enclosure (site)   Cropmark of oval enclosure visible on aerial photographs (GSI, S 143–4). Not visible on the ground.
24:38   28-8-1990

332 BECKFIELD/TINNACLOHY
OS 28:2:6 (437,521)   Hachured   OD 400–500
22960,18236
Enclosure (site)   Marked on the 1841 and 1908 eds. OS 6" map. Cropmark of circular enclosure visible on aerial photographs (GSI, S 76–7). Shown on 25" map as a bivallate enclosure (max. diam. *c.* 60m N–S). No visible surface traces.
28:10   12-9-1991

333 BELLEGROVE
OS   9:6:6   (434,319)   Hachured   OD 200
25859,20611

Enclosure (site) Not marked on the 1841 ed. OS 6" map but hachured as a small oval enclosure (dim. *c.* 20m NW–SE) on subsequent eds. Site levelled; no visible surface traces. Possibly a landscape feature.
9:13   24-7-1990

334 BLACKHILLS
OS 23:12:2 (772,241)   OD 300–400   24286,18593
Enclosure (site) A circular enclosure visible on aerial photograph (BKS, 601465). A slight rise in the ground surface indicates the site. No other visible surface traces.
23:28   17-8-1990

335 BOHERARD
OS 22:16:2 (797,77)   Hachured   OD 400–500   23338,18411
Enclosure A circular area (diam. *c.* 27.5m) defined by a low scarp (H *c.* 1.3m). No other visible surface traces.
22:26   19-6-1991

336 BOHERARD
OS 22:16:3 (863,119)   OD 300–400   23408,18455
Enclosure (site) Cropmark of circular enclosure visible on aerial photographs (GSI, S 74–5; S 110–11). Not visible on the ground.
22:28   19-6-1991

337 BOLEY (Ballyadams By.)
OS 25:8:4 (739,369)   OD 300–400   26200,18747
Enclosures (sites) Cropmark of subcircular conjoined enclosures visible on aerial photograph (CUCAP, ATA 23). Not visible on the ground.
25:21   23-8-1990

338 BOLEY UPPER
OS 23:10:2 (330,239)   OD 300–400   23819,18586
Enclosures (site) Cropmark of subcircular enclosures and linear features (No. 680) visible on aerial photographs (CUCAP, APA 30–1). Not visible on the ground.
23:20(01)   21-10-1991

339 BOLEY UPPER
OS 23:10:6 (390,193)   OD 400–500   23883,18538
Enclosure A subcircular enclosure marked on the 1890 ed. OS 6" map. Remains of a scarp at NE and E may represent the line of the enclosure. No other visible surface traces.
23:23   17-8-1990

340 BOLEY UPPER
OS 23:14:2 (351,78)   OD 200–300   23843,18417

Enclosure Marked on the 1841 ed. OS 6" map only. A circular area (max. diam. *c.* 40m N–S) defined by a low barely discernible bank (H *c.* 0.3m). No other visible surface traces.
23:34   17-8-1990

341 BORRIS GREAT
OS 13:6:5 (366,371)   OD 300–400   24819,20015
Enclosure (site) Marked on the 1841 ed. OS 6" map as a subcircular enclosure (max. diam. *c.* 70m E–W). Cropmark on aerial photograph (CUCAP, AVR 2). Not visible on the ground.
13:23   23-7-1990

342 BRISHA
OS 6:16:4 (766,27)   OD 1200–1300   23287,20278
Enclosure (possible) Not marked on any ed. of OS 6" maps but visible on aerial photographs (ACAP, V 300, 776–7) as a possible subcircular enclosure. Situated in afforested area on mountain top. Not located and may be levelled.
6:10   14-6-1991

343 BUNLACKEN
OS 35:9:3 (189,277)   OD 500–700   23682,17345
Enclosures (site) Circular enclosures and field banks (No. 104) are visible on aerial photographs (GSI, S 35–6; S 101–2). Not visible on the ground.
35:40(01)   22-9-1990

344 CAPARD
OS 7:6:1 (245,415)   OD 900–1000   23708,20691
Enclosure Visible on aerial photographs (ACAP, V 300, 736–7) as an embanked enclosure. The area surrounding the site is planted with young trees and is impenetrable with scrub, briars and gorse.
7:4   12-9-1990

345 CAPPALINNAN
OS 33:8:3 (912,404)   Indicated   OD 400–500   22493,17467
Enclosure Not marked on the 1841 ed. OS 6" map. A circular area (diam. *c.* 54.2m) defined by an earthen bank (Wth *c.* 2.4m, int. H *c.* 0.8m, ext. H *c.* 1.1m).
33:7   15-8-1991

**346 CAPPANARROW/KILLEEN
      (Upperwoods By.)**
OS 11:13:3 (221,94)   Hachured   OD 500–600   22717,19702
Enclosure (site) Marked on the 1841 and 1909 eds. OS 6" maps; a subcircular enclosure (max. diam. *c.* 110m NE–SW). No visible surface traces.
11:10   25-7-1991

Fig. 7—*Capard, enclosure* (**344**)

347 CARDTOWN
OS 11:10:5 (320,207)   Hachured   OD 500–600
22821,19823

Enclosure (site)   Marked on the 1841 and 1909 eds.
OS 6" maps; a subcircular enclosure (max. diam. *c.*
50m E–W). No visible surface traces.
11:9   25-7-1991

348 CARRIGEEN (Stradbally By.)
        Kilmurry ED
OS 14:5:5 (104,367)   Hachured   OD 400–500
25517,20019

Enclosure   A circular area (C *c.* 17m NW–NE)
defined by a bank (Wth *c.* 1m, ext. H *c.* 1.5m). No
other visible surface traces. Original entrance not
identifiable.
14:9   22-5-1990

349 CASHEL (Cullenagh By.)
OS 18:10:4 (238,156)   Hachured   OD 300–400
24692,19147

Enclosure (site)   Marked on the 1841 and 1909 eds.
OS 6" maps; a subcircular enclosure (diam. *c.*
37.8m). A slight rise in the ground level indicates the site.
18:19   8-5-1990

350 CASTLECUFFE
OS 2:14:1 (308,146)   Hachured   OD 500–600
22796,21038

Enclosure   An irregularly shaped platform (dims. *c.*
33m E–W, *c.* 26m N–S) situated on top of S side of
valley, and defined by a scarp (max. H 1m) from

E–W, and at NW by a slight scarp with remains of
stone wall on top.
2:15   31-10-1990

351 CASTLECUFFE
OS 6:2:1 (231,563)   OD 800–900   22717,20838

Enclosure (possible, site)   Not marked on any ed. OS
6" map but appears on aerial photograph (ACAP, V
300, 723–4) as a large enclosure. No visible surface
traces.
6:3   14-6-1991

352 CASTLEDURROW DEMESNE
OS 35:2:3 (435,601)   Hachured   OD 300–400
23939,17690

Enclosure (site)   Marked on the 1841 and 1908 eds.
OS 6" maps; a subcircular enclosure (max. diam. *c.*
40m NE–SW). No visible surface traces.
35:6   22-9-1990

353 CASTLETOWN (Clandonagh By.)
        Donaghmore ED
OS 28:10:1 (305,269)   Hachured   OD 300–400
22823,17968

Enclosure (site)   Marked on the 1841 and 1908 eds.
OS 6" maps; a roughly oval enclosure (max. dim. *c.*
30m NW–SE). Visible on aerial photographs (GSI, S
76–7). No visible surface traces.
28:43   29-9-1991

354 CLASHBOY
OS 19:13:5 (115,5)   Hachured   OD 400–500
25539,18996

Enclosure (site)   Marked on the 1841 and 1909 eds. OS 6" maps; a roughly oval enclosure (max. dim. *c.* 40m NW–SE). No visible surface traces.
19:17   4-5-1990

355 CLOGHOGE
OS 30:6:5 (337,320)   Hachured   OD 500–600
24807,18041
Enclosure (site)   Marked on the 1841 and 1908 eds. OS 6" map; a circular enclosure (max. diam. *c.* 50m). No visible surface traces.
30:22   21-6-1991

356 CLONARD or CAPPALOUGHLIN
OS 17:10:4 (245,214)   Hachured   OD 400–500
23723,19199
Enclosure (possible)   Possible subcircular enclosure visible on aerial photographs (GSI, S 161–2). Remains of low bank (Wth *c.* 2.5m, int. H *c.* 0.3m, ext. H *c.* 0.7m) survive from NW–NE. No other visible surface traces.
17:9   28-8-1990

357 CLONBANE
OS 23:2:5 (339,516)   Hachured   OD 200–300
23825,18879
Enclosure   A circular area (diam. *c.* 22m) defined by a low bank (Wth *c.* 3.2m, int. H *c.* 0.5m, ext. H *c.* 0.9m) with slight evidence of fosse.
23:1   15-8-1990

358 CLONBROCK
OS 31:15:2 (583,125)   Hachured   OD 500–600
26044,17847
Enclosure (site)   A small circular enclosure (max. diam. *c.* 15m) is hachured from N–SW on the 1906 ed. OS 6" map only. No visible surface traces.
31:7   2-7-1990

359 CLONCULLANE
OS 24:2:2 (359,555)   Hachured   OD 600–700
24821,18929
Enclosure (site)   Marked on the 1841 and 1909 eds. OS 6" maps; a D-shaped enclosure (max. dims. *c.* 60m NE–SW, 40m N–S). The site was bounded by slight banks and overgrown with scrub (OPW file). No visible surface traces.
24:9   27-8-1990

360 CLONCULLANE
OS 24:2:5 (364,520)   Hachured   OD 600–700
24827,18893
Enclosure   Marked on the 1841 and 1909 eds. OS 6" maps; a subcircular enclosure (max. diam. *c.* 80m N–S). Only faint traces of bank visible at S. No other

surface traces survive.
24:11   31-7-1990

361 CLONKEEN (Maryborough West By.)
OS 12:16:6 (870,3)   Hachured   OD 300–400
24379,19623
Enclosure   Not marked on the 1841 ed. OS 6" map. A subcircular area (dims. *c.* 16m E–W, 10.5m N–S) defined by a scarp (H *c.* 0.5–1m). No evidence of fosse.
12:7   9-8-1990

362 CLONLAHY CORPORATION LAND
OS 21:16:2 (816,129)   Hachured   OD 400–500
22383,18456
Enclosure   A subcircular area (dims. *c.* 37.5m NE–SW, *c.* 25.7m NW–SE) defined by a scarp (H *c.* 1.4m). No evidence of fosse or original entrance.
21:25   25-6-1991

363 CLONOGHIL (Upperwoods By.)
OS 16:5:4 (16,320)   Hachured   OD 400–500
22505,19299
Enclosure (site)   Marked on the 1841 and 1909 eds. OS 6" maps; a circular enclosure (max. diam. *c.* 40m). No visible surface traces.
16:10   24-7-1991

364 CLONOGHIL (Upperwoods By.)/ ROSSNACLONAGH OUTSIDE
OS 16:9:2 (91,301)   Hachured   OD 400–500
22584,19280
Enclosure   A circular area (diam. *c.* 35.5m) defined by a low bank (Wth *c.* 3.4m, int. H *c.* 0.5m, ext. H *c.* 1.4m) with traces of a fosse visible.
16:11   22-7-1991

365 CLOPOOK
OS 19:14:2 (366,114)   OD 500–600   25802,19114
Enclosure (possible, site)   Cropmark of part of enclosure visible on aerial photograph (CUCAP, AYP 62). Not visible on the ground.
19:20   16-8-1990

366 CLOPOOK
OS 19:14:6 (390,38)   OD 400–500   25829,19034
Enclosure (site)   A subcircular enclosure visible on aerial photographs (GSI, S 168–9). Not visible on the ground.
19:23   16-8-1990

367 COLT
OS 17:16:6 (849,38)   OD 300–400   24363,19019
Enclosure (site)   Cropmark of oval enclosure visible

on aerial photographs (GSI, S 163–4). Not visible on the ground.
17:21   28-8-1990

368 COLT
OS 18:13:1 (54,141) Hachured OD 300–400
24498,19130
Enclosure A semicircular enclosure hachured from SE–NW on 1909 ed. OS 6" map. Portion of a low bank (C *c.* 36.5m S–W) and external fosse survive at S and W. No other visible surface traces.
18:22   15-5-1990

369 CONES
OS 7:5:4 (68,343) OD 900–1000 23522,20614
Enclosure (possible) Possible enclosure visible on aerial photographs (ACAP, V 300, 737–8). Situated in valley bottom, close to river, in heavily wooded area. Site not reached because of inaccessibility due to tree-planting.
7:3   12-9-1990

370 COOLANOWLE
OS 26:13:5 (139,73) Hachured OD 200–300
26545,18437
Enclosure (site) Marked on the 1888 and 1909 eds. OS 6" map; a subcircular area (max. diam. *c.* 40m N–S). The site has been levelled but a circular area defined by vegetation change is visible on the ground.
26:17   24-7-1990

371 COOLANOWLE
OS 26:13:3 (188,132) Hachured OD 200–300
26596,18500
Enclosure (site) Marked on the 1888 and 1909 eds. OS 6" map; a circular area (diam. *c.* 35m). Now indicated by a slight rise in the ground level. No other visible surface traces.
26:18   23-7-1990

372 COOLNABOUL WEST
OS 28:14:6 (434,59) Indicated OD 300–400
22962,17748
Enclosure (site) Marked on the 1841 ed. OS 6" map; indicated on 1908 ed. as an irregular enclosure (max. dims. *c.* 30m N–S, 25m E–W). No visible surface traces.
28:58   6-9-1991

373 COOLNABOUL WEST
OS 28:14:6 (435,47) Hachured OD 300–400
22963,17735
Enclosure Marked on the 1841 and 1908 eds. OS 6" maps; a circular area (max. diam. *c.* 40m). Slight evidence of bank at S. No other visible surface traces.
28:59   6-9-1991

374 COOLTEDERY
OS 5:9:2 (130,274) Hachured OD 200–300
25533,21200
Enclosure (site) In a low-lying boggy area. Marked on the 1910 ed. OS 6" map as a circular enclosure (max. diam. *c.* 20m). No visible surface traces.
5:5   15-5-1990

375 CORBALLY (Tinnahinch By.) Meelick ED
OS 3:14:5 (350,4) OD 600–700 23818,20898
Enclosure Situated in upland area. Hachured as a subcircular enclosure (max. diam. *c.* 40m E–W) on the 1841 ed. OS 6" map. All that now remains of this site, at ground level, is a semicircular area defined by a scarp at N. Smaller embanked circle (diam. 2m) situated in N portion of site.
3:20   8-8-1990

376 CORRAUN
OS 22:12:4 (725,224) OD 300–400 23261,18565
Enclosure (site) Cropmark of circular enclosure visible on aerial photographs (GSI, S 150–1). Not visible on the ground.
22:19(21)   12-8-1991

377 CREELAGH
OS 34:2:1 (262,597) OD 300–400 22781,17674
Enclosures (site) Cropmark of subcircular enclosures visible on aerial photographs (GSI, S 39–9). Not visible on the ground.
34:6   1-7-1991

378 CREMORGAN
OS 18:11:3 (631,251) OD 500–600 25106,19251
Enclosure Marked on the 1841 ed. OS 6" map as a subcircular enclosure (max. diam. *c.* 60m N–S). A circular area defined by an earthen bank (Wth *c.* 2.5m) survives from S–NE. No other visible surface traces.
18:20   14-6-1990

379 CRUBEEN
OS 18:14:4 (274,32) OD 400–500 24731,19016
Enclosure (site) Cropmark of subcircular enclosure visible on aerial photograph (CUCAP, AYN 37). Not visible on the ground.
18:27   8-5-1990

380 CRUBEEN
OS 18:14:5 (336,42) OD 600–700 24797,19028
Enclosure (site) Part of a subcircular enclosure is visible from *c.* SW–E on aerial photographs (GSI, S 164–5). Not visible on the ground.
18:28   9-5-1990

381 CRUBEEN
OS 24:2:1 (295,598) Hachured OD 500–600
24754,18974
Enclosure (site) Marked on the 1841 and 1909 eds.
OS 6" maps; an irregularly shaped enclosure (max.
dims. *c.* 45m N–S, 40m E–W). No visible surface
traces.
24:7   27-8-1990

382 CRUBEEN
OS 24:2:1 (306,572) OD 500–600 24765,18947
Enclosure (possible, site) Cropmark of circular
enclosure visible on aerial photographs (GSI, S
145–6). No visible surface traces.
24:8(04)   27-8-1990

383 CUDDAGH
OS 16:16:6 (881,20) Indicated OD 400–500
23421,18991
Enclosure A circular area (diam. *c.* 44m) defined by a
low earthen bank (Wth *c.* 3.4m, int. H *c.* 0.3m, ext. H
c. 0.8m). No other visible surface traces.
16:27   17-9-1991

384 CULLENAGH (Cullenagh By.)
OS 18:14:2 (374,79) Hachured OD 600–700
24836,19067
Enclosure (site) Marked on the 1841 and 1909 eds.
OS 6" maps; a subcircular enclosure (max. diam. *c.*
60m NE–SW). No visible surface traces.
18:26   14-6-1990

385 CULLENAGH (Cullenagh By.)
OS 18:15:1 (499,110) Hachured OD 500–600
24968,19101
Enclosure (site) A subcircular enclosure (max. diam.
c. 40m E–W) marked on the 1909 ed. OS 6" map. No
visible surface traces.
18:29   14-6-1990

386 DAIRYHILL
OS 23:13:4 (38,10) OD 400–500 23513,18341
Enclosure Marked on the 1841 ed. OS 6" map only. A
subcircular area (dims. *c.* 79m E–W, *c.* 58m N–S)
defined by a scarp (H *c.* 0.9m). No evidence of fosse
or original entrance. Possibly a tree plantation.
23:30   19-8-1990

387 DAIRYHILL
OS 23:13:4 (71,10) OD 400–500 23548,18342
Enclosure (site) Cropmark of enclosure visible on
aerial photographs (GSI, S 73–4). Not visible on the
ground.
23:31   17-8-1990

388 DERRY (Maryborough East By.)/
KILCOLMANBANE/RATHLEAGUE
OS 13:15:5 (558,2) Indicated OD 300–500
25025,19628
Enclosure Visible on aerial photographs (GSI, S
224–5). A circular area (diam. *c.* 35m) defined by an
earthen bank (Wth *c.* 3.2m, int. H *c.* 0.9m, ext. H *c.*
1.4m). Scant remains of fosse survive at SW. No other
visible surface traces.
13:58   8-7-1990

389 DERRY (Tinnahinch By.) Meelick ED
OS 3:9:6 (227,180) OD 300–400 23686,21083
Enclosure (site) Evidence of subcircular enclosure on
aerial photographs (GSI, N 404–5). No visible surface
traces other than bend in field fence to N of site.
3:9   1-8-1990

390 DERRYGARRAN
OS 13:3:4 (467,466) Hachured OD 300–400
24924,20116
Enclosure A circular enclosure (max. diam. *c.* 20m)
marked on the 1909 ed. OS 6" map. It is defined by a
bank (ext. H 1.3m) at N and E. The site is overgrown
with trees and has been used as a dump.
13:6   18-6-1990

391 DERRYGARRAN
OS 13:7:1 (492,444) Hachured OD 300–400
24951,20095
Enclosure (site) Marked on the 1841 and 1909 eds.
OS 6" maps; a semicircular enclosure (max. diam. *c.*
40m NW–SE). No visible surface traces.
13:24   23-7-1990

392 DERRYKEARN
OS 23:3:6 (620,480) *'Raheendonnell'* OD 300–400
24123,18844
Enclosure (site) Marked on the 1841 and 1909 eds.
OS 6" maps; a roughly circular area (max. diam. *c.* 48m
N–S) with building shown at NE. Although site was
bulldozed in more recent times and a modern bunga-
low now occupies the greater part of it, the outline of a
bank and external fosse, defined by a strong growth of
nettles, is discernible running from SW–N. Tradition
of church formerly located within interior.
23:7(01)   27-5-1994

393 DERRYKEARN
OS 23:4:4 (717,525) Hachured OD 300–400
24225,18892
Enclosure A subcircular flat-topped low platform
(dims. *c.* 95m NW–SE, 51m NE–SW) defined by a
scarp (H *c.* 1–2.5m) with an external fosse from
SW–NE (Wth *c.* 3.5m, D *c.* 1m). Possible original
entrance at NNE.
23:10   16-8-1990

394 DERRYKEARN
OS 23:4:4 (720,504)   OD 300–400   24228,18870
Enclosure (site)   Cropmark of circular enclosure visible on aerial photographs (GSI, S 147–8). Not visible on the ground.
23:11   14-9-1990

395 DERRYNASEERA
OS 16:6:6 (446,325)   OD 300–400   22959,19309
Enclosure (possible, site)   Cropmark of oval-shaped enclosure visible on aerial photographs (GSI, S 158–9). Not visible on the ground.
16:13   22-7-1991

396 DONAGHMORE
OS 28:5:3 (184,400)   Hachured   OD 300–400
22694,18105
Enclosure (site)   Marked on the 1841 and 1908 eds. OS 6" maps; a subcircular enclosure (max. diam. *c.* 35m NE–SW). No visible surface traces.
28:20   16-9-1991

397 DOOARY
OS 24:2:5 (369,468)   Hachured   OD 500–600
24833,18838
Enclosure   A circular area (diam. *c.* 25m) defined by a low bank and barely visible fosse.
24:12   27-8-1990

398 DOOARY
OS 24:6:2 (380,448)   Hachured   OD 500–600
24845,18817
Enclosure   A large subcircular enclosure (dims. *c.* 100m E–W, 90m N–S) defined by a scarp (ext. H *c.* 1m) from S–N. The E half of the site is incorporated into a field fence. No evidence of fosse or original entrance.
24:20   31-7-1990

399 DOON (Maryborough West By.)
OS 17:15:3 (663,85)   Hachured   OD 300–400
24166,19067
Enclosure (site)   Marked on the 1841 and 1910 eds. OS 6" map; a circular enclosure (max. diam. *c.* 45m). No visible surface traces.
17:15   14-9-1990

400   DROUGHILL
OS 5:5:4 (71,330)   OD 200–300   25471,21258
Enclosure   Situated on a slight rise in a low-lying area E of the River Barrow. A dished area (max. diam. *c.* 30m N–S) surrounded by a possible degraded bank, most pronounced at S, defines the site. The N side is cut into the natural rise. Visible on aerial photograph (CUCAP, BDL 3); possibly a ringfort.
5:1   28-5-1990

401 DUNACLEGGAN
OS 28:5:4 (70,374)   Hachured   OD 300–400
22574,18077
Enclosure   A raised circular area (diam. *c.* 19.3m) defined by a scarp (H *c.* 1.2m). No other visible surface traces.
28:21   16-9-1991

402 DURROW TOWNPARKS
OS 35:2:3 (443,550)   Indicated   OD 300–400
23947,17635
Enclosure (site)   Marked on the 1841 ed. OS 6" map, and indicated on the 1908 ed. as a subcircular enclosure (max. diam. *c.* 45m NE–SW). No visible surface traces.
35:7   22-9-1990

403 DYSART
OS 13:15:3 (675,146)   Hachured   OD 400–500
25147,19782
Enclosure (site)   Marked on the 1841 ed. OS 6" map. Depicted as a subcircular enclosure (max. diam. *c.* 55m NE–SW) running from S–NE on the 1909 ed. A field wall curves around the site from NE–S. No visible surface traces.
13:57   31-5-1990

404 FALLOWBEG MIDDLE
OS 25:2:2 (316,577)   Hachured   OD 400–500
25752,18962
Enclosure (site)   Marked on the 1841 and 1909 eds. OS 6" map; a circular enclosure (max. diam. *c.* 40m). No visible surface traces.
25:4   28-8-1990

405 FISHERSTOWN
OS 9:12:5 (844,200)   OD 100–200   26294,20490
Enclosure (possible, site)   Possible enclosure not marked on any ed. of OS 6" maps but visible as oval cropmark on aerial photograph (GSI, N 344). No visible surface traces.
9:19   24-7-1990

406 GARRANBAUN
OS 15:3:6 (635,490)   Hachured   OD 600–700
22181,19476
Enclosure   A circular area (diam. *c.* 24.3m) defined by a low bank (Wth *c.* 3.2m, int. H *c.* 0.4m, ext. H *c.* 0.6m). No other visible surface traces.
15:5   12-9-1991

407 GARRANBAUN
OS 15:3:6 (640,464)   Indicated   OD 600–700
22187,19448
Enclosure (site)   Marked on the 1841 and 1909 eds.

OS 6" maps; a subcircular enclosure (max. diam. *c.* 45m E–W). No visible surface traces.

15:6   12-9-1991

408 GARRENDENNY
OS 36:7:3 (633,442)   OD 800–900   26100,17542
Enclosure (site) Cropmark of subcircular enclosure visible on aerial photographs (GSI, S 25–6). Not visible on the ground.
36:3   5-9-1990

409 GARROUGH
OS 32:15:1 (515,108)   OD 100–200   26948,17839
Enclosure (site) Circular enclosure visible on aerial photographs (GSI, S 22–3). Not visible on the ground.
32:21   15-8-1990

410 GARRYGLASS
OS 24:7:3 (685,387)   OD 500–600   25168,18755
Enclosure (possible, site) Cropmark of subcircular enclosure visible on aerial photographs (GSI, S 143–4). Not visible on the ground.
24:25   28-8-1990

411 GARRYGLASS
OS 24:8:1 (743,447)   Hachured   OD 500–600
25228,18820
Enclosure (site) Marked on the 1841 and 1909 eds. OS 6" map; a subcircular enclosure (max. dims. *c.* 80m NW–SE, *c.* 55m E–W). No visible surface traces.
24:26   21-10-1991

412 GORTAROATA
OS 16:13:4 (51,21)   OD 300–400   22545,18984
Enclosure (site) A circular enclosure visible on aerial photographs (GSI, S 156–7). Reference to a moat here (Carrigan 1905, vol. 2, 133–4). No visible surface traces.
16:21   16-9-1991

413 GORTEENNAHILLA
OS 35:13:3 (193,110)   OD 800–900   23689,17169
Enclosure (site) A subcircular enclosure visible on aerial photographs (GSI, S 101–2). Not visible on the ground.
35:56   23-9-1990

414 GORTEENNAMEALE/MOHER EAST
OS 11:2:5 (359,483)   Hachured   OD 900–1000
22859,20115
Enclosure A circular area (diam. *c.* 54m) defined by a bank (Wth *c.* 4.3m, ext. H *c.* 1.8m), except from NE–SE, and external fosse (Wth *c.* 6m) best preserved at N and NE. No evidence of original entrance.
11:2   25-7-1991

415 GORTNALEE
OS 28:5:1 (20,404)   Hachured   OD 300–400
22521,18108
Enclosure (site) Marked on the 1841 ed. OS 6" map as a circular enclosure. On the 1908 ed., hachures indicate the site from SE–W (C *c.* 50m). No visible surface traces.
28:19   13-9-1991

416 GRAIGUEADRISLY
OS 33:16:2 (828,121)   OD 400–500   22408,17168
Enclosure Indicated as an irregular enclosure (max. diam. *c.* 60m NW–SE) on the 1841 ed. OS 6" map. Remains of an earthen bank (Wth *c.* 1.4m, int. H *c.* 0.3m, ext. H *c.* 0.5m) at E and S.
33:18   17-8-1991

417 GRAIGUEARD
OS 34:2:6 (440,475)   OD 400–500   22970,17547
Enclosure (site) A circular enclosure visible on aerial photographs (GSI, S 38–9). Not visible on the ground.
34:8   9-10-1990

418 GRAIGUEAVOICE
OS 35:5:6 (182,364)   Hachured   OD 300–400
23675,17437
Enclosure A circular area (diam. *c.* 36m) defined by a scarp (ext. H *c.* 1m). No visible evidence of fosse or original entrance.
35:24   27-9-1990

419 GRAIGUEAVOICE
OS 35:5:6 (218,334)   Hachured   OD 400–500
23712,17405
Enclosure (site) The arc of an enclosure (C *c.* 50m NW–E) is marked on the 1908 ed. OS 6" map. No visible surface traces.
35:27   20-9-1990

420 GRAIGUEAVOICE
OS 35:6:1 (255,379)   Indicated   OD 300–400
23751,17453
Enclosure (site) A subcircular enclosure (max. dims. *c.* 35m NE–SW, 20m NW–SE) marked on the 1908 ed. OS 6" map. The site is indicated by a slight rise in the ground. No other visible surface traces.
35:28   27-9-1990

421 GRANGE (Ballyadams By.)
OS 26:15:6 (625,42)   OD 100–200   27059,18410
Enclosure (site) Cropmark of subcircular enclosure visible on aerial photographs (CUCAP, BDH 56, 58). Not visible on the ground.
26:23   3-8-1990

422 GRANGE (Ballyadams By.)
OS 26:15:6 (644,42)   OD 100–200   27078,18410
Enclosure (site)   Cropmark of subcircular enclosure visible on aerial photograph (CUCAP, BDH 56). Not visible on the ground.
26:24   3-8-1990

423 GRANGE MORE
OS 22:13:3 (218,151)   Hachured   OD 400–500
22726,18483
Enclosure   A circular area (diam. *c.* 21m) defined by a low bank (Wth *c.* 2.7m, int. H *c.* 0.3m, ext. H *c.* 0.8m) from NW–NE with slight evidence of fosse at N. The S half of the site is incorporated into the townland boundary field fence.
22:15   4-8-1991

424 GRANGE MORE
OS 22:10:4 (305,197)   Hachured   OD 400–500
22818,18532
Enclosure (site)   Marked on the 1909 ed. OS 6" map; a circular enclosure (diam. *c.* 10m). No visible surface traces.
22:16   4-8-1991

425 GRANGE UPPER
OS 13:16:6 (867,30)   OD 500–600   25351,19660
Enclosure   Marked on the 1841 ed. OS 6" map; a subcircular enclosure (max. diam. *c.* 60m NE–SW). Defined by a low bank (Wth *c.* 1.9m, int. H *c.* 0.9m, ext. H *c.* 0.5m) at W, N and E. Slight evidence of fosse.
13:66   5-6-1990

426 GREATHEATH (Maryborough East By.)
OS 13:4:1 (731,530)   Hachured   OD 300–400
25202,20188
Enclosure (site)   Marked on the 1841 and 1909 eds. OS 6" maps; a roughly circular enclosure (max. diam. *c.* 15m). No visible surface traces.
13:8   24-5-1990

427 GREATHEATH (Maryborough East By.)
OS 13:4:6 (855,502)   Hachured   OD 300–400
25334,20159
Enclosure (site)   Marked on the 1841 and 1909 eds. OS 6" maps; a subcircular enclosure (max. diam. 20m). No visible surface traces.
13:17   24-5-1990

428 GRENAN
OS 29:16:1 (766,87)   OD 400–500   24287,17791
Enclosure (site)   Cropmark of subcircular enclosure visible on aerial photograph (CUCAP, AJQ 53). Not visible on the ground.
29:47   8-7-1990

429 GRENAN
OS 35:4:4 (747,495)   OD 200–300   24270,17581
Enclosure (possible, site)   Cropmark of circular enclosure visible on aerial photograph (CUCAP, BDL 14). Not visible on the ground.
35:14   9-10-1990

430 GRENAN
OS 35:4:4 (766,514)   OD 200–300   24289,17601
Enclosure (site)   Cropmark of subcircular enclosure visible on aerial photograph (CUCAP, AJQ 49). Not visible on the ground.
35:15   10-10-1990

431 GRENAN
OS 35:4:5 (793,482)   OD 200–300   24318,17568
Enclosure (site)   Cropmarks of circular enclosure and part of a subrectangular enclosure (No. 581) visible on aerial photograph (CUCAP, ASW 45). Not visible on the ground.
35:16(01)   10-10-1994

432 GRENAN
OS 35:8:2 (808,421)   OD 200–300   24334,17503
Enclosure (site)   Cropmark of enclosure visible on aerial photograph (CUCAP, AJQ 51). Not visible on the ground.
35:38   11-10-1990

433 GUILEEN (Stradbally By.)
     Luggacurren ED
OS 19:14:2 (331,130)   Hachured   OD 500–600
25766,19130
Enclosure (site)   Marked on the 1841 and 1909 eds. OS 6" maps; a subcircular enclosure (max. diam. *c.* 60m NW–SE). No visible surface traces.
19:19   16-8-1990

434 HARRISTOWN (Clandonagh By.)
OS 34:1:1 (26,534)   OD 300–400   22532,17604
Enclosure (site)   Cropmark of subcircular enclosure visible on aerial photographs (GSI, S 39–40). Not visible on the ground.
34:2(02)   1-7-1991

435 HARRISTOWN (Slievemargy By.)
OS 32:15:1 (533,130)   OD 100–200   26967,17862
Enclosure (site)   Marked on the 1841 ed. OS 6" map as a subcircular enclosure. On the 1908 ed., a curving field boundary (C *c.* 40m) indicates the line of the site from E–S. No visible surface traces.
32:22   15-8-1990

436 HAYWOOD DEMESNE
OS 30:6:1 (239,385)   OD 500–600   24703,18109
Enclosure (site)   Cropmark of subcircular enclosure visible on aerial photographs (GSI, S 69–70). Not visible on the ground.
30:20   21-6-1991

437 INCH (Ballyadams By.)
OS 25:8:1 (715,387)   Hachured   OD 400–500
26175,18765
Enclosure   Marked on the 1909 ed. OS 6" map; a subcircular enclosure (max. dims. *c.* 60m E–W, 50m N–S). Faint traces of the bank survive at SE and S, and the fosse at NW. No other visible surface traces.
25:19   21-8-1990

438 INCHACOOLY
OS 5:12:5 (777,227)   Hachured   OD 200–300
26217,21157
Enclosure   Situated on W bank of the Black River. A subcircular enclosure (max. ext. diam. *c.* 30m N–S) defined by an inner bank (max. Wth *c.* 5.5m, ext. H 1.3m) best preserved from S–NNW, an intervening fosse (Wth at base 1.3m), and an outer bank which is only barely discernible from S–W but more pronounced at N. The site is badly overgrown, full of badger holes, and drainage spoil lies between it and the river. Possibly a ringfort.
5:9   12-6-1990

439 IRONMILLS or KILRUSH
OS 30:14:3 (445,109)   Hachured   OD 700–800
24923,17820
Enclosure   A circular area (diam. *c.* 28.7m) defined by a scarp (H *c.* 1.2m).
30:31   20-6-1991

440 KEELOGE SOUTH
OS 22:1:1 (29,568)   OD 300–400   22522,18921
Enclosure (site)   Enclosure visible on aerial photographs (GSI, S 153–4). Not visible on the ground.
22:1   5-8-1991

441 KILBREEDY
OS 28:11:1 (518,270)   Hachured   OD 300–400
23048,17971
Enclosure (site)   Marked on the 1908 ed. OS 6" map; a circular enclosure (max. diam. *c.* 70m). No visible surface traces.
28:47   29-9-1991

442 KILCOKE
OS 28:2:1 (264,554)   Hachured   OD 400–500
22777,18269

Enclosure (site)   Marked on the 1841 and 1908 eds. OS 6" maps; a subcircular enclosure (max. diam. *c.* 50m N–S). No visible surface traces.
28:4   11-9-1991

443 KILCOLMANBANE
OS 18:3:5 (558,473)   Hachured   OD 500–600
25026,19485
Enclosure   A circular area (diam. *c.* 25.8m) defined by a bank (Wth *c.* 2.5m, int. H *c.* 0.2m, ext. H *c.* 0.8m) and slight remains of a fosse. No evidence of original entrance.
18:3   12-6-1990

444 KILDELLIG
OS 22:14:5 (384,9)   Hachured   OD 400–500
22903,18334
Enclosure   A subcircular area (dims. *c.* 42.3m E–W, 33m N–S) defined by a scarp (H *c.* 0.8m). No evidence of fosse or original entrance.
22:21   8-8-1991

445 KILLADOOLEY DP
OS 27:4:6 (907,508)   OD 300–400   22481,18217
Enclosure (possible, site)   Cropmark of subcircular enclosure visible on aerial photographs (GSI, S 77–8). Not visible on the ground.
27:6   7-11-1990

446 KILLEANY
OS 23:10:2 (311,256)   OD 300–400   23799,18604
Enclosure (site)   Cropmark of subcircular enclosure visible on aerial photographs (CUCAP, APA 30–1). Not visible on the ground. A ringfort (No. 228) lies immediately to NW.
23:19(02)   21-10-1991

447 KILLEEN (Ballyadams By.)
OS 26:15:1 (481,79)   OD 200–300   26906,18448
Enclosure (site)   Cropmark of circular enclosure visible on aerial photographs (GSI, S 60–1). Not visible on the ground.
26:21   3-8-1990

448 KILLEEN (Ballyadams By.)
OS 26:15:4 (465,66)   OD 200–300   26889,18434
Enclosures (site)   Cropmark of a circular and irregular enclosure visible on aerial photographs (CUCAP, BGN 59–60). Not visible on the ground.
26:22   3-8-1990

449 KILLEEN (Stradbally By.)
OS 14:6:1 (254,404)   Hachured   OD 300–400
25675,20058

Enclosure Marked on the 1909 ed. OS 6" map as a subcircular enclosure (max. diam. *c.* 55m NE–SW). A bank (ext. H *c.* 1.8m) is visible from W–N. Old buildings run along the E side of site. No visible surface traces of fosse or original entrance.
14:13   22-5-1990

450 KILLEEN (Stradbally By.)
OS 14:6:1 (270,413) Hachured OD 200–300
25691,20069
Enclosure The arc of an enclosure (C *c.* 40m S–W) marked on the 1909 ed. OS 6" map is defined by a low bank (Wth *c.* 4.5m, int. H *c.* 0.1m, ext. H *c.* 0.4m). No other visible surface traces.
14:14   22-5-1990

451 KILLEEN (Stradbally By.)
OS 14:6:2 (325,453) OD 200–300 25750,20111
Enclosure (site) Cropmark of circular enclosure visible on aerial photograph (CUCAP, AYN 20). Not visible on the ground.
14:15   15-6-1990

452 KILMANMAN
OS 2:7:5 (540,332) OD 300–400 23039,21237
Enclosure (site) Circular cropmark, to NW of church (No. 767), visible on aerial photographs (CUCAP, ASU 98–9). Not visible on the ground.
2:2(05)   6-9-1990

453 KILMURRY
OS 14:1:3 (191,578) Hachured OD 200–300
25607,20242
Enclosure (site) Not marked on the 1841 ed. OS 6" map; a subcircular enclosure (max. diam. *c.* 20m NW–SE) on the 1909 ed. No visible surface traces.
14:2   15-6-1990

454 KILRORY
OS 14:6:5 (314,356) OD 200–300 25739,20009
Enclosures (site) Cropmark of two subcircular enclosures, one of which is marked on the 1841 ed. OS 6" map (C *c.* 50m SE–W), visible on aerial photographs (CUCAP, AYN 21–2). No visible surface traces.
14:17   15-6-1990

455 KNOCKAHAW
OS 27:14:6 (439,56) Hachured OD 500–600
21992,17735
Enclosure (site) Marked on the 1841 and 1907 eds. OS 6" maps; a circular area (max. diam. *c.* 40m). No visible surface traces.
27:18   7-10-1990

456 KNOCKARDAGANNON NORTH
OS 27:15:1 (515,89) Hachured OD 500–600
22072,17770
Enclosure A circular area (diam. *c.* 45m) defined by a low earthen bank (Wth *c.* 1.5m, max. H *c.* 0.5m), and a stone wall at SW. No other visible surface traces.
27:21   9-11-1990

457 KNOCKARDAGANNON SOUTH
OS 27:15:4 (512,33) Hachured OD 400–500
22069,17712
Enclosure (site) Marked on the 1841 and 1907 eds. OS 6" map; a circular area (max. diam. *c.* 36m). No visible surface traces.
27:20   7-10-1990

458 KNOCKARDAGUR
OS 30:3:5 (574,519) OD 800–900 25055,18254
Enclosure (site) Part of a large subcircular enclosure visible on aerial photographs (GSI, S 67–8). Not visible on the ground.
30:16   18-6-1991

459 KNOCKBAUN
OS 24:16:3 (904,97) OD 900–1000 25402,18452
Enclosure (site) An oval enclosure visible on aerial photographs (GSI, S 66–7). Not visible on the ground.
24:49(01)   19-7-1991

460 KNOCKBAUN
OS 24:16:6 (898,44) OD 900–1000 25396,18395
Enclosure A circular area (max. diam. *c.* 53m) defined by an inner bank (Wth *c.* 3m, int. H *c.* 0.15m, ext. H 0.6m), a shallow intervening fosse and an outer bank (Wth 1.3m, int. H *c.* 0.1m, ext. H *c.* 0.45m) except at S. It is cut by a field boundary at S and NNW. No trace of original entrance. This site is visible on aerial photographs (GSI, S 66–7).
24:54   19-7-1991

461 KNOCKNAGRALLY or KILLENNY BEG
OS 35:2:5 (316,501) OD 300–400 23814,17582
Enclosure (site) Cropmark of subcircular enclosure visible on aerial photographs (CUCAP, BDL 17; BGN 83). Not visible on the ground.
35:9   9-10-1990

462 KYLE (Clandonagh By.)
OS 34:9:4 (29,166) Hachured OD 500–600
22539,17217
Enclosure A subcircular area (dims. 48m E–W, 25.7m N–W) defined by a scarp (H *c.* 1.3m). No other visible surface traces.
34:24   3-7-1991

463 KYLETALESHA
OS 13:1:3 (200,594)   OD 200–300   24641,20249
Enclosure (site) Not marked on the 1841 or 1909 eds.
OS 6" maps. A D-shaped enclosure visible on aerial
photographs (GSI, N 230–1). No visible surface traces.
13:1   21-7-1990

464 KYLETILLOGE/OLDGLASS
OS 29:9:4 (51,154)   Indicated   OD 200–300
23532,17854
Enclosure (possible, site) Part of a circular enclosure
is visible on aerial photographs (GSI, S 35–6). No
visible surface traces.
29:28   13-9-1990

465 LACKEY
OS 15:15:2 (548,133)   Indicated   OD 500–600
22093,19097
Enclosure A subcircular area (dims. 25.7m N–S, 23m
E–W) defined by a scarp at E, and elsewhere by an
earthen bank (Wth *c.* 3.4m, int. H *c.* 0.2m, ext. H *c.*
0.8m). Slight evidence of fosse.
15:20   15-9-1991

466 LARRAGAN
OS 2:10:3 (458,281)   Hachured   OD 300–400
22954,21183
Enclosure A circular enclosure (max. diam. *c.* 40m)
marked on the 1910 ed. OS 6" map. The site has been
levelled but is visible as a cropmark on aerial
photographs (ACAP, V 300, 709–10). Possibly a
bivallate ringfort.
2:9   6-9-1990

467 LISBIGNEY
OS 29:8:6 (911,336)   Hachured   OD 300–500
24438,18054
Enclosure (site) Marked on the 1841 and 1906 eds.
OS 6" maps; a subcircular enclosure (max. diam. *c.*
60m N–S). No visible surface traces.
29:26   14-8-1990

468 LISBIGNEY
OS 30:9:2 (90,241)   Hachured   OD 300–400
24547,17955
Enclosure Marked on the 1908 ed. OS 6" map as a subcircular enclosure (max. diam. *c.* 50m NE–SW) which
has been quarried into at S. Remains of an earthen
bank (Wth *c.* 3.5m, int. H *c.* 0.5m, ext. H *c.* 1.1m)
survive from W–E. No other visible surface traces.
30:25   20-6-1991

469 LISDUFF
OS 27:14:6 (454,4)   Hachured   OD 400–500
22008,17681

Enclosure (site) Marked on the 1841 and 1907 eds.
OS 6" maps; a semicircular enclosure (C *c.* 30m
NW–SE). No visible surface traces.
27:19   7-10-1990

470 LISMURRAGHA
OS 33:7:2 (609,443)   Hachured   OD 400–500
22173,17505
Enclosure A subcircular area (dims. *c.* 38m N–S, 24m
E–W) defined by a scarp (H *c.* 1.2m). No other visible
surface traces.
33:5   14-8-1991

471 LISNAGOMMON
OS 24:14:3 (397,112)   Hachured   OD 600–700
24866,18462
Enclosure (site) Marked on the 1841 and 1909 eds.
OS 6" map; a subcircular enclosure (max. diam. *c.*
40m NW–SE, 30m NE–SW). No visible surface traces.
24:44   21-10-1991

472 LONGFORD
OS 16:2:2 (311,585)   Hachured   OD 400–500
22814,19582
Enclosure (site) Marked on the 1909 ed. OS 6" map;
a subcircular enclosure (max. diam. *c.* 40m NE–SW).
No visible surface traces.
16:5   23-7-1991

473 LOUGHTEEOG
OS 18:8:3 (862,435)   Hachured   OD 400–500
25347,19448
Enclosure (site) Marked on the 1841 and 1909 eds.
OS 6" maps; a subcircular enclosure (max. diam. *c.*
60m NE–SW). A road cut through the site at NNE and
SE. No visible surface traces.
18:13   12-6-1990

474 LOWRAN
OS 22:3:4 (510,483)   Hachured   OD 300–400
23031,18836
Enclosure A circular enclosure (diam. *c.* 27.6m) defined
by a low earthen bank (Wth *c.* 3.7m, int. H *c.* 0.7m, ext.
H *c.* 0.9m). No evidence of fosse or original entrance.
22:8   5-8-1991

475 LUGGACURREN
OS 25:2:3 (432,600)   'The Dun of Luggacurren'
OD 500–600   25874,18988
Enclosure A subcircular area (diam. 30m N–S) defined
by an earth and stone bank (Wth *c.* 3.5m, int. H *c.*
0.5m, ext. H *c.* 1.75m) at SW and W, and elsewhere by
a scarp. A shallow external fosse (Wth *c.* 2m) survives
from SW–N. No evidence of original entrance.
25:5(01)   28-8-1990

476 LUGGACURREN
OS 25:6:6 (415,347)   OD 700–800 25858,18720
Enclosure (site) Cropmark of subcircular enclosure visible on aerial photographs (GSI, S 141–2). Differential growth indicates the enclosing element at E and W. No other visible surface traces.
25:16   19-7-1990

477 MAIDENHEAD
OS 26:13:4 (38,45)   Hachured OD 500–600
26439,18406
Enclosure A subcircular area (diam. 19.8m N–S) defined by a low earthen bank (Wth *c*. 2.2m, int. H *c*. 0.2m, ext. H *c*. 1.05m), best preserved at W.
26:16   5-7-1990

478 MAYO
OS 36:4:1 (704,548)   OD 700–800 26174,17655
Enclosure (site) Cropmark of enclosure visible on aerial photographs (GSI, S 25–6). Not visible on the ground. A possible cairn (No. 61) lay to NE.
36:1(01)   5-9-1990

479 MIDDLEMOUNT or BALLYVOGHLAUN
OS 28:15:3 (667,109) Hachured OD 200–300
23207,17803
Enclosure (site) Marked on the 1841 and 1908 eds. OS 6" maps; a subcircular enclosure (max. dims. *c*. 70m NW–SE, 50m E–W). No visible surface traces.
28:64   4-9-1991

480 MOAT
OS 30:2:6 (408,508)   Hachured OD 500–600
24880,18240
Enclosure An oval area (dims. *c*. 25.2m E–W, 20.7m N–S) defined by a scarp (H *c*. 1.3m). No other visible surface traces.
30:13   18-6-1991

481 MONAVEA
OS 36:8:1 (750,436)   OD 800–900 26224,17538
Enclosure (site) A subcircular enclosure visible on aerial photographs (GSI, S 25–6). Not visible on the ground.
36:4   16-11-1990

482 MORETT
OS 9:13:5 (88,52)   Hachured OD 200–300
25497,20326
Enclosure (site) A circular enclosure (max. diam. *c*. 50m) is hachured on all eds. of OS 6" maps. Site now levelled. No visible surface traces.
9:23   20-7-1990

483 MORETT
OS 14:1:1 (20,583)   Indicated   OD 300–400
25426,20245
Enclosure A subcircular enclosure (dims. *c*. 27.8m N–S, *c*. 21.5m E–W) defined by a scarp (H *c*. 1.2m) from NE–NW. No evidence of fosse or original entrance.
14:1   15-6-1990

484 MOUNTEAGLE
OS 24:1:4 (61,502)   OD 300–400 24508,18871
Enclosure (site) Cropmark of subcircular enclosure visible on aerial photographs (GSI, S 184–5). Not visible on the ground.
24:4   8-8-1990

485 MOUNTEAGLE
OS 24:5:1 (56,402)   OD 300–400 24503,18765
Enclosure (site) Cropmark of subcircular enclosure visible on aerial photograph (CUCAP, AJQ 54). Not visible on the ground.
24:18   27-8-1990

486 MOUNTFEAD
OS 17:15:5 (541,4)   Hachured OD 300–400
24038,18980
Enclosure (site) Marked on the 1841 and 1909 eds. OS 6" map; a large subcircular enclosure (max. diam. *c*. 115m). Defined by a scarp (H *c*. 1m) from NW–NE, otherwise no visible surface traces.
17:16/23:3*   14-9-1990

487 NEWTOWN (Clarmallagh By.)
OS 35:1:3 (159,557)   Hachured OD 300–400
23648,17640
Enclosure (site) Marked on the 1841 and 1908 eds. OS 6" maps; a circular area (max. diam. *c*. 42m). No visible surface traces.
35:3   22-9-1990

488 NEWTOWN (Clarmallagh By.)
OS 35:5:3 (181,424)   OD 300–400 23672,17500
Enclosure (site) Cropmark of subcircular enclosure and linear features (No. 681) visible on aerial photograph (CUCAP, BGN 79). Not visible on the ground.
35:18(01)   10-10-1990

489 NEWTOWN (Stradbally By.)
OS 14:13:3 (226,123)   *'Rathmore'* OD 300–400
25648,19761
Enclosure (site) Marked on the 1841 and 1909 eds. OS 6" maps; an irregular enclosure (max. dims. *c*. 60m NW–SE, 50m E–W). No visible surface traces.
14:37   16-6-1990

Fig. 8—*Park Upper, enclosure sites* (**493**)

490 NEWTOWN or SKIRK
OS 21:16:2 (776,114)   Hachured   OD 500–600
22341,18439
Enclosure   The S portion of an enclosure (C *c.* 35m
E–SW) marked on the 1909 ed. OS 6" map is defined
by a low bank (Wth *c.* 1.7m, int. H *c.* 0.7m, ext. H *c.*
0.6m). No evidence of fosse or original entrance.
21:22   25-6-1991

491 OLDGLASS DP
OS 28:11:3 (670,235)   Hachured   OD 400–500
23209,17936
Enclosure   The S portion of an enclosure (C *c.* 45m
SE–SW) marked on the 1908 ed. OS 6" map is defined
by a low bank (Wth *c.* 1.8m, int. H *c.* 0.3m, ext. H *c.*
0.9m).
28:48   30-9-1991

492 OLDTOWN (Maryborough West By.)
OS 17:8:1 (759,406)   OD 300–400   24264,19407
Enclosure (site)   An oval enclosure is visible on aerial
photographs (GSI, S 226–7). Not visible on the
ground. Possible field system (No. 112) to N and NE.
17:8(01)   28-8-1990

493 PARK UPPER
OS 14:9:5 (100,170)   Hachured   OD 400–500
25515,19810
Enclosures (sites)   Cropmark of subcircular
enclosures, one of which is marked on the 1909 ed. OS
6" map (diam. *c.* 30m N–S), visible on aerial
photographs (CUCAP, AIF 74–75). No visible surface
traces. Linear features (No. 682) run to NE.
14:27(01)   6-6-1990

494 PARKBEG
OS 1:11:4 (497,194)   Hachured   OD 400–500
23964,21740
Enclosure (site)   Marked on the 1888 and 1909 eds.
OS 6" maps; an irregular enclosure (max. dim. *c.* 60m
ENE–WSW). No visible surface traces.
1:1   13-8-1990

495 PARKNAHOWN
OS 34:8:6 (881,310)   OD 300–400   23437,17378
Enclosures (site)   Cropmark of subcircular conjoined
enclosures visible on aerial photograph (CUCAP, BDL
30). Not visible on the ground.
34:23   25-9-1990

496 PARKNAHOWN
OS 34:12:2 (823,283)   OD 300–400   23376,17348
Enclosure (site)   Cropmark of part of subcircular enclosure visible on aerial photograph (CUCAP, ASW 49). Not visible on the ground.
34:27   26-9-1990

497 POWELSTOWN
OS 18:4:5 (788,458)   Hachured   OD 300–400 25269,19472
Enclosure (site)   Marked on the 1841 ed. OS 6" map as a circular enclosure; on the 1909 ed., hachures indicate the site from NE–S (C *c*. 60m). No visible surface traces.
18:5   4-5-1990

498 POWELSTOWN
OS 18:4:5 (788,482)   OD 400–500   25269,19497
Enclosure (site)   Cropmark of D-shaped enclosure visible on aerial photograph (CUCAP, AYN 36). Not visible on the ground.
18:6   4-5-1990

499 RAGGETTSTOWN
OS 30:1:2 (150,564)   OD 500–600   24607,18297
Enclosure   Marked on the 1841 ed. OS 6" map. An irregularly shaped enclosure (dim. 41m E–W) defined by a scarp from S–NW. The cropmark of a fosse (Wth *c*. 4m) is visible at E.
30:3   7-8-1990

500 RAHEEN (Maryborough East By.)
OS 13:8:6 (893,350)   OD 500–600   25376,19999
Enclosure (site)   Marked on the 1841 ed. OS 6" map; a roughly oval-shaped enclosure (max. dim. *c*. 50m E–W). Cropmark visible on aerial photographs (CUCAP, ATA 25; AYN 25). Not visible on the ground.
13:37   31-5-1990

501 RAHEEN (Maryborough East By.)
OS 13:8:6 (916,362)   Indicated   OD 600–700 25399,20012
Enclosure (site)   Marked on the 1909 ed. OS 6" map; an irregular enclosure (max. dim. *c*. 55m E–W). No visible surface traces.
13:38   10-6-1990

502 RAHEENANISKA
OS 14:7:1 (532,435)   OD 200–300   25968,20094
Enclosure (site)   Cropmark of circular enclosure visible on aerial photograph (CUCAP, AYN 11). Not visible on the ground.
14:20   15-6-1990

503 RAHEENANISKY
OS 18:4:3 (891,564)   OD 400–500   25377,19584
Enclosure (site)   Cropmark of subcircular enclosure visible on aerial photographs (CUCAP, AYN 33–4). Not visible on the ground.
18:4   4-5-1990

504 RAHEENANISKY
OS 18:4:6 (874,515)   Hachured   OD 400–500 25359,19533
Enclosure (site)   Marked on the 1841 ed. OS 6" map as a large irregular enclosure. On the 1909 ed., only the S half (max. dim. *c*. 50m E–W) is hachured. No visible surface traces. According to local information, this was an orchard.
18:9   4-5-1990

505 RAHEENDUFF (Stradbally By.)
OS 19:1:2 (84,543)   Hachured   OD 300–400 25501,19564
Enclosure   A subcircular enclosure (max. diam. *c*. 45m) marked on the 1909 ed. OS 6" map. It is defined by a bank at SW. No other visible surface traces.
19:1   15-7-1990

506 RAHEENLEAGH
OS 35:1:5 (103,480)   OD 300–400   23589,17558
Enclosure (site)   Cropmark of circular enclosure visible on aerial photographs (CUCAP, BDL 21–2). Not visible on the ground.
35:82   23-9-1990

507 RAHEENLEAGH
OS 35:1:5 (91,467)   OD 300–400   23577,17545
Enclosure (site)   Cropmark of circular enclosure visible on aerial photographs (GSI, S 35–6). Not visible on the ground.
35:83   23-9-1990

508 RAHEENNAHOWN
OS 25:3:1 (518,549)   OD 500–600   25965,18934
Enclosure (site)   Cropmark of subcircular enclosure visible on aerial photographs (GSI, S 169–70; S 141–2). Not visible on the ground.
25:7   23-8-1990

509 RAHEENNAHOWN
OS 25:3:2 (572,603)   OD 300–400   26021,18992
Enclosure (site)   Cropmark of oval enclosure visible on aerial photographs (GSI, S 169–70). Not visible on the ground.
25:8   23-8-1990

510 RAHIN

OS 25:4:3 (877,540)   OD 300   26344,18929

Enclosure (site) Cropmark of part of subcircular enclosure visible on aerial photograph (CUCAP, BGN 67). Not visible on the ground.

25:34   23-8-1990

511 RALISH

OS 24:13:6 (170,48)   OD 500   24628,18392

Enclosure (site) A circular enclosure visible on aerial photographs (GSI, S 145–6). Not visible on the ground.

24:43   28-8-1990

512 RATHCOFFEY

OS 3:9:4 (31,186)   'Raheen Fort'   OD 300–400
23479,21088

Enclosure (site) Situated on E–W ridge; marked on the 1910 ed. OS 6" map as a subcircular area (max. diam. *c.* 30m WNW–ESE). The site is now completely levelled with only cropmark of fosse visible at N (in suitable conditions).

3:7   8-8-1990

513 RATHCREA

OS 14:3:4 (485,468)   OD 200–300   25919,20128

Enclosure (site) An oval enclosure marked on the 1841 ed. OS 6" map. The area of the site is indicated by a hollow (dim. 44m E–W). No other visible surface traces.

14:5   13-6-1990

514 RATHCREA

OS 14:7:1 (500,451)   OD 200–300   25934,20111

Enclosure (site) Cropmark of circular enclosure visible on aerial photograph (CUCAP, AYN 14). Not visible on the ground.

14:19   15-6-1990

515 RATHDOWNEY

OS 28:14:2 (310,141)   OD 300–400   22829,17833

Enclosure (site) Not marked on the 1841 or 1908 eds. OS 6" maps. 135m NE of Rathdowney Protestant church was a circular flat-topped enclosure (diam. 22.5–27m, H *c.* 2.43m). It was levelled in 1840 and five cart loads of human bones were removed from it; possible site of ancient church (No. 792) (Carrigan 1905, vol. 2, 339–40). No visible surface traces.

28:55(03)   30-9-1991

516 RATHLEAGUE

OS 13:15:5 (558,2)   Hachured   OD 300–500
25025,19628

Enclosure Visible on aerial photographs (GSI, S 224–5). A circular area (diam. *c.* 35m) defined by an earthen bank (Wth *c.* 3.2m, int. H *c.* 0.9m, ext. H *c.* 1.4m). Scant remains of fosse at SW. No other visible surface traces.

13:58/18:1*   8-7-1990

517 RATHLEASH

OS 5:13:6 (166,20)   Hachured   OD 300–400
25573,20933

Enclosure (site) Marked on the 1841 and 1910 eds. OS 6" maps; a subcircular area (max. diam. *c.* 70m N–S). No visible surface traces apart from a slight depression in the area of the site. Visible as cropmark on aerial photographs (GSI, N 411–12).

5:13   15-5-1990

518 RATHMOYLE

OS 24:9:5 (93,200)   Hachured   OD 500–600
24545,18553

Enclosure (site) Marked on the 1841 and 1909 eds. OS 6" maps; a subcircular area (max. dims. 50m NW–SE, 40m NE–SW). No visible surface traces.

24:31   28-8-1990

519 RATHNALEUGH

OS 27:8:1 (714,421)   OD 300–400   22279,18123

Enclosure (site) Cropmark of enclosure visible on aerial photographs (GSI, S 78–9). Not visible on the ground.

27:9   7-11-1990

520 RATHPIPER SOUTH

OS 28:14:6 (433,33)   Hachured   OD 300–400
22961,17720

Enclosure The W half of an enclosure (C *c.* 75m SW–N) is marked on the 1908 ed. OS 6" map. Remains of an earthen bank (Wth *c.* 1.8m, int. H *c.* 0.5m, ext. H *c.* 0.9m) survive. There was a castle (No. 1004) in the interior at N.

28:60(02)   6-9-1991

521 RATHTILLIG

OS 32:2:4 (261,456)   Hachured   OD 200–300
26676,18203

Enclosure A circular area (diam. *c.* 28m) defined by a scarp (H *c.* 0.8m). No other visible surface traces.

32:6   14-8-1990

522 RINN

OS 3:15:3 (633,131)   Hachured   OD 200–300
24115,21035

Enclosure (site) Shown as a subcircular enclosure (diam. *c.* 30m NW–SE) on OS 6" maps. Site has been quarried out and back-filled.

3:19   1-8-1990

Fig. 9—*Scrub and Glenmacolla, enclosure site* (**530**)

523 ROSSBAUN
OS 15:7:5 (591,352) Hachured OD 900–1000
22136,19329
Enclosure (site) Marked on the 1841 and 1909 eds.
OS 6" maps; a circular enclosure (max. diam. *c*. 20m).
No visible surface traces.
15:9   12-9-1991

524 ROSSDARRAGH
OS 34:5:5 (130,333) OD 400–500 22644,17394
Enclosure (site) A subcircular enclosure visible on
aerial photographs (GSI, S 38–9; S 97–8). Not visible
on the ground.
34:15   8-10-1990

525 ROSSDARRAGH
OS 34 NPL
Enclosure (site) Reference to a large enclosure
surrounded by a stone wall which was probably the
site of an old building, perhaps a castle (Carrigan
1905, vol. 2, 281). No visible surface traces.
34:16   2-7-1991

526 ROSSMORE (Slievemargy By.)
OS 37:7:1 (499,417) OD 100–200 26934,17524
Enclosure (site) Indicated on the 1841 ed. OS 6"
map as a circular enclosure, and as an irregular
enclosure (max. dim. *c*. 45m NW–SE) on the 1908 ed.
No visible surface traces.
37:5   15-11-1990

527 ROUNDWOOD
OS 11:15:3 (630,148) Hachured OD 400–500
23149,19764
Enclosure (site) Described as an oval enclosure
(dims. *c*. 75m NW–SE, 54m NE–SW) defined by a
bank (max. H *c*. 1.5m) with evidence of an external
fosse at N (OPW file). No visible surface traces.
11:13   25-7-1991

528 SCOTCHRATH
OS 23:10:4 (237,183) Hachured OD 300–400
23722,18526
Enclosure Marked on the 1841 and 1909 eds. 6" OS
map; a subcircular enclosure (max. diam. *c*. 40m
NW–SE). Only slight evidence of bank survives.
23:22   21-10-1991

529 SCRUB and GLENMACOLLA
OS 34:12:3 (898,234)   OD 300–400   23456,17297
Enclosure (possible)   Cropmark of subcircular enclosure visible on aerial photographs (CUCAP, BGN 86–7). Not visible on the ground.
34:30   27-9-1990

530 SCRUB and GLENMACOLLA
OS 34:12:6 (888,213)   OD 400–500   23445,17275
Enclosure (site)   Situated on a hill. Cropmark of circular enclosure (diam. 44m) visible on aerial photograph (CUCAP, BGN 86). Not visible on the ground.
34:31   27-9-1990

531 SCRUB and GLENMACOLLA
OS 35:5:4 (28,308)   OD 300–400   23512,17376
Enclosure (site)   Cropmark of E half of a subcircular enclosure visible on aerial photograph (CUCAP, BGN 86). Not visible on the ground.
35:19   10-10-1990

532 SCRUB and GLENMACOLLA
OS 35:5:4 (30,317)   OD 300–400   23515,17385
Enclosure (site)   Cropmark of circular enclosure visible on aerial photograph (CUCAP, BGN 84). Not visible on the ground.
35:20   10-10-1990

533 SKEAGH
OS 22:12:2 (793,290)   OD 300–400   23332,18636
Enclosure (site)   Cropmark of oval enclosure visible on aerial photographs (GSI, S 150–1). Not visible on the ground.
22:19(18)   12-8-1991

534 SKEAGH
OS 22:12:3 (851,254)   OD 300–400   23394,18598
Enclosure (site)   A subcircular enclosure visible on aerial photographs (GSI, S 150–1). Not visible on the ground.
22:19(20)   12-8-1991

535 SLATT LOWER
OS 31:2:1 (281,567)   OD 600–700   25721,18311
Enclosure (possible)   Not marked on any ed. OS 6" maps. An oval area (dims. c. 21.6m N–S, 18.4m E–W) with slight evidence of bank from NW–E. No other visible surface traces.
31:21   12-8-1991

536 SPAQUARTER
OS 35:9:5 (92,192)   Indicated   OD 500–600
23580,17254
Enclosure   A semicircular enclosure (C c. 40m

WNW–E) defined by a low bank (Wth c. 2m, int. H c. 0.3m, ext. H c. 0.5m) from W–E. No evidence of fosse or original entrance. A field wall cuts the site at WNW and E and the area to the S of it has been reclaimed.
35:42   3-10-1990

537 SRAH
OS 34:3:4 (484,511)   OD 400   23016,17585
Enclosure (site)   A circular enclosure visible on aerial photographs (GSI, S 37–8). Not visible on the ground.
34:10(02)   8-10-1990

538 SRAH
OS 34:3:4 (501,460)   Hachured   OD 300–400
23035,17532
Enclosure   Marked on the 1908 ed. OS 6" map as a circular enclosure (max. diam. c. 30m). It is defined by a low bank (ext. H c. 0.8m). No evidence of fosse or original entrance.
34:11   22-10-1990

539 STRADBALLY
OS 19:2:2 (314,543)   Hachured   OD 200–300
25743,19567
Enclosure (possible, site)   The SW portion of a possible enclosure (max. dim. c. 60m NW–SSE) is marked on the 1909 ed. OS 6" map. No visible surface traces.
19:2   2-5-1990

540 TANKARDSTOWN
OS 26:7:2 (592,390)   OD 200–300   27021,18777
Enclosure (possible, site)   Cropmark of subcircular enclosure visible on aerial photographs (GSI, S 136–7). Not visible on the ground.
26:9(05)   3-8-1990

541 TANKARDSTOWN
OS 26:11:2 (544,299)   OD 200–300   26970,18681
Enclosure (possible, site)   Cropmark of subcircular enclosure visible on aerial photograph (CUCAP, BDH 59). Not visible on the ground.
26:12   5-7-1990

542 TIMAHOE
OS 18:16:3 (920,79)   Indicated   OD 400–500
25412,19073
Enclosure   An oval-shaped enclosure (dims. 52m SW–NE, 24m SE–NW) defined by a bank (Wth c. 3.5m, int. H c. 0.8m, ext. H c. 1.1m). No evidence of fosse. Visible on aerial photographs (GSI, S 167–8).
18:60/19:67*   10-9-1990

56

543 TIMOGUE
OS 19:5:5 (147,326)   Hachured   OD 300–400
25569,19335
Enclosure (site)   Marked on the 1841 and 1909 eds.
OS 6" map; part of a subcircular enclosure (max. diam.
c. 55m N–S) cut by a field wall at N and SSE. No
visible surface traces.
19:9   20-5-1990

544 TINNAHINCH
OS 3:13:2 (153,88)   OD 500–600   23609,20986
Enclosure   An almost circular area (int. diam. *c.* 76m
E–W) situated close to hilltop and defined by a much-
degraded bank/stone wall. Possibly the remains of
large cashel.
3:12(01)   1-8-1990

545 TINNAHINCH
OS 3:13:6 (170,60)   Hachured   OD 400–500
23626,20955
Enclosure   Situated at end of small ridge, SSE and
downslope from enclosure (No. 544). A circular area
(int. diam. *c.* 55m) rising towards the centre,
surrounded by a fosse and the remains of an outer bank
at N. Possible entrance with slight ramp at NNW.
3:12(03)   1-8-1990

546 TINNAHINCH
OS 6:4:3 (921,539)   OD 900–1000   23446,20820
Enclosure   Not marked on any ed. of OS 6" map;
located from aerial photographs (GSI, N 203–4;
ACAP, 738–9) and situated on mountain top. Large
circular enclosure (max. diam. 36m) defined by a bank
(Wth 5.5m, H *c.* 0.6m). Possible entrance (Wth 3.3m)
at NE.
6:5   15-12-1988

547 TINNASRAGH
OS 32:5:4 (65,358)   Indicated   OD 400–500
26470,18097
Enclosure (site)   Marked on the 1841 and 1908 eds.
OS 6" map; an irregular enclosure (max. dim. *c.* 45m
E–W). No visible surface traces.
32:10   23-8-1990

548 TINWEAR
OS 35:7:3 (621,453)   OD 500–600   24137,17535
Enclosure (site)   Cropmark of subcircular enclosure
visible on aerial photographs (GSI, S 33–4). Not
visible on the ground.
35:11   9-10-1990

549 TINWEAR
OS 35:3:6 (663,511)   OD 300–400   24181,17596
Enclosure (site)   Cropmark of part of subcircular

enclosure visible on aerial photograph (CUCAP, BDL
15). Not visible on the ground.
35:13   9-10-1990

550 TOBERBOE or KILLENNY MORE
OS 35:2:4 (291,482)   OD 300–400   23788,17563
Enclosures (site)   Cropmarks of circular enclosures
visible on aerial photograph (CUCAP, BGN 82). Not
visible on the ground.
35:8   9-10-1990

551 TOBERBOE or KILLENNY MORE
OS 35:6:1 (298,438)   OD 300–400   23795,17516
Enclosure (site)   Cropmark of circular enclosure
visible on aerial photographs (CUCAP, ASW 47–8;
BGN 80–1). Not visible on the ground.
35:30   11-10-1990

552 TOBERBOE or KILLENNY MORE
OS 35:6:2 (315,443)   OD 300–400   23814,17522
Enclosure (site)   Cropmark of W half of subcircular
enclosure visible on aerial photograph (CUCAP, BGN
80). Not visible on the ground.
35:33   11-10-1990

553 TOBERBOE or KILLENNY MORE
OS 35:6:4 (292,353)   Hachured   OD 300–400
23791,17427
Enclosure   A circular area (diam. *c.* 26.4m) defined by
a bank (Wth *c.* 3.2m, int. H *c.* 0.3m, ext. H *c.* 1.5m)
from N–S with an external fosse (Wth *c.* 4m) from
SW–W.
35:35   22-9-1990

554 TOBERBOE or KILLENNY MORE
OS 35:6:5 (355,335)   OD 400–500   23857,17408
Enclosure (possible, site)   Cropmark of possible
circular enclosure visible on aerial photographs (GSI,
S 34–5). Not visible on the ground.
35:36   22-9-1990

555 TOWLERTON
OS 31:16:2 (801,133)   Hachured   OD 700–800
26274,17859
Enclosure   An oval area (dims. *c.* 44m N–S, 34m
E–W) defined by a scarp (H *c.* 1m). No evidence of
fosse or entrance.
31:8   17-7-1990

556 TULLYROE
OS 23:16:2 (803,132)   OD 300–400   24320,18479
Enclosure (site)   Cropmark of circular enclosure
visible on aerial photograph (CUCAP, AYN 38). Not
visible on the ground.
23:37   17-8-1990

557 VICARSTOWN (COSBY)
OS 14:7:3 (644,402)   OD 200–300   26087,20061
Enclosure (possible, site)   Cropmark of subcircular enclosure visible on aerial photograph (CUCAP, AYN 19). Not visible on the ground.
14:21   12-6-1990

558 VICARSTOWN (DODD)
OS 14:8:3 (918,437)   Hachured   OD 100–200 26376,20101
Enclosure   Not marked on the 1841 ed. 6" OS map. A semicircular area (diam. 22m E–W) defined by a scarp (H *c.* 0.4m) from W–NE. Slight evidence of fosse at W. The River Barrow flows immediately to the E of the site.
14:23   15-6-1990

15. Rectilinear Enclosures

These monuments are classified solely on their morphology and may not all be of a comparable date. The majority included in this chapter are derived from aerial photographs and the current edition of the OS 6-inch maps. As none of these monuments have been even partially excavated, their function and date must remain supposition. However, the large upland subrectangular enclosure at Boley (No. 573) may be of prehistoric date, while that at Ballynahimmy (No. 569) may represent the remains of a tower house and bawn.

559 AGHNACROSS
OS 30:2:6 (450,494)   OD 600–700   24924,18226
Rectilinear enclosure (site)   Marked on the 1841 ed. OS 6" map; subrectangular enclosure (max. dim. *c.* 35m E–W). Slight evidence of bank at NW and N. No other visible surface traces; possibly a moated site.
30:14   13-8-1990

560 ARCHERSTOWN
OS 35:7:5 (556,325)   OD 500–600   24069,17399
Subrectilinear enclosure (site)   Cropmark of a large subrectangular enclosure visible on aerial photographs (GSI, S 103–4). Not visible on the ground.
35:37   11-10-1990

561 ASHFIELD
OS 32:1:6 (160,460)   OD 400–500   26570,18206
Subrectilinear enclosure   Marked as a subrectangular enclosure (max. dims. *c.* 50m N–S, 45m E–W) on the 1841 ed. OS 6" map only. The bank (Wth *c.* 3.5m, int. H *c.* 0.3m, ext. H *c.* 0.9m) and external fosse (Wth *c.* 2.8m) survive at S. Outline of bank visible at W and N. No other visible surface traces.
32:4   14-8-1990

562 BALLINTLEA
OS 19:11:2 (555,278)   Indicated   OD 400–500   26001,19288
Subrectilinear enclosure (site)   A subrectangular enclosure hachured on the 1841 ed. OS 6" map and indicated (max. dim. *c.* 60m NNE–SSW) on the 1909 ed. No visible surface traces.
19:12   3-5-1990

563 BALLYBUGGY
OS 34:1:2 (149,581)   OD 400–500   22662,17656
Rectilinear enclosure   A rectangular area (dim. 34m E–W) defined by a low bank (Wth *c.* 2m, H *c.* 0.4–0.5m). No other visible surface traces.
34:4(07)   27-9-1990

564 BALLYCOLLA HEATH
OS 29:5:6 (180,318)   Hachured   OD 337   23666,18028
Subrectilinear enclosure   A subrectangular enclosure (dims. *c.* 61m N–S, *c.* 52m E–W), on high ground in undulating terrain, defined by a low bank (Wth *c.* 3m,

int. H *c.* 0.5m, ext. H *c.* 0.7m) from W–E, and remains of possible fosse at N. No other visible surface traces.
29:19   13-9-1990

565 BALLYDAVIS
OS 13:7:2 (610,393)   Hachured   OD 400–500   25076,20041
Subrectilinear enclosure   Marked on the 1909 ed. OS 6" map as a subrectangular enclosure (max. dim. *c.* 60m NNE–SSW). Remains of a bank survive at NE, E and S. No other visible surface traces.
13:25   23-7-1990

566 BALLYDAVIS
OS 13:8:4 (732,331)   Hachured   OD 300–400   25205,19977
Subrectilinear enclosure (site)   Marked on the 1841 and 1909 eds. OS 6" maps as a subrectangular enclosure (max. dim. *c.* 45m NW–SW). No visible surface traces.
13:34   10-6-1990

567 BALLYFOYLE
OS 26:11:3 (642,242)   OD 100–200   27074,18621
Rectilinear enclosure (possible, site)   Cropmark of part of possible rectangular enclosure visible on aerial photograph (CUCAP, BGN 58). No visible surface traces.
26:15   5-7-1990

568 BALLYMADDOCK (Cullenagh By.)
OS 24:9:5 (129,186)   Hachured   OD 500–600   24583,18538
Subrectilinear enclosure (site)   Marked on the 1841 ed. OS 6" map. A subrectangular enclosure (max. dim. *c.* 40. NW–SE) bounded by a fosse (OPW file). No visible surface traces.
24:33   8-8-1990

569 BALLYNAHIMMY
OS 2:10:4 (276,165)   OD 500–600   22762,21058
Rectilinear enclosure   Marked on the 1841 and 1881 eds. OS 6" maps. Subrectangular area (dims. 58m E–W, 42m N–S) defined by a bank along W, N and E sides and by a scarp at S. A slight fosse survives along N side. Evidence of stone in bank material at N; possible entrance at NE. Internal N–S bank in E half of interior. What appears to be a circular structure, in NE

angle of enclosure, is visible on aerial photograph (CUCAP, V 300, 712); possibly the remains of a tower house and bawn.
2:7   31-10-1990

570 BALLYNOWLAN
OS 14:10:1 (239,237) OD 300–400 25661,19882
Subrectilinear enclosure (site) Cropmark of subrectangular enclosure visible on aerial photographs (GSI, S 221–2). Not visible on the ground.
14:28   16-6-1990

571 BALLYROAN (Cullenagh By.)
OS 24:2:2 (312,559) OD 500–600 24772,18934
Subrectilinear enclosure (site) Cropmark of subrectangular enclosure visible on aerial photographs (GSI, S 145–6; 165–6). Not visible on the ground.
24:8(01)   31-7-1990

572 BALLYROAN (Cullenagh By.)
OS 24:2:1 (302,554) Hachured OD 500–600 24761,18928
Subrectilinear enclosure Marked on the 1841 and 1909 eds. OS 6" maps; a subrectangular enclosure (max. dims. *c.* 50m NW–SE, 40m E–W). No visible surface traces.
24:8(02)   31-7-1990

573 BOLEY (Ballyadams By.)
OS 25:11:3 (684,270) OD 700–800 26144,18642
Subrectilinear enclosure (site) Cropmark of subrectangular enclosure visible on aerial photographs (GSI, 140–1). Not visible on the ground.
25:26   21-10-1991

574 BOLEYBEG
OS 24:15:5 (575,74) OD 500–600 25054,18424
Rectilinear enclosure (possible, site) Cropmark of rectangular enclosure visible on aerial photographs (GSI, S 68–9). Not visible on the ground.
24:46   18-7-1991

575 CLONOGHIL (Cullenagh By.)
OS 29:2:3 (400,568) Hachured OD 200–300 23896,18294
Subrectilinear enclosure A raised subrectangular enclosure (dims. 30m E–W, 23m N–S) defined by a bank (int. H *c.* 0.2m, ext. H *c.* 1m) at N, and elsewhere by a scarp. No other visible surface traces.
29:9   8-11-1990

576 COLT
OS 17:16:5 (839,38) Hachured OD 300–400 24352,19019

Subrectilinear enclosure (site) Marked on the 1841 and 1910 eds. OS 6" map; a subrectangular enclosure (max. dims. *c.* 45 NE–SW, 40m NW–SE). No visible surface traces.
17:20   28-8-1990

577 COOLOWLEY (PLOTT)
OS 27:8:5 (831,338) Indicated OD 300–400 22402,18037
Rectilinear enclosure Indicated on the 1907 ed. OS 6" map as a roughly rectangular enclosure (max. dims. *c.* 80m N–S, 50m E–W). A raised area (H *c.* 1m) enclosed by a wide shallow drain on E and S sides marks the site. Carrigan (1905, vol. 2, 140) suggests that this may be the burial ground associated with Coolowley church (No. 723). No grave-markers visible.
27:13   11-10-1990

578 DOOARY
OS 24:6:2 (374,409) OD 500–600 24839,18776
Rectilinear enclosure (site) Cropmark of an almost square enclosure visible on aerial photographs (GSI, S 144–5). Not visible on the ground.
24:21   28-9-1990

579 FARNANS
OS 31:4:2 (792,599) Hachured OD 600–700 26260,18350
Rectilinear enclosure Marked on the 1906 ed. OS 6" map as a square enclosure (max. dim. *c.* 40m). A slightly raised area enclosed by a fosse (Wth *c.* 6m) at N, NE and W survives. No other visible surface traces.
31:4(02)   12-9-1990

580 GRAIGUEAVALLAGH
OS 33:4:2 (808,591) OD 300–400 22382,17664
Rectilinear enclosure (site) Rectilinear enclosure visible on aerial photographs (GSI, S 41–42). Not visible on the ground.
33:3   14-8-1991

927 GRANGE MORE
OS 22:10:4 (305,172) Hachured OD 400–500 22818,18505
Rectilinear enclosure (site) Marked on the 1890 and 1909 eds. OS 6" maps; hachures indicate E and part of S sides of a rectangular enclosure (max. dim. *c.* 50m N–S), a drain lies to N; possibly a moated site. No visible surface traces.
22:17(01)   4-8-1991

581 GRENAN
OS 35:4:5 (792,484) OD 200–300 24317,17569
Subrectilinear enclosure (site) Cropmarks of part of a

subrectangular enclosure and circular enclosure (No. 431) visible on aerial photograph (CUCAP, ASW 45). Not visible on the ground.
35:16(02)   10-10-1990

582 IRONMILLS or KILRUSH
OS 30:10:3 (452,231) OD 500–600   24930,17949
Rectilinear enclosure A rectangular enclosure (dims. *c.* 32m E–W, 21.5m N–S), in low-lying wet land, defined by an earthen bank (Wth *c.* 2.8m, int. H *c.* 0.7m, ext. H *c.* 1.5m) and a wide shallow external fosse (Wth *c.* 3.7m).
30:27   20-6-1991

583 IRONMILLS or KILRUSH
OS 30:10:5 (378,154)   OD 600–700   24852,17867
Rectilinear enclosure (possible) Cropmark of rectangular enclosure visible on aerial photographs (GSI, S 30–1). Not visible on the ground.
30:28   20-6-1991

584 KILDELLIG
OS 22:15:4 (520,24)   OD 400–500   23047,18352
Subrectilinear enclosure (possible, site) Cropmark of subrectangular enclosure visible on aerial photographs (GSI, 375–6). Not visible on the ground.
22:27   19-6-1991

585 KILLEANY
OS 23:6:1 (292,407) Hachured OD 200–300 23777,18763
Rectilinear enclosure (site) Marked on the 1841 and 1909 eds. OS 6" map; a rectangular enclosure (max. dims. *c.* 60m N–S, 40m E–W). No visible surface traces. A tower house (No. 960) lies to E.
23:12(02)   17-8-1990

586 ORCHARD LOWER
OS 19:13:6 (167,32) Hachured OD 400–500 25593,19026
Rectilinear enclosure A subrectangular area (max. dim. *c.* 40m NE–SW) enclosed by a shallow fosse (Wth *c.* 3m, int. D *c.* 1.3m, ext. D 0.5m) from SE–ENE. Possible original entrance at ENE.
19:18   4-5-1990

587 RAHEEN (Maryborough West By.)
OS 17:16:5 (798,44) Hachured OD 300–400 24309,19025
Rectilinear enclosure (possible) Marked on the 1841 ed. OS 6" map as an almost square enclosure. On the 1906–7 revision, the S, W and N sides (max. dim. *c.* 50m N–S) are hachured. Vague outline of the bank and fosse visible.
17:19   14-9-1990

588 RATHCOFFEY
OS 3:9:4 (43,178)   OD 300–400   23492,21080
Subrectilinear enclosure (site) A subrectangular enclosure is visible on aerial photographs (GSI, N 403–4). The site has been levelled and a dish-shaped area indicates its location.
3:8   8-8-1990

589 SKEAGH
OS 22:12:2 (778,270) OD 300–400   23316,18614
Subrectilinear enclosure (site) A subrectangular enclosure visible on aerial photographs (GSI, S 150–1). Not visible on the ground.
22:19(19)   12-8-1991

590 VICARSTOWN (DODD)
OS 14:4:4 (705,466) Hachured OD 200–300 26151,20129
Rectilinear enclosure Immediately W of the Grand Canal. A rectangular enclosure is marked on the 1841 ed. OS 6" map. On the 1909 ed., only the E corner (C *c.* 35m NE–ESE) is marked. The site has been partially destroyed but remains of the bank survive at E and SE.
14:7   12-6-1990

16. Earthworks

The majority of the sites included in this chapter are derived from the 1st edition OS 6-inch maps. As almost all of them have been levelled in the interim, with no surviving surface traces, it is impossible to define their exact nature. They are therefore designated as 'Earthwork (site)' or, in the case of an upstanding monument which cannot be more precisely defined, simply as 'Earthwork'.

Within the entries the earthworks are subdivided into 'forts' and 'enclosures'. The term fort refers to sites designated as such on the 1st edition OS maps, while enclosure refers to an enclosed space of any shape. In the case of upstanding monuments, internal diameters are given; the maximum external diameter is given for levelled sites measured from the maps.

591 ARDATEGGLE
OS 37:1:1 (12,565) OD 900–1000 26418,17675
Earthwork (site) Marked on the 1841 ed. OS 6" map as a subcircular enclosure (max. diam. *c.* 40m E–W) clipped by a road from N–NNE. No visible surface traces.
37:1   15-11-1990

592 BALLINRAHIN
OS 32:6:2 (358,419) OD 200–300 26779,18165
Earthwork (site) Marked on the 1841 ed. OS 6" map as an irregular enclosure (max. dims. *c.* 90m NW–SE, 80m N–S). No visible surface traces.
32:11   23-8-1990

593 BALLYDAVIS
OS 13:7:3 (619,387) OD 400–500 25086,20035
Earthwork (site) The SE side and part of SW side of a possible rectangular enclosure (C *c.* 30m E–S) is marked on the 1841 ed. OS 6" map. No visible surface traces.
13:26(01)   10-6-1990

594 BALLYDAVIS
OS 13:7:3 (622,387) OD 400–500 25088,20035
Earthwork (site) Marked on the 1841 ed. OS 6" map; a rectangular enclosure (max. dim. *c.* 30m NW–SE). No visible surface traces.
13:26(02)   10-6-1990

595 BALLYGEEHIN UPPER
OS 23:13:6 (224,68) OD 300–400 23709,18405
Earthwork (site) Marked on the 1841 ed. OS 6" map; a circular 'fort' (max. diam. *c.* 60m). No visible surface traces.
23:33   19-8-1990

596 BALLYHEGADON GLEBE
OS 28:5:5 (149,355) OD 300–400 22658,18058
Earthwork (site) Marked on the 1841 ed. OS 6" map; a circular 'fort' (max. diam. *c.* 50m). No visible surface traces.
28:22   16-9-1991

597 BALLYHIDE
OS 37:7:5 (547,364) OD 100–200 26985,17469
Earthwork (site) Marked on the 1841 ed. OS 6" map; a subcircular enclosure (max. diam. *c.* 40m N–S). No visible surface traces.
37:6   15-11-1990

598 BALLYKING
OS 24:10:6 (450,206) OD 400–500 24921,18562
Earthwork (site) Marked on the 1841 ed. OS 6" map; a circular enclosure (max. diam. *c.* 45m). No visible surface traces.
24:37   28-8-1990

599 BALLYMADDOCK (Cullenagh By.)
OS 24:13:5 (110,67) Hachured OD 500–600
24564,18412
Earthwork (possible) Marked on the 1841 and 1909 eds. OS 6" maps as a tree-covered mound (max. dim. 60m N–S). A fosse (Wth *c.* 5m, int. D *c.* 1.8m, ext. D *c.* 1m) survives at SE, with faint traces at N. Remains of an external bank (Wth *c.* 4.8m, ext. H *c.* 1.6m) survive at SE. No other visible traces. Quarried at E, W and interior. Possible remains of a landscape feature.
24:40   28-8-1990

600 BALLYMULLEN
OS 30:1:1 (44,596) OD 400–500 24495,18329
Earthwork (possible, site) Indicated on the 1841 ed. OS 6" map; a circular enclosure (max. diam. *c.* 20m). No visible surface traces.
30:1   17-6-1991

601 BALLYTARSNA (Upperwoods By.)
OS 22:6:2 (343,450) OD 400–500 22855,18800
Earthwork (site) Marked on the 1841 ed. OS 6" map; a subcircular enclosure (max. diam. *c.* 35m NW–SE) clipped by field wall at NE. No visible surface traces.
22:4   5-8-1991

602 BOLEYBAWN/IRONMILLS or KILRUSH
OS 30:10:3 (443,301) OD 600–700 24919,18023
Earthwork (site) Marked on the 1841 ed. OS 6" map; an irregular enclosure (max. dims. *c.* 50m N–S, 25m

E–W). No visible surface traces.
30:24   21-6-1991

603 BORRIS LITTLE
OS 13:10:1 (307,294) OD 200–300 24757,19934
Earthwork (site) Marked on the 1841 ed. OS 6" map;
a circular 'fort' (max. diam. *c.* 45m) clipped by field
fence from SW–NW. No visible surface traces.
13:42   11-6-1990

604 CAPPAKEEL
OS 9:13:3 (188,98) OD 200–300 25602,20375
Earthwork (site) Marked on the 1841 ed. OS 6" map;
a circular enclosure (diam. *c.* 20m). No visible surface
traces.
9:20   20-7-1990

605 CAPPANACLOGHY
OS 23:7:5 (559,347) OD 300–400 24060,18703
Earthwork (site) Marked on the 1841 ed. OS 6" map;
a circular 'fort' (max. diam. *c.* 35m). Known locally as
the 'rath field'. No visible surface traces.
23:14   17-8-1990

606 CAPPANASHANNAGH
OS 30:2:4 (244,511) OD 500–600 24707,18242
Earthwork (site) Marked on the 1841 ed. OS 6" map;
a subrectangular enclosure (max. dim. *c.* 40m E–W)
cut by a NE–SW running field wall. No visible surface
traces.
30:9   18-6-1991

607 CASTLEFLEMING or HEATH
OS 27:11:2 (616,254) OD 400–500 22176,17946
Earthwork (site) Marked on the 1841 ed. OS 6" map;
a circular 'fort' (max. diam. *c.* 50m) clipped by road at
SE. No visible surface traces.
27:15   22-10-1990

608 CASTLETOWN (Clandonagh By.)
   Moneymore ED
OS 21:4:1 (702,566) OD 400–500 22258,18917
Earthwork (site) Indicated on the 1841 ed. OS 6"
map; a circular enclosure (max. diam. *c.* 25m). No
visible surface traces.
21:6   24-6-1991

609 CLOGRENAN
OS 37:6:6 (402,332) OD 300–400 26832,17433
Earthwork (site) Marked on the 1841 ed. OS 6" map;
a circular 'fort' (max. diam. *c.* 20m). No visible
surface traces.
37:4   15-11-1990

610 CLONAGEERA/CAPPONELLAN
OS 35:7:1 (534,453) OD 500–700 24045,17535
Earthwork (site) Marked on the 1841 ed. OS 6" map;
a subcircular enclosure (max. diam. *c.* 40m NW–SE)
with a possible mound in the interior at W. No visible
surface traces.
35:10   22-9-1990

611 CLONANNY
OS 5:11:4 (505,154) 'Kalladodgara Fort (Site of)'
OD 200 25930,21078
Earthwork (site) Marked on the 1841 ed. OS 6" map
as a circular 'fort' (max. diam. *c.* 20m) clipped by a
field wall at NE. No visible surface traces.
5:8   12-6-1990

612 CLONBARROW
OS 17:1:2 (147,584) OD 300–400 23616,19589
Earthwork (site) Marked on the 1841 ed. OS 6" map;
a subrectangular enclosure (max. dims. *c.* 40m E–W,
25m N–S). No visible surface traces.
17:1   29-10-1990

613 CLONDUFF
OS 3:2:5 (320,484) OD 200–300 23781,21405
Earthwork (site) Marked on the 1841 ed. OS 6" map;
a subcircular enclosure (max. diam. *c.* 20m NE–SW).
No visible surface traces.
3:1   13-8-1990

614 CLONEEB
OS 34:1:1 (35,558) OD 300–400 22541,17631
Earthworks (site) Earthworks visible on aerial
photographs (GSI, S 39–40) to SW of church and
graveyard (No. 712). No visible surface traces.
34:1(04)   28-9-1990

615 CLONMEEN NORTH
OS 33:7:5 (551,369) OD 400–500 22113,17426
Earthwork (site) Marked on the 1841 ed. OS 6" map;
a circular 'fort' (max. diam. *c.* 30m). No visible
surface traces.
33:6   14-8-1991

616 CLONMORE (Clandonagh By.)
OS 27:3:1 (497,578) OD 300–400 22047,18287
Earthwork (site) Marked on the 1841 ed. OS 6" map;
a circular 'fort' (max. diam. *c.* 35m). No visible
surface traces.
27:2   6-10-1990

617 CLONMORE (Clandonagh By.)
OS 27:3:5 (550,517) OD 300–400 22104,18223
Earthwork (site) Marked on the 1841 ed. OS 6" map;

a small circular enclosure (max. diam. *c.* 15m); possibly a mound. No visible surface traces.
27:3   6-10-1990

618 CLONREHER
OS 13:1:5 (81,462)   OD 200–300   24517,20109
Earthwork (site) Marked on the 1841 ed. OS 6" map; a circular enclosure (max. diam. *c.* 25m). No visible surface traces.
13:2   18-6-1990

619 CLOONALOO
OS 32:9:5 (151,163)   OD 400–500   26563,17892
Earthwork (site) Indicated on the 1841 ed. OS 6" map; a subcircular enclosure (max. diam. *c.* 40m NW–SE). No visible surface traces.
32:13   23-8-1990

620 COOLKERRY
OS 28:11:4 (496,157)   OD 300–400   23026,17851
Earthwork (site) Marked on the 1841 ed. OS 6" map; a subrectangular enclosure (max. dims. *c.* 50m NE–SW, 45m E–W). No visible surface traces.
28:49   30-9-1991

621 COOLTEDERY
OS 5:9:2 (134,294)   OD 200–300   25537,21222
Earthwork (site) Marked on the 1841 ed. OS 6" map as a subcircular enclosure (diam. *c.* 40m NW–SE) enclosing two smaller enclosures at NW and SE; possibly a double motte and bailey. No visible surface traces .
5:4   15-5-1990

622 COOPERHILL DEMESNE
OS 32:10:1 (237,256)   OD 300–400   26652,17991
Earthwork (site) Marked on the 1841 ed. OS 6" map; a circular 'fort' (max. diam. *c.* 45m). No visible surface traces.
32:14   23-8-1990

623 CUDDAGH
OS 22:4:3 (864,563)   OD 300–400   23404,18925
Earthwork (site) Marked on the 1841 ed. OS 6" map; a circular enclosure (max. diam. *c.* 30m). No visible surface traces.
22:9   6-8-1991

624 CULLAHILL MOUNTAIN
OS 35:9:6 (204,156)   OD 800–900   23699,17217
Earthwork (site) Marked on the 1841 ed. OS 6" map; a suboval 'fort' (max. dims. *c.* 50m E–W, 45m NW–SE) cut by field wall from NW–N. No visible surface traces.
35:43   22-9-1990

625 DERRIN
OS 22:1:5 (102,485)   OD 300–400   22600,18834
Earthworks (site) Carrigan (1905, vol. 2, 129) refers to extensive traces of foundations around 'Derrin Castle' (No. 1034). No visible surface traces.
22:3(02)   5-8-1991

626 DERRINDUFF
OS 16:1:3 (157,566)   OD 400–500   22651,19560
Earthwork (site) Marked on the 1841 ed. OS 6" map; an irregular enclosure (max. dims. *c.* 65m NW–SE, 60m E–W). No visible surface traces.
16:1   23-7-1991

627 DERRINSALLAGH/DOON (Clandonagh By.)
OS 22:9:4 (74,170)   OD 400–500   22574,18501
Earthwork (site) Indicated on the 1841 ed. OS 6" map; a subcircular enclosure (max. diam. *c.* 50m NE–SW) cut by road at S and NW. No visible surface traces.
22:12   6-8-1991

628 DERRYKEARN
OS 23:3:5 (608,478)   OD 300–400   24110,18841
Earthworks (site) Earthworks visible on aerial photographs (GSI S 147–8). Not visible on the ground.
23:7(05)   17-8-1990

629 DYSART
OS 13:16:4 (696,63)   OD 500–600   25170,19694
Earthwork (site) Marked on the 1841 ed. OS 6" map; a rectangular enclosure (max. dims. *c.* 50m N–S, 30m E–W) cut by an internal wall at ENE and WNW. No visible surface traces. 'Pigott's Castle' (No. 935) lies on the line of the site at WNW.
13:61(02)   6-6-1990

630 FARRANVILLE
OS 28:3:4 (521,476)   Hachured   OD 300–400   23049,18189
Earthwork (possible, site) Marked on the 1908 ed. OS 6" map only; an irregular line of hachures indicates part of a possible earthwork (C *c.* 85m SSE–SW). A slightly raised area is visible at the location of site.
28:13   12-9-1991

631 GARRANMACONLY
OS 21:15:2 (594,94)   OD 500–600   22148,18417
Earthworks (site) Earthworks visible on aerial photographs (GSI S, 79–8) to SE of tower house (No. 955). Not visible on the ground.
21:13(02)   24-6-1991

632 GARRINTAGGART
OS 24:16:4 (748,67) Hachured OD 600–700
25238,18419
Earthwork (site) Not marked on the 1841 ed. OS 6"
map; on the 1909 ed., hachures indicate a narrow
earthwork (dims. *c.* 40m NE–SW, 15m NW–SE)
clipped by field boundary at SW. No visible surface
traces.
24:47   18-7-1991

633 GARRYMORE
OS 3:8:2 (808,421) OD 200–300 24296,21344
Earthwork (site) Indicated on the 1841 ed. OS 6"
map; a circular enclosure (max. diam. *c.* 25m). No
visible surface traces.
3:6   13-8-1990

634 GRAIGUEADRISLY
OS 34:13:4 (30,72) OD 500–600 22542,17118
Earthwork (site) Marked on the 1841 ed. OS 6" map;
a small subcircular enclosure (max. diam. *c.* 15m
E–W); possibly a mound. No visible surface traces.
34:33   3-7-1991

635 GRAIGUEAVOICE
OS 35:5:6 (191,366) OD 300–400 23684,17438
Earthwork (site) Marked on the 1841 ed. OS 6" map;
a circular 'fort' (max. diam. *c.* 40m). A field wall
curved around the site from S–NW. No visible surface
traces.
35:25   27-9-1990

636 GREATHEATH (Maryborough East By.)
OS 13:8:1 (742,450) OD 300–400 25215,20103
Earthwork (site) Immediately SW of ring-barrow
(No. 58). Marked on the 1841 ed. OS 6" map; a very
small circular enclosure (max. diam. *c.* 10m). No
visible surface traces; probably removed when the road
to W was built. Possibly a ring-barrow.
13:30(02)   24-5-1990

637 GREATHEATH (Maryborough East By.)
OS 13:8:2 (772,451) Hachured OD 300–400
25246,20105
Earthwork (site) A D-shaped area (dims. 37.5m E–W,
15m N–S) defined by a large quarry trench from
SW–NE with an unexcavated baulk at WNW. A bank
visible immediately inside the line of the trench from
WNW–NE consists of graded spoil material from the
quarry. From NE–E a bank (Wth 3m, ext. H 1.2m)
with a shallow external fosse (D 0.2–0.5m), outside of
which is a berm (Wth 10m), is similar in form to that
of ringforts. A roadway runs from E–SW. Possibly the
remains of a ringfort.
13:32   18-5-1994

638 GURTEEN
OS 26:13:6 (226,75) OD 200–300 26637,18441
Earthwork (site) Marked on the 1841 ed. OS 6" map;
a subcircular enclosure (max. diam. *c.* 40m E–W). No
visible surface traces.
26:20   4-7-1990

639 INCHANISKY
OS 11:7:4 (482,373) OD 600–700 22990,20000
Earthwork (site) Marked on the 1841 ed. OS 6" map;
a circular enclosure (max. diam. *c.* 25m) with a lime
kiln in the interior at NE. No visible surface traces.
11:4   23-7-1991

640 JOHNSTOWN GLEBE
OS 28:9:2 (112,231) OD 300–400 22620,17926
Earthwork (site) Marked on the 1841 ed. OS 6" map;
a subcircular 'fort' (max. diam. *c.* 50m N–S). No
visible surface traces.
28:37   17-9-1991

641 KILCOKE
OS 28:2:2 (368,578) OD 400–500 22887,18295
Earthwork (site) Marked on the 1841 ed. OS 6" map;
a subrectangular enclosure (max. dims. *c.* 35m E–W,
25m N–S). No visible surface traces.
28:5   11-9-1991

642 KILLEEN (Upperwoods By.)
OS 11:14:4 (296,66) OD 400–500 22797,19674
Earthwork A rectangular enclosure (max. dims. *c.*
35m NW–SE, 30m NE–SW) marked on the 1841 ed.
OS 6" map. No visible surface traces.
11:12   25-7-1990

643 KILNASHANE
OS 30:2:5 (312,466) Hachured OD 500–600
24780,18195
Earthwork (site) Shown on the 1908 ed. OS 6" map
and the 25" map as a mound (diam. *c.* 20m) with a
raised area (*c.* 60m E–W) around it from E–NNW.
Possible landscape feature. No visible surface traces.
30:12   18-6-1991

644 KILRORY
OS 14:10:1 (295,301) OD 200–300 25720,19950
Earthwork (site) Marked on the 1841 ed. OS 6" map;
an almost square enclosure (max. dim. *c.* 30m
NE–SW). A field wall clips the site at E. No visible
surface traces.
14:30   15-6-1990

645 KILRORY
OS 14:10:2 (351,266) OD 200–300 25779,19914
Earthwork (site) Marked on the 1841 ed. OS 6" map;

a subrectangular enclosure (max. dims. *c.* 30m E–W, 20m N–S). No visible surface traces.
14:31   15-6-1990

646 KILRORY
OS 14:10:5 (336,219)   OD 200–300   25763,19864
Earthwork (site)   Marked on the 1841 ed. OS 6" map; an irregular enclosure (max. dim. *c.* 45m NE–SW). No visible surface traces.
14:32   7-6-1990

647 KILRORY
OS 14:10:5 (346,209)   OD 200–300   25774,19854
Earthwork (site)   Marked on the 1841 ed. OS 6" map; an irregular enclosure (max. dims. *c.* 75m N–S, 65m E–W). No visible surface traces.
14:33   7-6-1990

648 KNOCKFIN
OS 28:15:5 (544,50)   OD 300–400   23078,17740
Earthwork (site)   Marked on the 1841 ed. OS 6" map; a subcircular enclosure (max. diam. *c.* 55m NW–SE). No visible surface traces.
28:67   4-9-1991

649 KNOCKPHILIP
OS 14:14:6 (446,68)   OD 300–400   25882,19706
Earthwork (site)   Marked on the 1841 ed. OS 6" map; a circular 'fort' (max. diam. *c.* 50m). No visible surface traces.
14:41   7-6-1990

650 LOUGHAKEO
OS 13:16:6 (848,24)   OD 500–600   25331,19654
Earthwork (possible, site)   The arc of a possible earthwork (max. dim. *c.* 60m SE–SW) is marked on the 1841 ed. OS 6" map. No visible surface traces.
13:65   5-6-1990

651 LYROGE
OS 28:13:1 (25,118)   OD 300–400   22529,17805
Earthwork (site)   Marked on the 1841 ed. OS 6" map; a small circular enclosure (max. diam. *c.* 20m); possibly a mound. No visible surface traces.
28:52   30-9-1991

652 MILLTOWN
OS 25:8:2 (783,400)   OD 300–400   26247,18780
Earthworks (site)   Reference to earthen mounds at Milltown tower house (No. 961) (O'Hanlon and O'Leary 1907, vol. 1, 303). No visible surface traces.
25:20(02)   23-7-1990

653 MORETT
OS 8:16:2 (775,109)   OD 300–400   25247,20384
Earthwork (site)   Hachured as a very large circular enclosure (max. diam. *c.* 70m) on the 1841 ed. OS 6" map. No visible surface traces.
8:16   20-6-1990

654 MORETT
OS 8:16:6 (895,8)   'Rathnalulagh (Site of)' OD 300–400   25374,20277
Earthwork (site)   The S portion of a possible rectangular earthwork (C *c.* 50m SE–SW) is hachured on the 1841 ed. OS 6" sheet, and indicated only as a field fence on later eds. No visible surface traces.
8:20   20-7-1990

655 MOUNTEAGLE
OS 24:1:4 (24,522)   OD 300–400   24468,18892
Earthwork (site)   Marked on the 1841 ed. OS 6" map as a subcircular enclosure (max. diam. *c.* 25m N–S). No visible surface traces.
24:2   8-8-1990

656 MOUNTEAGLE
OS 24:1:4 (11,488)   OD 300–400   24455,18856
Earthwork (site)   Marked on the 1841 ed. OS 6" map as a subcircular enclosure (max. diam. *c.* 40m NW–SE). No visible surface traces.
24:3   8-8-1990

657 MOUNTEAGLE
OS 24:5:1 (49,409)   OD 300–400   24496,18773
Earthwork (site)   Hachured on the 1841 ed. OS 6" map as a large irregular enclosure (max. dim. *c.* 70m NW–SE), clipped by field wall from NW–E. No visible surface traces.
24:17   28-9-1990

658 NEWTOWN (Clarmallagh By.)
OS 35:1:1 (66,556)   OD 200–300   23550,17639
Earthwork (site)   A circular 'fort' (max. diam. *c.* 40m) marked on the 1841 ed. OS 6" map. No visible surface traces.
35:2   8-11-1990

659 RAGGETTSTOWN
OS 30:1:2 (112,531)   OD 400–500   24567,18261
Earthwork (site)   Marked on the 1841 ed. OS 6" map; a circular 'fort' (max. diam. *c.* 30m). No visible surface traces.
30:6   17-6-1991

660 RAHEENANISKY
OS 18:4:5 (791,520)   OD 400–500   25272,19537

Earthwork (site) Marked on the 1841 ed. OS 6" map; a subcircular enclosure (max. diam. *c.* 40m NE–SW). No visible surface traces.
18:7   4-5-1990

661 RAHEEN UPPER
OS 28:6:4 (234,363)   OD 300–400   22748,18067
Earthwork (site) Marked on the 1841 ed. OS 6" map; a circular 'fort' (diam. *c.* 40m). No visible surface traces.
28:29   16-9-1991

662 RALISH
OS 24:13:5 (153,21)   OD 400–500   24609,18364
Earthwork (site) Marked on the 1841 ed. OS 6" map; a suboval enclosure (max. dim. *c.* 40m NW–SE). No visible surface traces.
24:42   28-8-1990

663 RATHMILES
OS 5:14:4 (249,48)   OD 300–400   25661,20963
Earthwork (possible, site) An irregular enclosure (max. dim. *c.* 50m N–S) hachured on the 1841 ed. OS 6" map. Possibly a landscape feature. No visible surface traces .
5:15   20-9-1990

664 RATHNAMANAGH
OS 13:6:2 (367,450)   OD 300–400   24819,20099
Earthwork (site) Marked on the 1841 ed. OS 6" map; a subcircular enclosure (max. diam. *c.* 35m NW–SE). No visible surface traces.
13:21   26-5-1990

665 ROSSBAUN
OS 15:7:5 (596,310)   OD 800–900   22143,19285
Earthwork (site) Marked on the 1841 ed. OS 6" map; a subcircular enclosure (max. dims. *c.* 70m E–W, 60m NW–SE) hachured from NNE–NW. A field boundary indicates the line of the site from NW–NNE. A trackway cuts through it at E and WSW. No visible surface traces.
15:10   12-9-1991

666 ROSSDARRAGH
OS 34:5:5 (149,319)   OD 400–500   22664,17379
Earthwork (site) Marked on the 1840 ed. OS 6" map; a roughly trapezoidal enclosure (max. dims. *c.* 75m NE–SW, 40m NW–SE). No visible surface traces.
34:18   4-7-1991

667 SHANGANAGH BEG
OS 20:15:1 (462,91) Hachured   OD 100–200
26880,19100
Earthwork (site) Marked on the 1841 ed. OS 6" map as a small circular enclosure (max. diam. *c.* 15m). On the 1909 ed., the site is depicted as a mound. No visible surface traces.
20:6   10-7-1990

668 SLATT UPPER
OS 31:6:4 (264,369)   Hachured   OD 500–600
25704,18101
Earthwork (site) Not marked on the 1841 ed. OS 6" map; on the 1906 ed., hachures indicate the line of an earthwork (C *c.* 100m) from SSW–NW. No visible surface traces.
31:6   17-7-1990

669 TINNAHINCH
OS 7:1:2 (140,565)   OD 600–700   23597,20849
Earthwork (possible, site) Shown as a circular mound or platform (diam. *c.* 25m) on the 1841 and 1888 eds. OS 6" maps. No visible surface traces.
7:1   8-8-1990

670 TOBERBOE or KILLENNY MORE
OS 35:6:2 (353,434)   Hachured   OD 300–400
23854,17512
Earthwork A circular area (diam. *c.* 10.3m) defined by a low scarp (H 0.3m) from SE–NE. No evidence of fosse or entrance.
35:34   20-9-1990

671 TOMOCLAVIN
OS 19:14:6 (454,56)   OD 400–500   25897,19053
Earthwork (site) Marked on the 1841 ed. OS 6" map; an irregular enclosure (max. dim. *c.* 40m NE–SW). No visible surface traces.
19:24   3-5-1990

672 TURFARNEY
OS 28:15:5 (544,50)   OD 300–400   23078,17739
Earthwork (site) Indicated on the 1841 ed. OS 6" map; a subcircular enclosure (max. diam. *c.* 40m NW–SE). No visible surface traces.
28:66   4-9-1991

673 TURFARNEY
OS 34:3:2 (567,588)   OD 300–400   23103,17668
Earthwork (site) Marked on the 1841 ed. OS 6" map; a subrectangular enclosure (max. dims. *c.* 60m NE–SW, 40m E–W). No visible surface traces.
34:14   1-7-1991

674 WATERCASTLE
OS 29:12:1 (729,286)   OD 300–400   24247,17999
Earthwork (site) Marked on the 1841 ed. OS 6" map; a circular enclosure (max. diam. *c.* 25m). No visible surface traces.
29:36   13-8-1990

17. Linear Features

This chapter includes a variety of linear features most of which appear only on aerial photographs. Some are possibly field or drainage systems of medieval date or later. Others appear to be associated with ringforts or enclosures of an earlier period.

675 AGHMACART
OS 34:8:4 (759,363)   OD 300–400   23308,17432
Linear features   Linear features, possibly field systems, visible on aerial photograph (CUCAP, AYP 5) to NW of priory (No. 689). Not visible on the ground.
34:19(11)   8-10-1990

676 BALLAGHARAHIN
OS 33:3:3 (680,602)   OD 400–500   22247,17674
Linear feature   Linear feature visible on aerial photographs (GSI, S 40–1) to SSW of ringfort (No. 135). A flat-topped bank (Wth *c.* 5m) curving gently from SSW–NNE (C *c.* 52.3m) is visible on the ground.
33:1*/27:28(02)   26-10-1990

677 BALLYADAMS
OS 19:16:3 (857,109)   OD 200–300   26321,19113
Linear features (site)   Cropmark of linear features visible on aerial photograph (CUCAP, BGN 69), to SW of enclosure site (No. 294), and cutting it at SE and NNW. Not visible on the ground.
19:29(02)   3-5-1990

678 BALLYFOYLE
OS 26:11:5 (612,204)   OD 200–300   27044,18580
Linear features (site)   Cropmarks of linear features, possibly old field systems, visible on aerial photographs (CUCAP, BGN 56–7). Not visible on the ground.
26:14(02)   1-8-1990

679 BALLYROAN (Cullenagh By.)
OS 24:1:2 (136,590)   OD 300–400   24586,18964
Linear features (site)   Cropmarks of linear features and enclosure with annexe (No. 321) visible on aerial photographs (CUCAP, AJQ 55–6). Not visible on the ground.
24:1(02)   27-8-1990

680 BOLEY UPPER
OS 23:10:2 (336,231)   OD 300–400   23825,18578
Linear features (site)   Cropmark of linear features, close to enclosure site (No. 338), visible on aerial photographs (CUCAP APA 30–1). Not visible on the ground.
23:20(02)   21-10-1991

681 NEWTOWN (Clarmallagh By.)
OS 35:5:3 (184,432)   OD 300–400   23675,17508
Linear features (site)   Cropmarks of linear features, possibly field systems, and enclosure (No. 488), visible on aerial photograph (CUCAP BGN 79). Not visible on the ground.
35:18(02)   10-10-1990

682 PARK UPPER
OS 14:9:5 (103,172)   OD 400–500   25519,19812
Linear feature (site)   Linear features, running NE from enclosures (No. 493), visible on aerial photographs (CUCAP, 74–5). Not visible on the ground.
14:27(02)   6-6-1990

683 SHRULE
OS 32:7:3 (688,414)   OD 100–200   27128,18164
Linear features (site)   Cropmark of linear features visible on aerial photographs (CUCAP BDH 51–3). Not visible on the ground.
32:12(02)   14-8-1990

18. Ecclesiastical Sites

The introduction of Christianity to Ireland in the fifth century lead to the development of numerous monastic foundations throughout the country. By the eight century a standardised form had emerged characterised by the enclosing bank or vallum which was often a double enclosure; the inner enclosure surrounded the church and graveyard, and the outer one enclosed the domestic dwellings and workshops of the community (Ryan 1991, 136). Buildings of this period were generally wooden, it was not until the eleventh/twelfth centuries that stone became the predominant building material, and as a result no traces survive above ground level. However, the enclosures may survive as low earthworks or cropmarks, or may be indicated by curving field boundaries or roadways.

Early ecclesiastical remains   Many of the early monastic foundations were used continuously over time and, in many cases, the churches were rebuilt or incorporated into later ones. Within this chapter, the term early ecclesiastical remains refers to sites where there is evidence of an Early Christian foundation (*c.* AD 500–1200) as well as a later church. Apart from an enclosure, features indicative of such sites include churches with projections or antae at the W end of the side-walls, bullaun stones, fonts, graveslabs and round towers. Romanesque art is also a feature. This art is characterised by the use of chevron and zigzag ornament, animal motifs and human heads with intertwined hair. The finest examples in the county are the doorway of the church (No. 765) at Killeshin and the doorway of the round tower (No. 804) at Timahoe.

Medieval churches   These churches (*c.* AD 1200–1600) may be divided into two groups: nave and chancel churches of the twelfth–thirteenth centuries, and simple rectangular churches of the fourteenth–sixteenth centuries. Features associated with the later parish churches include the placing of a doorway in one or both of the side-walls but generally in the south, bellcotes over the W gable, two-centred arches and ogee-headed windows.

Medieval monasteries   A more organised system of monastery-building was introduced to Ireland, from Europe, in the late twelfth century by the Cistercian, Augustinian, Dominican and Franciscan orders. These monasteries were centred about an open square or rectangle, with the church on one side and the various domestic buildings, such as the refectory and dormitories, on the other sides. Only a few examples are known in County Laois. The majority are concentrated in the south-western part of the county with a few outliers in the north-east and south-east. Most survive in a much-ruined condition.

684 ABBEYLEIX DEMESNE
OS 23:15:6 (692,0)   OD 200–300   24204,18338
Church (site)   Not marked as an antiquity on any OS 6" map. The old Protestant church stands on the site of the pre-Reformation church (Carrigan 1905, vol. 2, 389). No visible surface traces.
23:36(01)/29:11(01)*   14-9-1990

685 ABBEYLEIX DEMESNE
OS 29:3:3   NPL
Abbey (site)   Not marked on any OS 6" map. A Cistercian abbey was founded here in 1183/1184 by Cucogry O'More, Lord of Leix (Carrigan 1905, vol. 2, 387–9, 392; *JRSAI* 1948, 63–4). No visible surface traces survive. Altar-tomb (No. 811), granite font (No. 812) and graveslab (No. 813) nearby. (Stalley 1987, 241)
29:13(01)   4-7-1990

686 ACRAGAR
OS 8:10:1 (237,261) 'Foy Church (Site of), Grave Yard'   OD 200–300   24678,20539
Church (site)   Marked on the 1841 ed. OS 6" map as 'Foy Church (in Ruins)' but on the 1910 ed. as 'Site of'. No surface evidence of any structural remains other than a raised area in centre of graveyard. Simple incised cross-slab in roadside ditch, opposite entrance to graveyard. (*JKAS* 1904, 193)
8:8   11-6-1990

687 ADDERGOOLE
OS 34:8:2 (822,434)   OD 300–400   23374,17508
Nunnery (site)   Not marked on any ed. of OS 6" maps. A convent was granted to the prioress and nuns of Kilculliheen *c.* 1240 by David FitzMilo; no record of it being occupied after this. However, the nuns still owned 60 acres here in 1541 (Gwynn and Hadcock 1970, 312). According to Carrigan (1905, vol. 2, 234–5), the convent was situated in the 'Kiln Field', NW of Belmont House. No visible surface traces survive.
34:22(01)   25-9-1990

688 AGHABOE
OS 22:12:1 (737,238) 'Aghaboe Abbey (in Ruins), Font, Grave Yd.'   OD 300–400   23274,18580
Monastic complex   An Early Christian monastery was founded here in the sixth century by St Cainnech (Canice). It was plundered and burnt a number of times, and in 1234 was rebuilt as an Augustian priory (Harbison 1970, 139). A Dominican friary, founded by Florence MacGillapatrick, Lord of Ossary, was built

Fig. 10—*Aghaboe, ceiling of bell-tower* (**688**)

close by in 1382. It was suppressed in 1540 (Gwynn and Hadcock 1970, 221).

The present Protestant church stands on the site of the Augustinian church. Some of its windows are from the nearby Dominican church (Harbison *ibid.*). The belfry tower, with its original plinth, dates to the thirteenth century, and has been refaced and added to in modern times. Its two-centred arched sandstone doorway probably dates to the fifteenth century. There is a medieval head on E side of doorway; two other similar heads are on the adjoining façade of the church. Medieval stonework is visible inside doorway to W. A horizontal graveslab, dated 1675, lies at E end of church and an octagonal font lies outside entrance.

The Dominican church, to W, consists of a nave and chancel (L *c.* 32m, Wth *c.* 21m, Wall T *c.* 1.1m) with a transept at W end of S wall. Constructed mainly of rubble and limestone, its main features include a three-light window in E gable, a blocked-up doorway in W end of S wall, a similar doorway in N wall, which accessed the cloister, and a late medieval doorway in W wall. Within the church, set in E end of S wall, is an ogee-headed piscina with a scalloped bowl and six drain-holes. The transept has a three-light tracery window in S wall, and remains of a piscina in E wall. Grass-covered remains of the cloister are visible to N

of the church. Site of St Canice's Well (No. 849) lies *c.* 180m to the SW.
22:19(01)   12-8-1991

689 AGHMACART
OS 34:8:1 (760,380) '*Castle and Priory* (in Ruins), Grave Yard' OD 300–400 23308,17450

Priory A monastery is said to have been founded here in 550 (Carrigan 1905, vol. 2, 235). Records indicate that it was burnt in 1156 and that an Augustinian priory was established before 1168 by MacGillapatrick, Lord of Ossory (Gwynn and Hadcock 1970, 156). Only the NE angle of a medieval building (dims. 10.4m E–W, 7.2m N–S, wall T 1m) with a base-batter and built of limestone blocks survives. A modern building is attached to it. Pieces of masonry and architectural fragments are visible just N of the Protestant church which lies to SSW. A burial vault to SE is possibly of seventeenth-century origin (Carrigan 1905, vol. 2, 239) but has been modernised. Originally a gateway to the priory was situated to NW and a well to SW (*ibid.*). The church tower depicted by Grose (*ibid.*, 236) appears to have been misconstrued as a castle, and was thus recorded on the OS maps.
34:19(03)   8-10-1990

Fig. 11—*Aghaboe, detail on doorway of bell-tower* (**688**)

690 AGHNACROSS
OS 30:2:3 (434,533) 'Dysart Ch. (in Ruins), Grave Yd.' OD 400–500 24907,18267
Church Marked on the 1563 map of Leix and Offaly (Hore 1863, f.p. 345). Associated with St Monahan who died in 648 (Comerford 1886, vol. 3, 105–6). Within a roughly triangular graveyard, which is defined by an earthen bank (Wth *c.* 1m, int. H *c.* 1.1m, ext. H *c.* 0.5m) from NE–SE, is a nave and chancel church (L *c.* 12.7m, Wth *c.* 6.6m, wall T *c.* 0.9m) built of roughly coursed limestone. Doorway and ope in N and S walls, and ope in W gable. The segmental chancel arch (Wth *c.* 2.5m) is constructed of sandstone. All visible headstones postdate 1700. Reference to a cross-base built into a wall at the roadside (*ibid.*) of which there is no visible trace.
30:11(01)   18-6-1991

691 AHARNEY
OS 35:11:4 (483,164) 'Aharney Church (in Ruins), Grave Yd.' OD 400–500 23994,17229
Church Dedicated to St Bridget. Only the featureless W gable survives but Carrigan (1905, vol. 2, 308)

mentions that half of E gable and portions of S wall of the church (L *c.*12.75m, Wth *c.* 5.1m) were to be seen *c.* 1900. No early grave-markers visible .
35:47   27-9-1990

692 AKIP
OS 28:6:2 (339,420) OD 300–400 22857,18128
Church (site) and graveyard (site) Marked on the 1841 ed. OS 6" map. According to Carrigan (1905 vol. 2, 353), the church and graveyard were uprooted and tilled *c.* 1830. No visible surface traces.
28:27   16-9-1991

693 ANATRIM
OS 16:10:3 (438,239) 'Anatrim Church (in Ruins)' OD 300–400 22952,19218
Church and graveyard Reputedly the site of an early foundation established by St Mochaemhog in the late sixth century. A much-modified long rectangular late medieval parish church, largely rebuilt in the eighteenth century, with a sacristy formerly adjoining its NE end, and a belfry added to W end at a later date.

The church (int. dims. 16.9m E–W, 6.7m N–S, wall T 0.78m) is constructed of randomly coursed sandstone rubble, rendered with plaster internally. The original entrance (dims. 2.15m x 1.15m) at W end of N wall was blocked up, together with a rectangular ope at E end of same wall, during rebuilding. Three rectangular windows visible in corresponding S wall. The E gable contains a central round-headed window flanked by two long narrow rectangular lights, this arrangement having replaced the earlier traceried E window, three sidestones of which are incorporated into the later window base. A further three fragments of it are visible in graveyard S of church. Two large mid-eighteenth-century memorials are incorporated into W end of S wall and E end of N wall respectively. A barrel-vaulted sacristy (original ext. dims. 9m N–S, 7.18m E–W, int. H 2.75m), aligned N–S, is at a right angle to E end of N wall of church. Constructed of randomly coursed small flat pieces of sandstone, it is rendered with plaster internally. Blocked rectangular light in E wall. The sacristy was detached from N wall of church, reduced in size (present int. dims. 6m x 4.15m) and modified for use as the mausoleum of Sharp of Roundwood and Flood of Middlemount in the early nineteenth century. A square belfry (int. dims. 4.3m x 4.3m, wall T 0.6m) was added on to W end of church, perhaps in the eighteenth century, and was accommodated by breaching W gable wall. Two halves of two separate quernstones and late medieval architectural fragments, including three moulded jambstones and a window sidestone, were found in the graveyard. St Kaban's Well (No. 832) lies 130m to NNW.
16:16(03)   8-5-1991

694 BALLINTUBBERT

OS 19:11:3 (681,288) 'G. Yd.'   OD 300–400
26133,19301

Church (site)   Marked on the 1841 ed. OS 6" map. Reference to a church site here (Comerford 1886, vol. 3, 127); no visible surface traces survive. Uninscribed grave-markers in graveyard and holy well (No. 833) to SE.
19:14(01)   15-8-1990

695 BALLYADAMS

OS 19:16:5 (773,56) '*Ballyadams Church* (in Ruins), G. Yd., *Stone Apheaka Bowen's Tomb*'   OD 400–500
26233,19056

Church   Originally known as Kilmackeady, the church of MacAedh (O'Hanlon and O'Leary 1907, vol. 1, 182). A medieval limestone-built church (L *c.* 19.6m, wall T *c.* 0.9m) with a nave (Wth *c.* 5.3m) and chancel (Wth *c.* 5.6m). Entrance in S wall, probably not original. Opes in N and S walls and in W gable. Within church is an altar-tomb, erected in 1631 to Robert Bowen and his wife Alice Harpole by their son. Its S face depicts an arcade of four rounded arches containing four figures, two female, two male, in seventeenth-century costume with an incised inscription above

them. The effigies of Robert Bowen and his wife were originally on the covering slab of the tomb but these are now destroyed (*JKAS* 1912, 21–2). Above the altar-tomb is a mural tablet and above this an armorial panel. A late medieval limestone slab (L *c.* 2m, Wth *c.* 0.8m) with the effigy of Walter Harpole, Dean of Leighlin 1587–1597, carved in low relief, lies in SE corner of chancel. Numerous uninscribed grave-markers visible in surrounding subrectangular graveyard.
19:31(01)   10-9-1990

696 BALLYADDING

OS 9:7:4 (507,360) '*Church* (in Ruins), Grave Yd.'
OD 200–300   25937,20656

Church   Small late medieval parish church (dims. 12.9m E–W, 7.6m N–S, wall T 0.8m), built of rubble limestone, situated within a subrectangular graveyard. Small single-light window with broken ogee-head visible in E gable. Similar windows in N and S walls, opposite each other. Walls of church survive to roof level except E end of S wall, and S end of W gable. Remains of doorway (Wth 0.85m) with hammer-dressed and chamfered limestone blocks in W gable. (*JKAS* 1904, 192)
9:14   24-7-1990

697 BALLYBOODIN

OS 29:13:4 (73,19) 'Keeloge Burial Gd.'
OD 300–400   23556,17711

Early ecclesiastical remains   This is the church of St Aedhog, Maedhog or Mogue (Carrigan 1905, vol. 2, 229–30). Rectangular church (dims. *c.* 9.2m N–S, *c.* 6.2m E–W) constructed of rough limestone boulders. The S wall (T *c.* 0.6m) is best preserved with only the foundations of the other walls visible. A large granite stone font (Wth *c.* 0.3m, D *c.* 0.18m) with a central perforation, which was recovered from the Goul River (Carrigan 1905, vol. 2, 229), is situated in SW angle of church. Ecclesiastical enclosure visible on aerial photographs (CUCAP, BDL 23–4). Slight evidence of the enclosing bank survives at W, N and NE.
29:41(01)   8-7-1990

698 BALLYBUGGY

OS 34:1:2 (149,584) '*Church* (in Ruins), Grave Yard, St. Bridget's Stone'   OD 400–500   22661,17659

Church (site)   Situated within ringfort (No. 140). Tradition of a nunnery here (Carrigan 1905, vol. 2, 6 intro.). No standing remains survive but Carrigan (*ibid.* 342) refers to S wall of a church (int. dim. *c.* 7m) which was situated inside the D–shaped graveyard. Dressed limestone blocks and the top of an ogee-headed twin-light window referred to by Carrigan (*ibid.*) are still to be seen. Bullaun stone (Wth *c.* 0.8m, H *c.* 1m, T *c.* 0.6m) with depression (diam 0.3m, D 0.13m) in E face, and known as St Bridget's stone, lies in S end of graveyard.
34:4(01)   27-9-1990

Fig. 12 —*Ballyadding, church* (**696**)

699 BALLYNAGALL

OS 32:1:3 (188,536) OD 400–500 26598,18287

Chapel (site) Reference to a thatched chapel built in 1686 by a member of the Hartpole family (O'Hanlon *et al.* 1914, vol. 2, 579). It was subsequently replaced by the modern church. No early grave-markers visible.

32:1(01)   14-8-1990

700 BALLYNAHOWN

OS 2:13:1 (21,138) 'Church (in Ruins), Grave Yard' OD 400–500 22493,21027

Church In a low-lying area. An undifferentiated church within an almost circular graveyard which is delimited by a stone wall. The church (max. dims. *c.* 18.7m E–W, 8m N–S, wall T 0.8m) is built of rubble and sandstone, and was recently partially rebuilt with W wall in wrong position. Featureless, but some large sandstone quoins remain in place in NE and SE angles. Quernstone-base (diam. 0.43m) with small central hole lies on wall of graveyard. Early Christian cross-slabs (No. 818) originally located here have been moved to Clonaslee church.

2:13(01)   31-10-1990

701 BAUNAGHRA

OS 33:16:1 (755,115) '*Church* (in Ruins), *The Sconces*' OD 400–500 22331,17160

Early ecclesiastical remains The E and W gables, both with a single-light window, and part of S wall survive of this rectangular church (12.9m x 7.4m, T 0.8m) built of roughly coursed limestone blocks. No trace of entrance. A piscina is situated in E end of S wall. Carrigan (1905, vol. 2, 282) refers to an altar with cut-stone sides within church, no trace survives. Graveyard destroyed before 1905 (*ibid.*). Probably a late medieval parish church. The outline of an enclosure around the site can be seen on aerial photographs (GSI, S 96–7), and on the ground is visible in places as a scarp. Probably an early ecclesiastical enclosure. A coin dated AD 747 was found when a portion of the enclosure was levelled (*JRSAI* 1867, 72–3).

33:17(01)   25-10-1990

702 BOLEY LOWER

OS 23:11:5 (557,165) '*Templeshankyle* (in Ruins), Grave Yard' OD 300–400 24059,18510

Church Reference to a church and ancient burial

ground here (Comerford 1886, vol. 3, 338). Remains of a nave and chancel church survive, built of roughly coursed limestone, with a narrow slit ope in E gable and doorway in S wall. No other features visible.
23:25   17-8-1990

703 BORDWELL BIG
OS 28:7:3 (667,383) '*Bordwell Church* (in Ruins), Grave Yd.' OD 400–500 23205,18092
Early ecclesiastical remains An Early Christian foundation was established here (Carrigan 1905, vol. 2, 58). In the thirteenth century the church was granted to the Augustinians of St Thomas's Abbey, Dublin by Thomas de Hereford (*ibid.*). A nave (L *c.* 17m, Wth *c.* 8.5m) and chancel (L *c.* 7.6m, Wth *c.* 7.3m, wall T *c.* 0.9m) church, constructed of roughly coursed limestone, with a pointed arch doorway in W end of S wall, and a round arch doorway opposite in N wall. Remains of ope in N and S walls. The E gable is partly destroyed. All visible headstones postdate 1700. A short stretch of a bank and fosse at W, and a shallow fosse (Wth *c.* 10m, D *c.* 0.3m) from NW–NE, outside the graveyard wall, indicate the line of an early enclosure around the site.
28:34(01)   18-9-1991

704 BORRIS GREAT
OS 13:6:5 (328,363) 'Church (Site of)' OD 300–400
24779,20007
Church (site) Marked as 'Site of' on the 1841 and 1909 eds. OS 6" maps. Reference to a church indicated by a heap of stones (O'Hanlon and O'Leary 1907, vol. 1, 192–3). No visible surface traces. Holy well (No. 838) lies to *c.* 45m to SW.
13:22(01)   23-7-1990

705 CARRICKSALLAGH
OS 19:2:3 (387,542) '*Oughaval Church* (in Ruins)'
OD 300–400 25820,19566
Church St Coleman founded a monastery here in the sixth century. The later medieval church, constructed of roughly coursed limestone, was subsequently greatly modified by the Cosbys who built their family burial vault within the nave (O'Hanlon and O'Leary 1907, vol. 1, 324–6). As a result, the ground-floor level of the chancel (L *c.* 10.45m, Wth 9.15m) is now higher than that of the nave (L *c.* 17.4m, Wth 6.75m, wall T *c.* 1.9m). A three-light window, with later nineteenth-century insertions, survives in E wall of chancel. Evidence of drafting is visible on three windows in N and S walls. Over the chancel lies a barrel-vault and loft, with a possible wall-walk on N and S walls. A two-storey square tower projects from NW angle of nave. Within nave, a nineteenth-century doorway leads to the Cosby vault. The circular enclosure defining the graveyard was removed by the Poor Law Guardians and replaced by modern square one (*ibid.*).
19:3(01)   2-5-1990

706 CASHEL (Upperwoods By.)
OS 22:2:1 (278,537) OD 400–500 22786,18891
Church (site) Carrigan (1905, vol. 2, 179) refers to the site of a church and graveyard, dedicated to St Garadh, within N end of a substantial drystone rectangular enclosure (dims. *c.* 22.5m N–S, 14.4m E–W) which was destroyed in 1835. Also a rough limestone bullaun (diam. 0.32m, D 0.13m). No visible surface traces survive.
22:5(01)   5-8-1991

707 CASTLEBRACK
OS 1:15:2 (574,102) '*Church* (in Ruins), Grave Yard' OD 404 24047,21645
Church Situated in an elevated position in a rectangular graveyard to NNW of tower house (No. 947). Featureless and undifferentiated church (dims. 24.7m E–W, 8m N–S), in poor condition, built of roughly coursed rubble. Except for S wall which stands to its full height, only the foundations remain. Some architectural fragments are inserted in graveyard wall, and S wall of church.
1:4(03)   13-8-1990

708 CASTLEDURROW DEMESNE/
    DURROW TOWNPARKS
OS 29:15:5 (543,43) OD 200–300 24052,17742
Monastery (possible, site) Not marked on the 1841 or 1906 eds. OS 6" maps. The foundations of what was traditionally known as 'Durrow Monastery', founded by St Finlan, survived until 1835 (Carrigan 1905, vol. 2, 213). No visible surface traces survive.
29:42   12-7-1990

709 CASTLEQUARTER (Clarmallagh By.)
OS 35:5:4 (64,331) 'R.C. Chapel (in Ruins)'
OD 300–400 23550,17401
Church The private church of the Catholic Lords of Upper Ossory, situated *c.* 100m W of tower house (No. 954). It is roofless since Cromwellian times, and no burials have taken place here since the mid-nineteenth century (Carrigan 1905, vol. 2, 233). A late sixteenth-century nave and chancel church (L *c.* 19.7m, Wth *c.* 9.2m), built of roughly coursed limestone with an external base-batter. Remains of a doorway survive in S wall, as well as two single-light windows with splayed opes, and a dressed limestone piscina. Single-light ogee-headed window visible in W gable, and in E gable a two-light dressed limestone window with a rounded head on the inner face. Corbels, which carried a loft, project from the side-walls.
35:21(01)   27-9-1990

710 CHURCHTOWN
OS 16:12:5 (834,164) '*Church* (in Ruins), Grave Yard' OD 400–500 23371,19142
Church St Cedus is the patron Saint of Churchtown

Fig. 13—*Clonenagh, cross-slabs* (**714**)

and is commemorated on the 20th November (Carrigan 1905, vol. 2, 174). A late medieval parish church (L *c.* 16.2m, Wth *c.* 9m, wall T *c.* 0.85m) built of roughly coursed limestone. Remains of a doorway survive in W end of S wall. A window jamb, possibly belonging to the destroyed E window, lies in SW angle of church. Carrigan (*ibid.*, 172–3) describes a late medieval doorway in E end of N wall, and within graveyard, a roughly cut circular greenstone font (Wth *c.* 0.3m, D *c.* 0.9m) and a holed stone. These are no longer visible.
16:18(01)   16-9-1991

711 CLONAGH (Slievemargy By.)
OS 32:3:1 (482,546) '*Monastery* (in Ruins)'
OD 200–300   26909,18300
Monastery Unclassified religious house (Gwynn and Hadcock 1970, 364); associated with St Fintan (O'Flanagan 1933, vol. 2, 16–17). Very fragmentary remains of a late medieval limestone building survive. The entrance with a partly destroyed arch is in E wall (T *c.* 1.5m) with a chamber to N and S. Small barrel-vaulted area at S, and remains of stair tower in W wall.
32:7(01)   14-8-1990

712 CLONEEB
OS 34:1:1 (41,565) '*Church* (in Ruins) Grave Yard'
OD 368   22547,17638
Church (site) Marked on the 1841 and 1906 eds. OS 6" map. According to Carrigan (1905, vol. 2, 342), there was formerly a monastery here. Fragments of a church (L *c.* 23m), with traces of a doorway and credence near E end of S wall, survived until the early 1900s. Outside the graveyard, foundations of several buildings were visible. No surface traces survive. Earthworks (No. 614) to SW.
34:1(01)   28-9-1990

713 CLONENAGH
OS 17:2:3 (395,557) '*Church* (in Ruins) Grave Yard'
OD 400–500   23878,19563
Church A sixteenth-century nave (Wth *c.* 8.6m) and chancel (L *c.* 8.9m, Wth *c.* 6.4m) church built of roughly coursed sandstone and limestone rubble. The nave is only discernible at the cross-wall. The E gable contains a two-light limestone window with tracery. It is lightly hammer-dressed and has bar-holes and grooves. The sandstone chancel arch (Wth *c.* 3.55m, wall T *c.* 1.4m) has a central rib of finely hammer-

Fig. 14—*Clonenagh, cross-slabs* (**714**)

dressed limestone. Immediately above the apex of the arch is a sandstone rectangular-shaped window with a flat chamfered head. No original opes visible in N or S walls. A large number of uninscribed grave-markers and headstones, post 1700 in date, are visible in the surrounding subrectangular graveyard; also a block of sandstone with a skull and cross-bones in relief, and a corbel with a human face. (Comerford 1886, vol. 3, 291–9)
17:3(01)   31-8-1990

714 CLONENAGH
OS 17:2:3 (414,568) 'Burial Gd.' OD 400–500
23898,19574

Graveyard and cross-slabs Reference to a monastery founded by St Fintan *c.* 548 (O'Byrne 1856, 55–6). No visible surface traces survive. Within the graveyard are some Early Christian cross-slabs, rectangular in shape, carved in false relief or simply cross-incised. Also a block of sandstone decorated with Romanesque art. St Fintan's well (No. 842) and site of holy tree lie to SSE. Burial ground (No. 879) to S.
17:3(07)   31-8-1990

715 CLONENAGH
OS 17:2:3 (445,594) 'Church (Site of)'
OD 300–400 23930,19602

Church (site) Apart from a low mound, with a rectangular hollow area in the centre, no visible surface traces survive of this church. A hawthorn bush is growing on the spot marked 'thorn' on the 1841 ed. OS 6" map.
17:4(01)   31-8-1990

716 CLONKEEN (Maryborough West By.)
OS 17:4:5 (808,466) 'Church (Site of)'
OD 300–400 24315,19471

Church (site) An ancient church, formerly called Cluainchaoin, was traditionally remembered to have stood here, at a place called Churchfields, where an old burial ground was in use until the early 1800s (O'Hanlon and O'Leary 1907, vol. 1, 210–11). Reference to a church in the Ecclesiastical Taxation of 1302–6 (Sweetman 1875–80, vol. V, 250). Around 1616 the church was in a ruineous state but the chancel was kept in repair. No visible surface traces.
17:7(01)   28-8-1990

717 CLONKEEN (Cullenagh By.)

OS 29:8:6 (877,355) 'Clonkeen Church (in Ruins), Grave Yard' OD 300–400 24401,18074

Church Dedicated to St Fintan (Comerford 1886, vol. 3, 106–7). A ruined nave (Wth *c.* 6.55m) and chancel (Wth *c.* 5.3m) church (L *c.* 13.4m, wall T *c.* 0.8m) with dividing wall, built of roughly coursed limestone blocks. An ope in E end of S wall may represent the doorway. Remains of an ope in centre of N wall.

29:25   13-8-1990

718 CLONMEEN SOUTH

OS 33:8:4 (718,339) 'Abbey (in Ruins)' OD 400–500 22290,17396

Abbey Unclassified religious house (Gwynn and Hadcock 1970, 364). Carrigan (1905, vol. 2, 344–5) refers to extensive remains of monastic buildings enclosed by a stone wall or caiseal and fosse. Remains now consist of a wall (L 6m) running NW–SE with an extensive length of wall-footing continuing from SE end. There is also another piece of standing masonry (Wth *c.* 1.6m) at SE. No other visible surface traces.

33:9(01)   25-10-1990

719 CLONMEEN SOUTH

OS 33:8:4 (715,318) 'Church (in Ruins)' OD 400–500 22287,17375

Church (site) Situated about 200m S of abbey site (No. 718). Described as a church (L *c.*11.7m, Wth *c.* 10.65m) with doorway in S wall (Carrigan 1905, vol. 2, 345). No visible surface traces except for a rubble limestone wall (L 10m) running E–W. Modern farm buildings immediately to E of site.

33:10   25-10-1990

720 CLOPOOK

OS 19:14:5 (383,51) 'Church (in Ruins), Grave Yd.' OD 400–500 25822,19047

Church A nave (L *c.* 11m, Wth *c.* 6.45m) and chancel (L *c.* 8.85m, Wth *c.* 4.5m) church built of rough limestone blocks randomly coursed. A segmental arch divides nave from chancel. Surviving features include two opes in S wall of nave, with broken entrance at W end, and one ope in N wall. The E window is badly damaged. All visible headstones postdate 1700. (Comerford 1886, vol. 3, 127–8)

19:22   16-8-1990

721 COOLBANAGHER

OS 8:15:6 (680,52) 'Coolbanagher Church (in Ruins), Grave Yard' OD 300–400 25147,20322

Church A nave and chancel church (dims. 19.1m E–W, 6.5m N–S, wall T 0.75m) built of roughly coursed limestone blocks. The dividing wall retains possible basal remains of a Romanesque chancel arch. Blocked-up Romanesque doorway of one order visible in W gable. Its sandstone arch is decorated with incised line mouldings. Font (No. 827) may originally have been located here. Coolbanagher tower house (No. 952) lies *c.* 100m to NE. (O'Hanlon and O'Leary 1907, vol. 1, 221)

8:14(01)   20-6-1990

722 COOLKERRY

OS 28:15:1 (485,87) 'Coolkerry Church (in Ruins), Grave Yard' OD 300 23015,17778

Church Circa 70m NE of site of Coolkerry Castle (No. 989). Marked on the Down Survey map as 'ruined church, weir, cabin'. A rectangular church (L *c.* 17m, Wth *c.* 7.3m, wall T *c.* 0.9m) with standing remains of W gable. The N, E and S walls are indicated by grass-covered banks. (Carrigan 1905, vol. 2, 340–1)

28:61   4-9-1991

723 COOLOWLEY (PLOTT)

OS 27:8:5 (834,352) Indicated OD 300–400 22405,18052

Church Rectangular nave and chancel church (L *c.* 14.7m, Wth *c.* 7.4m, wall T *c.* 0.95m) built of roughly coursed rubble limestone. Featureless, apart from a rectangular window in W gable. (Carrigan 1905, vol. 2, 140)

27:12   11-10-1990

724 CORBALLY (Ballyadams By.)

OS 25:3:6 (675,512) 'Tecolm Church (in Ruins), Grave Yard' OD 300–400 26131,18897

Church Marked on the 1563 map of Leix and Offaly (Hore 1863, f.p. 345). Associated with St Colman of Oughaval (Comerford 1886, vol. 3, 131). Constructed of roughly coursed limestone, only W gable (Wth *c.* 6.65m, wall T *c.* 1m) with segmental arched doorway remains standing. No headstones visible.

25:10   19-7-1990

725 COURSE

OS 29:15:3 (656,107) 'Monastery (in Ruins)' OD 300–400 24171,17811

Monastery (site) Reference to a large quadrangular area (dims. *c.* 80m NNW–SSE, 70m ENE–WSW) enclosed by an earthen rampart, and traditionally believed to be the site of an ancient monastery (Carrigan 1905, vol. 2, 222). In 1901 Lord Ashbrook and others cleared the site exposing the remains of the foundations of a group of buildings (L *c.* 19m N–S), including a possible refectory and church (L *c.* 9m) running W, from N end of buildings (*ibid.*, 222–3). No visible surface traces survive.

29:46(01)   12-7-1990

726 COURSE

Subrectilinear enclosure (site) Incorporated with entry No. 725.

Fig. 15—*Coolbanagher, church doorway* (**721**)

727 CREMORGAN
OS 18:11:6 (687,223) '*Church* (in Ruins), Grave Yard'
OD 500–600   25165,19223
Church   Associated with St Colman (O'Hanlon and
O'Leary 1907, vol. 1, 246). Nave and chancel church
(L *c*. 13.75m, Wth *c*. 8m), built of roughly coursed
limestone and sandstone, within a rectangular
graveyard. Surviving features include a single-light
tracery window in E gable, and a pointed arch
doorway, with a later brick arch insertion, in S wall. A
cut-stone dressed capital with a chamfered outer edge
is visible on N jamb. Buttress to S of doorway.
Remains of an aumbry at E end of S wall. This was the
burial place of the O'Moores of Cremorgan
(Comerford 1886, vol. 3, 375). An earthen bank (Wth
c. 2.55m, int. H *c*. 0.4m, ext. H *c*. 1.25m), retained by a
stone wall externally, defines the graveyard from
NW–SE.
18:21(01)   14-6-1990

728 CROMOGE
OS 17:14:6 (450,18) '*St. Fintan's Church* (in Ruins),
Grave Yard'   OD 300–400   23942,18995
Church   Dedicated to St Fintan who resided here
before moving to Clonenagh (Comerford 1886, vol. 3,
337). A nave and chancel church (L *c*. 36m, Wth *c*.

11.4m), built of roughly coursed rubble limestone,
with a round segmental chancel arch. The chancel is
destroyed except for its SW angle. Comerford (*ibid.*)
mentions a small E window, a round-headed doorway
in W gable and a later square tower placed at W end;
only an ope in E gable is now visible. The N and S
walls are featureless. All visible inscribed headstones,
within subrectangular graveyard, postdate 1700. Holy
well (No. 850) lies *c*. 180m to SSW.
17:14   28-8-1990

729 CUFFSBOROUGH
OS 28:4:2 (815,531) '*Church* (Site of)'   OD 300–400
23359,18250
Church (site)   Reference to the foundations of a
church (dims *c*. 15.24m x 9.14m) and a community of
men dependent on Aghaboe (Carrigan 1905, vol. 2,
58). No visible surface traces survive.
28:15(01)   13-9-1991

730 CULLENAGH (Cullenagh By.)
OS 18:15:2 (587,97) '*Kilfailan Church* (in Ruins)'
OD 600–700   25061,19089
Church   Marked Cullenagh Abbey on the 1841 ed. OS
6" map. Remains of a nave and chancel church (L *c*.

18.7m, Wth *c.* 9.4m, wall T *c.* 0.9m) built of rubble limestone roughly coursed. Doorway in E end of N wall, and evidence of blocked-up opes in N and S walls. No other visible features.
18:30(01)   14-6-1990

731 CURRACLONE
OS 14:11:5 (592,186) '*Church* (in Rns.), Grave Yd.'
OD 200–300 26034,19832
Early ecclesiastical remains   Church marked on the 1563 map of Leix and Offaly (Hore 1863, f.p. 345). Present remains consist of a later church; only W gable with doorway is clearly visible, the N and S walls are indistinguishable due to heavy overgrowth. A family vault of the Walshes of Ballykilcavan, dated 1794, lies at E end. An earlier church once stood here (O'Hanlon and O'Leary 1907, vol. 1, 223). An Early Christian cross-slab with a simple Latin cross on E face was found among uninscribed gravestones in W half of graveyard. A gravestone immediately N of it is a reused architectural fragment, possibly from the earlier church. A substantial earthen enclosure, retained by an external stone wall, surrounds the graveyard. A further earthen bank with a shallow external fosse to N, enclosing the Glebe land on 1841 ed. OS 6" map, may be the remains of an outer enclosure (FitzPatrick 1991, 213–5).
14:35(01)   23-5-1994

732 DAIRYHILL
OS 29:1:2 (141,556) 'Kyle-cruttia' OD 300–400
23623,18279
Church (possible, site)   Carrigan (1905, vol. 2, 57) refers to a church site and graveyard, within which were numerous uninscribed headstones, enclosed by a large earthen bank. Not marked on the 1841 ed. OS 6" map, and no surface traces of a church or graveyard survive. The enclosing bank is visible from NNW–E. The S half is partly levelled and is indicated by a slight rise in ground level.
29:5   4-7-1990

733 DANGANS
OS 8:3:4 (463,462) '*Church* (in Ruins), Grave Yard'
OD 200–300 24913,20753
Church (site)   Old church in ruins mentioned here (O'Hanlon and O'Leary 1907, vol. 1, 180). No upstanding remains which might be considered part of a medieval church survive. The N gable of a mortuary chapel lies in NE part of the rectangular graveyard.
8:2   28-5-1990

734 DERRYKEARN
OS 23:3:5 (603,473) '*Kyletabreehren* (in Ruins), Grave Yd. (Disused)' OD 300–400 24105,18837
Church   Featurless church (L *c.* 15.9m, Wth *c.* 6.8m), consisting of a chancel and collapsed nave within a

large subrectangular graveyard. The interior of the church was also used for burial and contains post-1700 headstones.
23:7(03)   17-8-1990

735 DONAGHMORE
OS 28:5:6 (187,323) 'Grave Yd.' OD 300–400
22698,18024
Church (site)   According to Carrigan (1905, vol. 2, 352), the medieval church was destroyed in 1821. References to it date from the fifteenth century. The present church was built on its site.
28:25   29-9-1991

736 DUNMORE
OS 29:11:3 (638,250) OD 200–300 24151,17961
Church and graveyard (site)   Not marked on the 1841 or 1907 eds. OS 6" maps. Church, known as St Tachan's, and graveyard said to be situated under Dunmore House and its tennis court (Carrigan 1905, vol. 2, 223–4). No visible surface traces.
29:35   14-8-1990

737 DURROW TOWNPARKS
OS 29:15:5 (556,40) OD 293 24066,17738
Church (site)   Marked on the 1841 ed. OS 6" map and on the Down Survey map. Dedicated to St Fintan, it was demolished before 1731 and the site is now occupied by the Protestant church (Carrigan 1905, vol. 2, 213). No visible surface traces.
29:45   12-7-1990

738 DYSART
OS 13:15:6 (680,17) '*Church* (in Ruins), Grave Yd.'
OD 500–600 25153,19645
Church   Dysart is associated with Angus who founded a cell here. Sir Charles Coote, in 1801, described Dysart church as standing on a lofty hill with a square tower or steeple (O'Hanlon and O'Leary 1907, vol. 1, 229). This comparatively modern church is now ruined but traces of the foundations of an older church are incorporated within its walls. Reference to an ancient graveyard (*ibid.*).
13:59(01)   6-6-1990

739 EGLISH
OS 27:16:3 (882,128) 'Grave Yard' OD 300–400
22459,17815
Church (site)   Reference to a church site (L c. 14.4m) associated with St Nicholas. Only the foundations survived in the early 1900s, with further building foundations around it. Tradition of a monastery here. No grave-markers were visible in the graveyard which had been disused for a long period of time. (Carrigan 1905, vol. 2, 66). No visible surface traces.
27:30(01)   8-11-1990

740 EMO PARK
OS 9:5:4 (2,335) *'Killeenatogher Church (Site of)'*
OD 200–300   25403,20623
Church (site)   In a slightly elevated position. This church has been levelled and no surface traces are visible.
9:5   21-6-1990

741 ERRILL
OS 27:15:3 (634,130) *'St Kieran's Monastery (Site of)'*
OD 400   22197,17815
Monastery (site)   Marked 'Friary' on the 1841 ed. OS 6" map. Said to have been founded by St Kieran (Carrigan 1905, vol. 2, 346). Only some pieces of masonary remain within a raised square-shaped enclosure (dims. *c.* 54m sq.) defined by a scarp (H 1–1.5m). Possible original entrance at SE. Some stone is evident in the enclosure. No other visible surface traces. Medieval church (No. 742) *c.* 220m to SE.
27:22(02)   9-11-1990

742 ERRILL
OS 27:15:3 (650,117) *'St Kieran's Ch.* (in Ruins), Grave Yard'   OD 300–400   22214,17802
Church   A late medieval church (dims. 16.9m E–W, 8.8m N–S, wall T 1.1m). Features include a doorway towards W end of S wall, and a splayed chamfered round-headed window at E end. Some pieces of cut stone have been reused as grave-markers in the surrounding subrectangular graveyard. National monument No. 113 (Harbison 1970, 139–40).
27:24   9-11-1990

743 FARRANEGLISH GLEBE
OS 23:13:2 (82,122) *'Church* (in Ruins)'
OD 300–400   23560,18460
Church   In a low-lying area, immediately N of roadway. Incorrectly marked, to S of road, on 1909 ed. OS 6" map. A rectangular late medieval church (dims. 14.7m x 6.6m), aligned NW–SE, compsed of randomly coursed limestone and heavily overgrown with ivy. Upstanding remains include S wall (ext. H 1.1m), clipped at SE during construction of roadway, W gable (ext. H 3.8m), and N wall (ext. H 1.5m) with pronounced base-batter and large window at W end. Nothing visible of E gable at ground level. The interior of the church is full of collapsed masonry and foliage. Architectural fragments visible at base of N wall and within field boundary wall to SE. According to local information, there was a graveyard in the field known as 'the Church Field', to N of church. Large quantities of human bones were uncovered here, during ploughing, in the 1950s.
23:29   27-5-1994

744 FOSSY LOWER
OS 19:13:4 (27,1) *'Fossy Church* (in Ruins), Grave Yd.'   OD 400–500   25446,18991
Church   A late sixteenth-century parish church (L *c.*

13.8m, Wth *c.* 7.7m), built of uncoursed rubble, with a slight base-batter. Broken-out doorway (Wth *c.* 1.4m) in W gable. Five windows visible in S wall and four in N wall. In both walls one window is much larger than the others. The window dressings had been removed prior to repairs by the OPW in 1945 (OPW file). The smaller windows are simple rectangular opes which are chamfered and have glazing-bar-holes and grooves. Four are placed very high above the ground level. Piscina in SE angle. An Early Christain cross-slab was recently found in the graveyard (pers. comm. D. Delaney).
19:16/25:1*   4-5-1990

745 GARRYDUFF (Clandonagh By.)
OS 27:2:6 (450,466)   'Clonmeen Burial Ground'
OD 400–500   21999,18168
Church (possible, site)   Carrigan (1905, vol. 2, 138–9) refers to a church here but stated there were no traces of it in the graveyard. He also refers to the bullaun stone which has a bowl-shaped hollow (diam. *c.* 0.36m, D 0.15m) cut into a large limestone rock. It lies outside graveyard to NE.
27:1   6-10-1990

746 GLEBE (Clarmallagh By.) Durrow ED
OS 35:4:6 (882,508)   OD 100–200   24412,17596
Church (possible,site)   According to tradition, there was formerly and old church where the present church is now situated (O'Flanagan 1933, vol. 1, 40). No trace survives.
35:17   23-9-1990

747 GLEBE (Claremallagh By.) Durrow ED/ GRENAN
OS 35 NPL
Church (site)   Reference to a substantial ruined nave and chancel church (L *c.* 24.4m) with a three-light tracery window in E gable, and a pointed arch doorway and window in S wall. The nave, erected in 1646, was apparently older than the chancel and separated from it by the chancel arch (O'Hanlon and O'Leary 1907, vol. 1, 308). Not located.
                                                                35:74

748 GRAIGUEADRISLY
OS 33:16:3 (920,130) *'Colbally Church* (in Ruins)'
OD 500–600   22505,17178
Church   Known as Thomple-a-Churravolla or Corbally Church (Carrigan 1905, vol. 2, 282). A rectangular church (L *c.* 19.2m, Wth *c.* 5.7m, wall T *c.* 0.9m) constructed of roughly coursed limestone. The N wall is destroyed. Remains of ope in E end of S wall. Otherwise featureless.
33:23   17-8-1991

749 GRANGE (Ballyadams By.)
OS 32:3:6 (665,519) *'Monksgrange Church* (in Ruins), Grave Yard' OD 100–200 27102,18274
Church (site) Described as a large church surmounted by a square tower, although photographs dated *c.* 1906 show a featureless rectangular building without the tower (O'Hanlon and O'Leary 1907, vol. 1, 289–90). No surface evidence of church survives. Some uninscribed grave-markers visible in the surrounding subrectangular graveyard.
32:9   14-8-1990

750 GREATHEATH (Maryborough East By.)
OS 13:8:1 (725,448) OD 300–400 25197,20100
Chapel (site) Not marked in gothic on the 1841 ed. OS 6" map. Reference to a thatched chapel at Loughshinahawn and a font which was used as a cure for warts and growths (O'Hanlon *et al.* 1914, vol. 2, 586). No visible surface traces of chapel survive. The font was removed to a farmyard. Not located.
13:29(01)   23-7-1990

751 KILBREEDY
OS 28:7:4 (516,308) *'St. Bridget's Church* (in Ruins), Grave Yd.' OD 300–400 23046,18011
Church A late medieval parish church constructed of roughly coursed limestone. The E gable (Wth *c.* 6.6m), and part of S wall (L *c.* 14.2m, wall T *c.* 0.95m) with a chamfered doorway jambstone at W end survive. No other features visible. Some uninscribed grave-markers visible in surrounding rectangular graveyard. (Carrigan 1905, vol. 2, 59–60)
28:35   19-9-1991

752 KILBRICKAN
OS 17:13:6 (176,11) *'Church* (in Ruins)' OD 300–400 23653,18984
Church Situated in a low-lying area on S bank of the River Nore. Reference to the church of St Brocan or Brogan (Carrigan 1905, vol. 2, 176). A rectangular church (L *c.* 19m, Wth *c.* 9.8m, wall T *c.* 1.2m) with the base of the doorway (Wth *c.* 0.85m) at W end of S wall, and remains of a window at E end. Otherwise featureless. The E gable is destroyed. An inscribed stone (No. 823) on S wall was moved to Kilbrickan House (*ibid.*).
17:12(01)   31-8-1990

753 KILCOLMANBANE
OS 18:3:4 (512,470) *'Church* (in Ruins), Grave Yard' OD 500–600 24978,19481
Church St Colman Ban may have founded an early church here and he is commemorated on the 19th October (O'Hanlon and O'Leary 1907, vol. 1, 244–5). A late medieval nave (L *c.* 11.1m, Wth *c.* 6.6m) and chancel (L *c.* 6.55m, Wth *c.* 4.5m, wall T *c.* 1.4m) church built of rough limestone blocks randomly

coursed. The E window has been replaced by a modern entrance. The original doorway was possibly in S wall. Plain rectangular window in W gable. The nave and chancel are divided by a segmental rounded arch (Wth *c.* 2.4m), and the ground-floor level of the nave is 1.2m lower than that of the chancel. All visible headstones, in surrounding irregularly shaped graveyard, postdate 1700.
18:2   4-5-1990

754 KILCORAN
OS 28:14:5 (1337,46) OD 300–400 22860,17733
Church (possible, site) Not marked on the 1841 or 1908 eds. OS 6" maps. Human bones were discovered, in 1889, in Kilcoran rath (No. 221) which is thought to have been the site of a church associated with St Cobhran (Carrigan 1905, vol. 2, 341). No visible surface traces.
28:57(01)   6-9-1991

755 KILCRONAN
OS 30:10:1 (266,254) *'Kilcronan Church* (in Ruins), G. Yd.' OD 400 24733,17971
Church On W bank of the Owenbeg River. A monastery is said to have been founded here by St Cronan (O'Byrne 1856, 50–1). The church (dims. 12.8m x 5.18m) was almost levelled by 1907 but traces of wall foundations were visible; part of the graveyard was washed away by flood waters (O'Hanlon and O'Leary 1907, vol. 1, 235). Only a portion of W gable (H *c.* 1.3m) and E end of S wall now remain. No architectural features visible. Headstones in the surrounding subtriangular graveyard postdate 1700.
30:26   21-6-1991

756 KILDELLIG
OS 22:15:1 (508,78) *'Kildellig Church* (Site of), Grave Yd.' OD 400–500 23033,18408
Church St Ernan or Senan is the patron saint of Kyledellig and is commemorated on the 1st January. It is recorded as the 'Rectoria de Delgy' in thirteenth- and fourteenth-century entries in the Red Book of Ossory (Carrigan 1905, vol. 2, 64). According to Carrigan (*ibid.*), it was a very small church (L *c.* 11m), and in 1862 its E gable and S wall were knocked down and the material used in the construction of the surrounding rectangular graveyard wall. The foundations of a rectangular church, now barely visible, survive. A slight curve in the field bank E of the graveyard may indicate the remains of an enclosure.
22:22(02)   9-8-1991

757 KILDRINAGH
OS 16:14:2 (375,102) OD 300–400 22887,19072
Church (possible, site) Not marked on the 1841 or 1909 eds. OS 6" map. Reference to a church and

graveyard within a rath (No. 224). Four bronze daggers and burials were discovered (Carrigan 1905, vol. 2, 180). No visible surface traces.

16:23(01)   16-9-1991

758 KILGORY
OS 36:3:4 (489,459) '*Church* (Site of), Grave Yard' OD 700–800   25948,17559
Church (site) Marked 'Church (in Ruins)' on the 1841 ed. OS 6" map. Possibly the site of an early foundation associated with St Lony (Comerford 1886, vol. 3, 197). Only W gable, partially reconstructed, survives; a modern low wall was built on the line of the church foundations. Uninscribed grave markers visible in the surrounding subtriangular graveyard. Holy well (No. 859) and hawthorn bush festooned with rags lie to NW.
36:2(01)   5-9-1990

759 KILLABBAN
OS 26:11:4 (477,187) '*Killabban Church* (in Ruins), Grave Yd.'   OD 200–300   26901,18561
Church Founded by St Abban in 650 (O'Hanlon and O'Leary 1907, vol. 1, 247–9). Present remains consist of a nave (ext. dims. 15.4m x 9m) and chancel (ext. dims. 10.45m x 8.3m) church, of coursed limestone rubble, dating to the thirteenth century, with later fifteenth-/sixteenth-century alterations. The original two-light E window, which had granite jambs, was replaced by a single light of moulded and chamfered limestone. Entrance at W end of S wall, with later doorway in W wall. Ground level of chancel is presently 1m above that of nave. Remains of broken sarcophagus in chancel and numerous pieces of medieval cut stone visible in graveyard.
26:13(02)   4-8-1990

760 KILLINURE
OS 11 NPL
Church (site) Reference to a church site (Carrigan 1905, vol. 2, 152). Font (No. 826) originally located in churchyard (*ibid.*).
11:23

761 KILLEEN
OS 21: NPL
Church (site) Reference to church site in a field known as the 'Burying Meadow' and, within graveyard, a children's burial ground (No. 883). Font (No. 825) is said to be originally from this church (Carrigan 1905, vol. 2, 151).
11:21(03)

762 KILLEEN or
KILLEENLYNAGH (Portnahinch By.)
OS 8:11:1 (494,251) 'Killeen Grave Yd. (Disused)' OD 200   24949,20531

Church (possible, site) According to O'Hanlon *et al.* (1914, vol. 2, 574), this is the site of the ancient church of Killeen. No surface traces visible; the site has been levelled. A granite holy water font was moved from the church and placed at the 'Mass Pit', one field to N (*ibid.*). Not located.
8:9(01)   11-6-1990

763 KILLENNY (Stradbally By.)
OS 13:4:6 (893,487) '*Killenny Ch.* (in Ruins), Grave Yd.'   OD 300–400   25374,20144
Early ecclesiastical remains Associated with St Eithne (O'Hanlon and O'Leary 1907, vol. 1, 254). In 1615 it was in repair and used for Protestant service (Comerford 1886, vol. 3, 282). The church (L *c.* 27m, Wth *c.* 16.4m, wall T *c.* 0.9m) is built of roughly coursed limestone blocks. A narrow ope, splaying inwards, is visible in E gable. The S wall is almost completely destroyed and the remaining walls are obscured by ivy. Uninscribed grave-markers visible in the surrounding subtriangular graveyard. The enclosure visible on aerial photographs (GSI, N 227–8) from NW–NNE is indicated by low bank.
13:18(01)   25-5-1990

764 KILLERMOGH
OS 29:6:6 (407,362) '*Killermogh Church* (in Ruins), Grave Yard'   OD 200–300   23905,18077
Church The patron saint of Killermogh was St Muicin (Carrigan 1905, vol. 2, 65). Church (L *c.* 13.7m, Wth *c.* 5.7m, wall T *c.* 0.8m) built of roughly coursed limestone and rubble, and now in very poor condition. The E gable contains a single-light ope, otherwise featureless. There are some uninscribed grave-markers in the surrounding roughly rectangular graveyard.
29:22   13-8-1990

765 KILLESHIN
OS 32:14:5 (310,56) '*Ch.* (in Ruins), *Round Tower*, Grave Yard'   OD 300–400   26732,17781
Early ecclesiastical remains St Dermot founded an Early Christian church here but the patron is St Comhdan or Comgan who is commemorated on 27th February. Killeshin was plundered and the oratory demolished in 1041, and it was burnt in 1077 (*JKAS* 1910, 185–205). Only W end of nave and E end of chancel survive of this twelfth-century church (int. L *c.* 28.3m) composed of sandstone with granite quoins. The W gable (ext. Wth 13m), with anta at N end, contains an elaborately decorated Romanesque doorway which has four receding orders with capitals bearing human heads with intertwined hair. The arch, surmounted by a hood, is decorated with animal and foliage motifs, and its keystone, carved in relief, also bears a human head. Two inscriptious are visible; one on N side reads 'a prayer for Diarmait, King of Leinster' (Harbison 1970, 140). A granite window, pointed externally and round-headed internally, lies

Fig. 16—*Kilmanman, church* (**767**)

above doorway; a similar but larger window is visible in the adjoining section of N wall (int. L 11.9m). The S end of the adjoining S wall (int. L 5.4m) has a later buttress.

The later chancel (ext. Wth 8.25m) has a slight base-batter. The original E window has been replaced by a square two-light ogee-headed window, probably dating to the sixteenth century. An aumbry is visible in SE corner. Surviving sections of the adjoining N wall (int. L 5.2m) and S wall (int. L 1.4m) are featureless. Some cut and dressed stone lie in NE and SE angles. Modern burials have been placed within the church, and headstones in the surrounding graveyard postdate 1700. A round tower, to NW of church, was destroyed in 1703 (*JKAS* 1910, 189, 198). To N of doorway lies a circular undecorated granite font (diam. *c.* 0.8m) with a cone-shaped basin and central hole. A small socket in the rim of the font is probably associated with a cover. (Crawford and Leask 1925, 83–94; O'Hanlon and O'Leary 1907, vol. 1, 257–64)
32:20(02)   14-8-1990

766 KILMAINHAM
OS 8:6:2 (340,385) '*Friary* (in Ruins), Grave Yd.'
OD 200–300   24784,20670
Friary   Unclassified monastic establishment (Gwynn and Hadcock 1970, 369) also known as Triogue. Built

of poorly coursed limestone rubble, remains consist of E gable of church (max. dims. 20.6m E–W, 5.5m N–S), with only the foundation level of its other walls surviving. A barrel-vaulted building (max. dims. 7.3m N–S, 5.3m E–W) is attached to S wall of nave. Simple slit ope with glazing-bar-holes visible in E gable, which apparently was 'trefoil-headed' (*JKAS* 1904, 194). Probably a late medieval parish church.
8:3   11-6-1990

767 KILMANMAN
OS 2:7:5 (546,327) '*Kilmanman Church* (in Ruins), Grave Yd.'   OD 300–400   23046,21232
Church   Situated in an elevated position on N side of valley. Church (19.8m E–W, 9m N–S, wall T 0.9m) built of roughly coursed rubble, mainly sandstone. Featureless N wall; two-light tracery sandstone window visible in E gable. The S wall is almost completely destroyed, no evidence of doorway but evidence of window at E end. Remains of bellcote on top of W gable; also a rectangular window. Late medieval parish church, probably dating to the second half of the sixteenth century. Several fragments of dressed sandstone visible in surrounding subrectangular graveyard. Holy well (No. 860) to SSW.
2:2(01)   6-9-1990

768 KILMINFOYLE
OS 29:1:4 (64,517) 'Burial Gd. (Disused)' OD 300
23541,18237
Church (possible, site) Possibly the site of the church
of St Maoilpoil (Dowling 1981, 16). A low earthen
mound (diam. *c.* 28m, H *c.* 1.5m), destroyed at N,
marks the site. No visible grave-markers .
29:2(01)   4-7-1990

769 KILMURRY
OS 14:1:6 (199,472) '*Church* (in Ruins)'
OD 300–400 25617,20130
Church Marked on the 1563 map of Leix and Offaly
(Hore 1863, f.p. 345). Possibly dedicated to the
Blessed Virgin Mary (O'Hanlon and O'Leary 1907,
vol. 1, 273). Church (L *c.* 36m, Wth *c.* 16.1m, wall T
c. 0.9m) constructed of roughly coursed limestone
blocks with remains of a doorway in ruined N wall,
and a broken-out window and aumbry in E end of S
wall. Otherwise featureless.
14:3   15-6-1990

770 KILTEALE
OS 13:12:6 (909,218) '*Kilteale Ch.* (in Ruins), Grave
Yard' OD 400–500 25394,19860
Church Possibly associated with St Tiedil. Used for
Protestant service in the seventeenth century
(Comerford 1886, vol. 3, 280–1). A medieval church
(max. L *c.* 11m, Wth *c.* 7.7m, wall T *c.* 0.8m) built of
roughly coursed limestone blocks. Remains consist of
E gable with a segmental arched doorway (Wth *c.*
1.1m, wall T *c.* 0.68m) and a rectangular window
overhead. No architectural features visible in surviving
portions of N and S walls. Irregularly shaped
uninscribed grave-markers visible in graveyard.
13:53(01)   25-7-1990

771 KILVAHAN
OS 18:10:3 (455,240) 'Burial Ground'
OD 400–500 24920,19239
Church (site) An old ruined church, possibly
associated with St Meathon, stood within an almost
circular graveyard until the early 1900s, however, not
a trace of it survives (O'Hanlon and O'Leary 1907,
vol. 1, 189–90). The Poor Law Guardians built a wall
around the graveyard which was originally enclosed
by a fosse (*ibid.*). Headstones postdate 1700.
Architectural fragments (No. 1051) from the church
are incorporated in a nearby tuck mill.
18:17(01)   12-6-1990

772 KNOCKSEERA
OS 22:9:3 (185,244) '*Church* (Site of), Grave Yard'
OD 500–600 22691,18580

Church (site) Associated with St Kieran of Ossory.
Only the foundations of the church (L *c.* 15m, Wth *c.*
7.5m, wall T *c.* 0.96m) survive. Reference to remains
of an ancient altar, said to have been built against E
gable, and St Kieran's Bush (Carrigan 1905, vol. 2,
129–30). No trace of altar visible. St Kieran's Bush is
a hawthorn bush in NW angle of subrectangular
graveyard. Headstones postdate 1700.
22:13(01)   7-8-1991

773 KYLE (Clandonagh By.)
OS 15:16:5 (776,50) '*Abbey* (in Ruins), *St. Molua's
Grave*' OD 300–400 22335,19012
Early ecclesiastical remains St Molua founded a
monastery here in the sixth century (O'Hanlon and
O'Leary 1907, vol. 1, 277). The present church is
medieval in date but within the surrounding D-shaped
graveyard, a variety of features associated with the
earlier foundation survive. These include St Molua's
Grave, two Early Christian cross-slabs, the decorated
capital of a Romanesque doorway, another stone
bearing Romanesque decoration incorporated in the
graveyard wall, and St Molua's trough (No. 816)
which was originally located in E end of graveyard
under a rag tree now no longer extant. St Molua's
stone, a weathered limestone bullaun (L 1.6m, Wth
1.1m, H 0.6m) with five depressions, originally lay in
field across road to SSW. It was recently pushed up
against W end of N boundary of that field. Remains of
a possible ecclesiastical enclosure lie *c.* 200m to SE.
The church (dims. 13m N–S, 6.5m E–W, wall T
1m) is constructed of randomly coursed sandstone. In
poor condition, only the lower courses of E and S
walls survive, and the grassed-over wall-footings of
W and N walls. Featureless, but some cut and dressed
stone from it is incorporated in the graveyard wall and
architectural fragments, some of which were reused as
grave-markers, are visible in graveyard. Most graves
date from 1700–1900. The Teehan family vault, at N
end of E wall of church, has reused window facing-
stones, with identical crosses, from the earlier twelfth-
century church. (FitzPatrick 1993)
15:23(01)   22-7-1994

774 KYLE (Tinnahinch By.)
OS 3:13:4 (63,56) '*Church* (Site of)' OD 400–500
23513,20950
Church (site) On flat ground in upland area. No
surface evidence of church survives.
3:11(01)   8-8-1990

775 KYLECLONHOBERT
OS 13:1:6 (184,513) OD 200–300 24625,20164
Church (site) Marked on the 1841 ed. OS 6" map.
The site of this church was indicated by a heap of
stones (O'Hanlon and O'Leary 1907, vol. 1, 192). No
visible surface traces survive.
13:3   18-6-1990

776 LISMORE
OS 22:10:2 (331,244) 'Church (in Ruins), Grave Yard' OD 400–500 22845,18582
Church Dedicated to St Canice and known as Kilkennybeg, the little church of St Canice (Carrigan 1905, vol. 2, 131–2). A church (L *c.* 19m, Wth *c.* 14m, wall T *c.* 0.9m) with evidence of a narrow ope in E gable, and remains of a broken-out doorway in W gable with a narrow flat-headed ope overhead. Only the foundations of N wall survive. Headstones in the surrounding subrectangular graveyard postdate 1700. No other features visible; remains appear to be that of an early church (Carrigan 1905, vol. 2, 131–2).
22:18(01)   5-8-1991

777 LOUGHMANSLAND GLEBE
OS 5:10:2 (335,268) 'Lea Church (Site of)' OD 200–300 25749,21196
Church In a low-lying area. Little evidence of church survives except for a featureless wall fragment (dims. 4m E–W, 1.5m N–S) at W side of graveyard. Wall foundations visible to E of centre of the graveyard, but with no obvious pattern.
5:7   15-5-1990

778 MARYBOROUGH
OS 13:10:4 (265,213) OD 300–400 24713,19848
Church The church, constructed *c.* 1556 (O'Hanlon and O'Leary 1907, vol. 1, 436), consists of N wall of nave (L *c.* 18m) and W tower (dims. *c.* 5.3m x 5.2m) built of roughly coursed mixed stone. Features of the tower include a rectangular ope in E wall, and a blocked-up ope in W wall on ground-floor level. An external string course indicates first floor. Flat-topped window visible in E wall of second floor, and round-headed window on each wall of third floor.
13:41(02)   11-6-1990

779 MONDREHID
OS 16:13:4 (62,15) 'Eglish Friary (Site of)' OD 300–400 22557,18977
Church (site) Reference to the foundations of an old church (dims *c.* 9.14m x 3.6m) surrounded by an ancient cemetery and several associated small fields here. Not visible *c.* 1907. (O'Hanlon and O'Leary 1907, vol. 1, 297). No surface traces survive. Possibly an early monastic foundation (Gwynn and Hadcock 1970, 398).
16:22(01)   16-9-1991

780 MORETT
OS 9:13:4 (8,38) 'Morett Church (in Ruins)' OD 200–300 25413,20309
Church Only part of W wall of the church (max. L 8m, wall T 0.8m), built of rubble limestone, and a fragment of S wall with remains of a segmental arch, indicating a S aisle, survive. The N jambstone of a possible doorway is visible in W wall. A graveslab with a sim-

ple incised cross is built into the style of the stone wall of the lane, to W of church. (*JKAS* 1904, 194)
9:21(04)   21-6-1990

781 MOYANNA
OS 14:6:3 (455,402) 'Church (in Ruins), Grave Yd.' OD 200–300 25888,20059
Early ecclesiastical remains St Monenna may have founded a religious house here in the seventh or ninth century (O'Byrne 1856, 46). A church is marked on the 1563 map of Leix and Offaly (Hore 1863, f.p. 345). The surviving rectangular church (L *c.* 14.2m, Wth *c.* 7.7m) is built of roughly coursed limestone and has a round-headed doorway in W gable and a segmental round-headed narrow ope in E gable. Remains of N and S walls are featureless. Some uninscribed grave-markers visible in graveyard. A substantial circular enclosure (diam. *c.* 72.5m) defined by an earthen bank (Wth *c.* 2.5m, int. H *c.* 0.7m, ext. H *c.* 1.1m) survives from SE–NW.
14:16(01)   12-7-1990

782 NEWTOWN (Clarmallagh By.)
OS 35:1:1 (51,559) 'Kileaderry Nunnery (in Ruins)' OD 200–300 23533,17641
Nunnery Upstanding remains consist of portions of W and N walls of church (dims. 8m N–S, *c.* 7m E–W) with evidence of a doorway in W wall. Elevated area to E and S. Reference to a nunnery and possible enclosure here (Carrigan 1905, vol. 2, 229).
35:1(01)   8-11-1990

783 NEWTOWN or SKIRK
OS 21:12:4 (738,158) 'Church (in Ruins)' OD 500–600 22299,18486
Church This church, deciated to the Blessed Virgin, collapsed in 1835, and only E gable and portion of S wall survived (Carrigan 1905, vol. 2, 135). Constructed of rubble, the E gable (L *c.* 6.5m, wall T *c.* 0.9m) with a blocked-up ope, and a short fragment of S wall still stand. Carrigan (*ibid.*) also refers to a cut-stone slab, with chamfered edges and an inscription dated 1612, which was reused as a graveslab. It originally came from the chimney-piece of a building known as Skirke Castle. Not located.
21:10(01)   24-6-1991

784 OLDCOURT
OS 26:5:6 (156,349) 'Abbey (in Ruins)' OD 200–300 26560,18730
Abbey Formerly an episcopal residence of the Bishops of Leighlin dating from the late thirteenth century, this monastery is believed to have been founded by the O'Moore family (O'Hanlon and O'Leary 1907, vol. 1, 251, 302). Constructed of roughly coursed limestone rubble, remains consist of S wall (L *c.* 24.8m) and W gable (L *c.* 7.4m) of probable

Plate 1a—*Carrowreagh, bowl-barrow* (**45**)

Plate 1b—*Greatheath, ring-barrow* (**59**)

Plate 2a—*Clonenagh, cross-slabs* (**714**)

Plate 2b—*Aghaboe, motte and bailey* (**900**)

nave and chancel church which was later fortified, as evidenced by seven slit opes in S wall and two in W gable. Low banks at N indicate evidence of further possible buildings.
26:7(01)   4-8-1990

785 OLDTOWN (Clarmallagh By.)
OS 34:12:6 (853,188) 'Abbey (Site of)'
OD 400–500 23409,17248
Abbey (site) Reference to a church (dims. 12m E–W, 6.3m N–S) situated within an enclosure (Carrigan 1905, vol. 2, 233–4). No visible surface traces. Possibly an early monastic site.
34:32(01)   27-9-1990

786 PARKNAHOWN
OS 34:12:2 (832,277) OD 300–400 23385,17342
Church (possible, site) Not marked on the 1841 or 1906 eds. OS 6" maps. Reference to a possible church site called Kilmurry within rath (No. 246). No local tradition of one (Carrigan 1905, vol. 2, 240). No visible surface traces.
34:28(02)   26-9-1990

787 PORTNAHINCH
OS 4:14:3 (453,89) 'Church (in Ruins), Grave Yard'
OD 200–300 24901,20998
Church Situated on raised ground close to the River Barrow. Church (dims. 13m E–W, 6.7m N–S, wall T 0.9m), in fair condition, built of roughly coursed rubble limestone. The E window, with diagonally tooled and punch-dressed jambs, has a simple splayed ope with a rounded segmental head internally. Splayed slit ope also at E end of S wall. Doorway, now broken out, in W gable. Probably fourteenth century based on stone-dressing.
4:4   28-5-1990

788 RAHANAVANNAGH
OS 24:6:5 (321,308) 'Church (Site of)' OD 500
24784,18669
Church (site) Possibly a religious establishment founded by the O'Moores (O'Byrne 1856, 52). No visible surface traces of church. Uninscribed grave-markers in NE quadrant of graveyard.
24:23   31-7-1990

789 RAHIN
OS 26:1:4 (40,490) 'Church (in Ruins), Grave Yard'
OD 200–300 26436,18877
Church Church (L *c.* 15.6m, Wth *c.* 7.15m) constructed of roughly coursed limestone. The E gable contains evidence of a splayed window with a segmental arch. Rectangular-shaped window in W gable with double bellcote above it. The N and S walls are partly destroyed. Evidence of doorway in W

section of S wall. Some cut-stone fragments have been used as grave-markers in NE section of graveyard. (O'Leary and O'Hanlon 1907, vol. 1, 250)
26:3   20-7-1990

790 RATHASPICK
OS 25:8:5 (791,311) OD 300–400 26255,18686
Church (site) Shown on the 1563 map of Leix and Offaly (Hore 1863, f.p. 345). Reference to a church possibly founded by the O'Moore family (O'Hanlon and O'Leary 1907, vol. 1, 301–2). According to Comerford (1886, vol. 3, 132), the ivy-clad walls of the church, which had a high belfry and large E window, were pulled down to supply stone for the modern church erected nearby. He also mentions three vaults under the ruins of the church which were destroyed in 1813.
25:23(01)   23-7-1990

791 RATHDOWNEY
OS 28:14:1 (304,137) OD 300–400 22824,17828
Church (site) The pre-Reformation parish church, dedicated to the Most Holy Trinity, was demolished in 1818 (Carrigan 1905, vol. 2, 340). No visible surface traces. Its site is now occupied by the modern Protestant church.
28:55(01)   30-9-1991

792 RATHDOWNEY
OS 28:14:2 (310,141) OD 300–400 22829,17833
Church (possible, site) Reference to a possible church site situated within enclosure (No. 515). No visible surface traces.
28:55(02)   30-9-1991

793 RATHMORE (Clandonagh By.)
OS 28 NPL
Church (site) and graveyard Reference to a church site and obsolete graveyard enclosed by an almost levelled bank and fosse (Carrigan 1905, vol. 2, 141). Not located.
28:123   22-8-1990

794 RATHNALEUGH
OS 27:4:4 (716,473) 'Burial Ground (Disused)'
OD 300–400 22280,18178
Church (site) Reference to a church site associated with St Patrick, and a churchyard within which burials took place until 1780 (Carrigan 1905, vol. 2, 139). The churchyard was known locally as the Yew Tree Graveyard from a venerable yew tree which grew, *c.* 18m to W, over the Yew Tree Well (No. 869) *(ibid.)*.
27:4   30-9-1991

795 REARYMORE
OS 3:5:4 (61,348) 'Rearymore Ch. (in Ruins), Grave Yd.' OD 300 23509,21258

Fig. 17—*Sleaty, cross* (**799**)

Church and graveslabs   Only W gable and N wall
survive of this featureless rubble limestone-built
church (dims. 20.3m E–W, 8.6m N–S). Three Early
Christian graveslabs (No. 830) formerly located
against NW angle of church are now in Rosenallis RC
church. (O'Hanlon and O'Leary 1907, vol. 1, 307;
O'Flanagan 1933, vol. 2, 204)
3:3(01)   13-8-1990

796 ROSENALLIS
OS 3:15:4 (499,60)   '*Round Tower* (Site of)'
OD 400–500   23974,20960
Early ecclesiastical remains (site)   Situated on hilltop.
Reference to an old church in ruins and a possible
round tower (O'Hanlon and O'Leary 1907, vol. 1,
309–10), no traces of which survive; probably located
within enclosure. The tower which was pulled down
before 1838 was described as a narrow steeple of
rough masonry only one third as high as Timahoe (No.
804) (*ibid.*). The modern Protestant church now
occupies the site of the earlier church. During a
graveyard clean-up in 1991 some pieces of medieval
stonework were found, as well as a fine cross-inscribed
slab and a sheela-na-gig (No. 1015). Holy well (No.
870) lies to SW.
3:16   1-8-1994

797 ROSSDARRAGH
OS 34:5:6 (161,369) '*Kyleaderry Church* (in Ruins)'
OD 400–500   22677,17432
Church (site)   Reference to the foundations of a
church (dims. *c.* 17.67m x 9.45m) known as
Kyleaderry or Church of the Oak Grove (Carrigan
1905, vol. 2, 281). No visible surface traces survive.
34:17(01)   4-7-1991

798 SHRULE
OS 32:8:1 (694,399)   '*Burial Gd.* (Disused)'
OD 100–200   27134,18148
Church (site)   Reference to the ruins of an 'old chapel'
in a graveyard to N of 'Shrule Castle' (No. 965).
Within its nave were the tombs of the Hartpole family,
owners of the castle. Many of the tomb inscriptions
were defaced or illegible but a lithograph in the Royal
Irish Academy records the detail of Sir Robert
Hartpole's effigy-tomb, dated 1594. The church was
demolished after 1657 (O'Hanlon and O'Leary 1907,
vol. 1, 315–6). No surface traces survive.
32:12(04)   14-8-1990

799 SLEATY
OS 32:11:6 (690,169) '*Church* (in Ruins), Grave Yard,
Crosses'   OD 100–200   27132,17905

Early ecclesiastical remains Associated with St Fiacc, Sleaty was formerly of great importance and the residence of the chief Bishop of Leinster (Comerford 1886, 249–65). The present medieval church (ext. dims. 14.25m E–W, 8.9m N–S, wall T 0.86m) is composed of coursed limestone blocks, apart from E gable which was rebuilt and is of sandstone. Dressed stone is incorporated in some of the walls. The church is featureless apart from the splayed embrasure of a broken window at E end of S wall, and a semi-pointed doorway at W end. Its granite jambs are probably from the earlier church. A large octagonal granite font (Wth 0.81m, D 0.48m, T 0.12m) lies within church to W of doorway. Most of the headstones in the surrounding subrectangular graveyard postdate 1700. Numerous uninscribed and cut-stone granite grave-markers occur. There are also two granite crosses associated with the early foundation. One tall undecorated cross (H 2.8m, armspan Wth 0.74m, base Wth 0.35m, T 0.25m) lies almost opposite NW corner of W gable. The other smaller squatter cross (H 1.45m, armspan Wth 0.73m, base Wth 0.4m, T 0.26m) is among headstones to S of doorway. Its W face is decorated with a barely visible ringed cross. A small uninscribed modern sandstone cross stands outside church at SE. Holy well (No. 861) is associated with the site (O'Flanagan 1933, vol. 2, 39).

32:18(01)   14-8-1990

800 SRAHANBOY

OS 10:16:3 (892,105)   OD 700–800   22451,19711

Early ecclesiastical remains Reference to a church site and graveyard which was used for the burial of unbaptized children (No. 888) and within which was a bush known as the 'Burying Bush'. Close by lay a holy water stone, a font or bullaun stone (Carrigan 1905, vol. 2, 150). Substantial remains of an ecclesiastical enclosure defined by a low earthen stone bank survive.

10:2(01)   12-9-1991

801 STRABOE

OS 13:3:1 (493,597) '*Straboe Ch.* (in Ruins), Grave Yd.'   OD 300–400   24950,20255

Church Marked on the 1563 map of Leix and Offaly (Hore 1863, f.p. 345). A nave (L *c.* 12.25m, Wth *c.* 7.25m) and chancel (L *c.* 5.6m, Wth *c.* 6.5m, wall T *c.* 0.63m) church, built of limestone, with a round segmental chancel arch (Wth *c.* 1.7m), now blocked up. Rectangular slayed ope visible in E gable, and two doorways in N wall of nave. The W gable is featureless, as is S wall except for a blocked window. Numerous pieces of cut stone were reused as grave-markers.

13:5(01)   25-7-1990

802 STRADBALLY

OS 14:14:4 (303,8) 'Site of *Abbey*'   OD 200–300   25731,19641

Abbey (site) A Franciscan monastery was founded here in 1447 by O'More. It was destroyed, *c.* 1575, by Francis Cosby who constructed a house with its material. Traces of the monastery were visible at the end of the eighteenth century but were removed by the nineteenth century (O'Hanlon and O'Leary 1907, vol. 1, 327–9, 333–4, 410–11). (Gwynn and Hadcock 1970, 259)

14:39(01)   7-6-1990

803 TANKARDSTOWN

OS 26:7:2 (606,397) '*Tankardstown Church* (in Ruins), Grave Yd.'   OD 200–300   27034,18785

Church Marked on the Down Survey Barony Map. A nave and chancel church (L *c.* 18.9m, Wth *c.* 6.1m), built of roughly coursed limestone blocks, with traces of a segmental chancel arch. Doorway at W end of S wall. Evidence of window in E gable. All visible headstones postdate 1700. St Thomas's well (No. 872) lies to N.

26:9(04)   3-8-1990

804 TIMAHOE

OS 18:16:6 (869,30) '*Castle* (in Ruins) on Site of *Abbey, Round Tower*'   OD 300–400   25359,19021

Early ecclesiastical remains St Mochua, who died *c.* 657 founded an Early Christian monastery here. It was plundered and burnt in 919 and 1142 (Gwynn and Hadcock 1970, 45). In later medieval times, the O'Mores refounded the monastery, and in 1609 it was granted to Richard Cosby. The round tower is the only surviving feature of the early foundation. It probably dates to the twelfth century, though its base may be earlier. Built of sandstone and limestone, it is six storeys high (H 29.26m) and is roofed with a conical cap (Barrow 1979, 135–9). No floors survive. It is renowned for its Romanesque doorway, visible at first-floor level, which has four receding orders, in two pairs, and is finely decorated with human heads with intertwined hair. A window decorated in a similar style is visible at second-floor level. Slit, square-headed and pointed windows are on the other floors.

The fifteenth-century church, to SE of tower, was transformed in the sixteenth century into a tower house (No. 967) (Harbison 1970, 141), probably by one of the Cosbys. The only surviving feature of this church is a large arch (Wth 3.95m), possibly the chancel arch, which was blocked up and incorporated into the E wall of the castle. It is composed of punch-dressed chamfered limestone with evidence of diagonal tooling. (Petrie 1845, 234–43; Crawford 1924, 31–42)

18:31(01)   13-6-1990

805 TIMOGUE

OS 19:5:5 (132,358) 'Grave Yd.'   OD 300–400   25553,19369

Church (site) The Protestant church, within this 'very ancient cemetery' was probably built on the site of an earlier church associated with St Maedoc (O'Hanlon and O'Leary 1907, vol. 1, 338). No trace of it survives but within the Protestant church is an early medieval octagonal limestone font (int. Wth *c.* 0.44m, int. D *c.* 0.16m). On its E side is a human head, carved in relief, with a crown of thorns and a perforation (*JRSAI* 1947, 81).

19:7(02)   2-5-1990

806 TINTORE

OS 29:5:4 (19,304)   '*Eglish Church* (in Ruins)'
OD 344   23496,18011

Church (site) This church was dedicated to St Nicholas (Carrigan 1905, vol. 2, 371). A low rectangular mound of rubble, with wall-facing visible at W end, indicates its site.

29:16   14-8-1990

807 TIRHOGAR

OS 5:13:3 (188,110) '*Church* (in Ruins) Grave Yard'
OD 200–300 25596,21028

Church Simple single cell church (dims. 19.4m E–W, 6.8m N–S) built of roughly coursed limestone blocks and rubble. In poor repair with no cut stone left in situ. The doorway appears to have been at W end but is broken out, and there seems to have been two windows in both N and S walls. Architectural fragments and pieces of cut stone, of late medieval origin, are visible in the graveyard (pers. comm. E. FitzPatrick).

5:11   15-5-1990

808 TOBERBOE or KILLENNY MORE

OS 35:6:1 (296,424) '*Church* (in Ruins) Grave Yard'
OD 300–400 23794,17501

Early ecclesiastical remains A nave (L *c.* 15.5m, Wth

c. 8.1m, wall T *c.* 0.75m) and chancel (L *c.* 9.5m, Wth *c.* 5.3m) church constructed of roughly coursed limestone. The W gable and adjoining portion of N wall are levelled, and only the foundations of the chancel remained at the beginning of this century (Carrigan 1905, vol. 2, 227). Round-headed doorway visible at W end of S wall of nave, and blocked-up ope at E end. Uninscribed grave-markers visible in surrounding subrectangular graveyard. Gateway with rebated entrance (Wth *c.* 5.1m, D *c.* 3.3m, T *c.* 1m) lies to SW of church. Large subcircular enclosure surrounding site is visible on aerial photographs (CUCAP, BDL 18, 27–8). Evidence of possible bank at E and S, no other surface traces survive.

35:31(01)   20-9-1991

809 TULLOMOY

OS 19:15:2 (569,81)   '*Church* (Site of)'
OD 400–500 26017,19081

Church (site) The side-walls of this church were standing in 1838 (O'Hanlon and O'Leary 1907, vol. 1, 341). No surface traces survive other than a small slightly raised area consisting of earth and stone.

19:26   10-8-1990

810 VICARSTOWN (DODD)

OS 14:7:3 (659,419) '*Kylemahoe Church* (Site of)'
OD 216 26103,20079

Early ecclesiastical remains Reference to the site of an old church and disused graveyard here (O'Hanlon and O'Leary 1907, vol. 1, 294). The cropmark of an enclosure is visible around the site on aerial photograph (CUCAP, AYN 17) but no visible surface evidence survives.

14:22(01)   12-6-1990

19. Ecclesiastical Miscellanea

The monuments listed in this chapter, including altar-tombs, fonts, bullaun stones, graveslabs, cross-slabs, a wayside cross and a trough, are either isolated ecclesiastical objects, that is, not associated with a particular religious foundation, or ecclesiastical objects which were moved from one location to another, for example, the cross-slabs at Clonaslee (No. 818)

811 ABBEYLEIX DEMESNE

OS 29:3:3 (680,595) 'O'More's Tomb' OD 300–400
24191,18326

Altar-tomb Marked only on the 1907 ed. OS 6" map. Situated in the demesne garden is the altar-tomb of Melaghlin O'More with the effigy of an knight. He is covered by chain and plate armour, one of his hands is holding a sword and the other is resting on his thigh. It bears the following inscription 'Here lies Melaghlin, son of Owny O'More, who caused this tomb to be made, AD 1502. On whose soul may God have mercy. Amen'. (Stalley 1987, 241)
29:12   4-7-1990

812 ABBEYLEIX DEMESNE

OS 29:3:3 (680,595) OD 300–400 24191,18326

Font Not marked on the 1841 or 1907 eds. OS 6" maps. Recently placed with altar-tomb (No. 811). A large circular granite font (diam. *c.* 0.8m, D *c.* 0.4m, T *c.* 0.15m) with a central drain-hole (D *c.* 0.1m). Site of abbey (No. 685) nearby.
29:13(02)   4-7-1990

813 ABBEYLEIX DEMESNE

OS 29:3:3 (680,595) OD 300–400 24191,18326

Graveslab Not marked on the 1841 or 1907 eds. OS 6" map. Recently placed beside altar-tomb (No. 811). A rectangular-shaped slab (H *c.* 2m) with a simple cross in relief and inscription. It commemorates William O'Kelly who died in 1531. Site of abbey (No. 685) nearby.
29:13(03)   4-7-1990

814 ANATRIM

OS 16:10:3 (434,250) 'St. Kaban's Well and Stone'
OD 300–400 22947,19230

Incised stone Projecting inward from S side of St Kaban's Well (No. 832), and filling the greater part of its mouth, is a large limestone flag (dims. 1.6m x 1.15m, T 0.45m) decorated on its smooth upper surface with an incised circle (diam. 0.87m) and two elliptical depressions (dims. 0.11m x 0.05m, D 0.04–0.06m). Anatrim church (No. 693) lies to SSE.
16:16(01)   8-5-1991

815 BALLAGHARAHIN

OS 27:15:3 (645,106) 'Stone Crosses' OD 300–400
22209,17790

Wayside cross Remains of a cross shaft (H *c.* 0.85m, Wth *c.* 0.38m, T *c.* 0.21m) on a cut-stone chamfered

pedestal. On the upper part of E face is a shield with a coat-of-arms sculptured in relief. On the lower part are inscriptions, dated 1613 and 1622, to the Baron of Upper Ossory, his wife Kathrin More and their son and daughter-in-law (*JRSAI* 1924, 147–51).
27:25   8-10-1990

816 BALLINLA

OS 15:15:4 (515,40) OD 400–500 22060,18999

St Molua's trough Originally located at E end of graveyard (No. 773) under a hawthorn tree traditionally said to have been festooned with rags; it is now mounted in concrete in the yard of Ballaghmore Catholic church. The sandstone trough (L 0.95m, Wth 0.48m, ext. D 0.4m, int. D 0.25m, wall T 0.13m), rectangular in shape, is lipped on three sides of its mouth as if to receive a lid. Considering the pervious nature of this stone and the fact that there is no perforation for water outflow, it is unlikely that it functioned as a trough. The indications that it had a lid suggest it may have been used to contain precious objects (pers. comm. E. FitzPatrick).
15:33*/15:23   22-7-1994

817 CASTLEDURROW DEMESNE

OS 29:15:5 (564,52) OD 200–300 24074,17751

Cross (base, site) Reference to the rough limestone pedestal of a small cross at the head of St Fintan's Well (No. 840) (Carrigan 1905, vol. 2, 212). No trace survives.
29:43(02)   12-7-1990

818 CLONASLEE

OS 2:11:6 (668,209) OD 371 23176,21109

Early Christian cross-slabs Two rectangular-shaped sandstone slabs, both incised with simple crosses, are set against N wall of modern churchyard. The upper portion of each slab is broken. A third slab (*JKAS* 1937, 108) could not be found. Originally from Carrigeen graveyard (No. 700) (*JRSAI* 1916, 166; *JKAS* 1939, 187)
2:12   10-9-1990

819 COOLTEDERY

OS 5:9:2 (80,276) OD 200–300 25480,21202

Altar-tomb Hartpole effigy now in the garden of Kilnacourt House was originally located in St Mary's Church, Carlow. It consists of an armoured knight on a rectangular limestone slab with his now broken hands resting on his chest. The head is missing and the arms

Fig. 18—*Clonaslee, cross-slabs* (**818**)

and legs are damaged. The feet are placed on a dog. Remains of inscription on dexter side of knight. (*JKAS* 1910, 335–6)
5:32   8-12-1990

820 CROSS
OS 22 NPL

Cross-shaped depression   To SE of Aghaboe Abbey (No. 688). Carrigan (1905, vol. 2, 48–50) refers to a peculiar cross-shaped depression known locally as The Cross or Kenny's Cross. Not located.
22:19(16)   12-8-1991

821 ERRILL
OS 23:15:3 (646,130) '*St. Kieran's Tree*'
OD 300–400   22210,17816
Holy tree (site) Reference to a venerable old ash tree on the roadside to E of St Kieran's monastery (No. 741) (Carrigan 1905, vol. 2, 347). No trace survives.
27:23   9-11-1990

822 HAYWOOD DEMESNE
OS 30:5:6 (215,336)   OD 400–500 24678,18056

Font In SW corner of churchyard of Protestant church is an undecorated octagonal font (ext. H *c.* 0.62m, int. D *c.* 0.45m) with a circular basin.
30:18(02)   17-6-1991

823 KILBRICKAN
OS 17:13:6 (160,13)   OD 300–400   23635,18986
Inscribed stone   An inscribed stone originally on S wall of Kilbrickan church (No. 752) was moved to Kilbrickan House and used as a hearth-stone (Carrigan 1905, vol. 2, 176). Not visible.
17:11   31-8-1990

824 KILFEACLE
OS 25:15:5 (552,73)   OD 600–700   26005,18432
Cross-inscribed slab   Reference to a broken slab, inscribed with a circle within which four segments of circles formed a rough Maltese cross; found in a stone-lined grave (No. 897) *JRSAI* 1932 119–20).
25:33(03)   22-8-1990

825 KILLEEN (Upperwoods By.)
OS 11:14:1 (270,93)   OD 500–600   22769,19702

Font (site) Rough stone with hollow (Wth 0.22m, D 0.7m), originally from Killeen church (No. 761) (Carrigan 1905, vol. 2, 151). No visible traces.

11:11   25-7-1991

826 KILLINURE (Upperwoods By.)/ MOUNTAINFARM

OS 11:7:5 (547,309)   OD 600–700   23060,19933

Font Not marked on the 1841 or 1909 ed. OS 6" maps. Originally in use in Killanure church (No. 760); it was moved during Penal times to Burke's cross-roads (Carrigan 1905, vol. 2, 152). A limestone subcircular font (dims. *c.* 0.65m NW–SE, *c.* 0.75m NE–SW, D *c.* 0.23m) with a central drain-hole.

11:5   16-7-1991

827 MORETT

OS 8:12:4 (768,168)   OD 300–400   25239,20445

Font Now located in St John's church; moved from the grounds of Emo Park demesne *c.* 1935. It may originally have been in Coolbanagher church (No. 721). The font, which has an octagonal basin (max. int. diam. 0.57m, max. D 0.25m, wall T 0.1m) with a central drain-hole, is set on a modern base. Its eight panels are elaborately decorated with carvings in relief of angels or foliage designs, and they are separated from each other by a twisted vine. Punch-dressing indicates a late medieval date. (*JKAS* 1904, 196–7; Roe 1947, 82–3)

8:10   21-6-1990

828 MOYNE

OS 29:11:1 (490,236)   OD 200–300   23994,17944

Bullaun stone To SE of Moyne House in large flat pasture field. A roughly oval-shaped earthfast limestone outcrop (dims. 2.1m E–W, 1.15m N–S, H 0.3m) containing two large basins and a third rudimentary one on N perimeter. The E basin (dims. 0.41m E–W, 0.34m N–S, D 0.23m) is oval-shaped, while the W basin (diam. 0.4m, D 0.21m) is almost circular (pers. comm. E. FitzPatrick).

29:72

829 REARYMORE

OS 3:5:5 (106,331)   'St. Fionan's Wells'   OD 300–400   23557,21241

Bullaun stone Rock outcrop with bullaun-type holes, probably of natural origin. No evidence of a well. (*JKAS* 1938, 109)

3:4(02)   13-8-1990

830 ROSENALLIS

OS 3:15:4 (488,56)   OD 300–400   23963,20955

Graveslabs Three Early Christian graveslabs decorated with incised and false relief geometrical designs. One slab has face-like features. Originally located in Rearymore church (No. 795).

3:25   13-8-1990

20. Holy Wells

Any location where a water source is used on a regular basis as a focal point of cure or devotion may be defined as a holy well. Such wells can range from unadorned natural springs to mortared stone well-chambers (No. 833). Votive offerings such as coins or rosary beads are commonly found at them. Most of the wells are associated with a particular saint, and in the past were visited on a pattern day, usually the saint's anniversary day.

The dating of holy wells is problematic. While they are regarded as Christian, their origin may be pre-Christian in date. Religious cults associated with water have a long tradition in this country, dating back to prehistoric times. Some may be of more recent origin, for example, Father O'Connor's Well (No. 837).

The majority of the holy wells included here are isolated wells dedicated to particular saints. Also included are holy wells associated with church sites, and wells indicated in Gothic script on the OS 6-inch maps. The traditions and beliefs associated with many of these are forgotten.

831 AHARNEY
OS 35:15:1 (493,148) 'St. Bridget's Well'
OD 300–400 24005,17212
Holy well Dedicated to St Bridget. Until the nineteenth century, pilgrims came here on the 1st February (Carrigan 1905, vol. 2, 309). Indicated by a wet patch in the ground.
35:48   27-9-1990

832 ANATRIM
OS 16:10:3 (434,250) 'St. Kaban's Well and Stone'
OD 300–400 22947,19230
Holy well Pattern day 3rd November (Carrigan 1905, vol. 2, 150). A subcircular spring well (dims. 2.2m x 2.1m, D 1.2m) lined internally with drystone masonry at N and W. Projecting inward from S side of the well is St Kaban's stone (No. 814). Anatrim church (No. 693) lies to SSE.
16:16(02)   8-5-1991

833 BALLINTUBBERT
OS 19:11:3 (684,287) OD 300–400 26137,19299
Holy well Not marked on the 1841 or 1909 eds. OS 6" maps. Situated SE of church site (No. 694). Demarcated by a stone wall, three courses high, at E and W. Entrance with three steps leading down to the well at N. Known as St Brigid's Well.
19:14(03)   15-8-1990

834 BALLYGOWDAN
OS 28:4:2 (784,533) 'Bishop's Well' OD 300–400 23327,18251
Holy well (site) Reference to a holy well known as Bishop's Well (Carrigan 1905, vol. 2, 58). No visible surface traces.
28:14   13-9-1991

835 BALLYLEHANE LOWER
OS 25:12:5 (771,212) 'Toberternoge' OD 400–500 26236,18581
Holy well Indicated by a shallow pool of water (D c. 0.5m). No known historical references.
25:29   28-8-1990

836 BALLYNAGALL
OS 32:1:6 (156,504) 'St. Abban's Well' OD 400–500 26564,18253
Holy well (site) Reference to St Abban's Well (O'Hanlon *et al.* 1914, vol. 2, 580). No visible surface traces.
32:5(01)   14-8-1990

837 BALLYROAN (Maryborough East By.)
OS 13:10:2 (369,259) 'Father O'Connor's Well'
OD 300–400 24823,19897
Holy well (site) Not marked on the 1841 ed. OS 6" map. No visible surface traces.
13:43   11-6-1990

838 BORRIS GREAT
OS 13:6:5 (323,362) OD 300–400 24773,20005
Holy well To SW of church site (No. 704). Indicated by wet patch. Formerly known as the Priest's Well, now known as Fr O'Connor's Well (O'Dooley n.d., 5).
13:22(02)   23-7-1990

839 CAPPAGH NORTH
OS 12:4:5 (846,493) 'Toberleheen' OD 200–300
24348,20140
Holy Well (site) Marked on the 1841 and 1909 eds. OS 6" maps. Now dry.
12:1   9-8-1990

840 CASTLEDURROW DEMESNE
OS 29:15:5 (564,52) 'St. Fintan's Well'
OD 200–300 24074,17751
Holy well Reference to a holy well with a cross pedestal (No. 817) at its head (Carrigan 1905, vol. 2, 212). It comprises a horseshoe-shaped area (Wth c. 3.5m) surrounded by a stone wall.
29:43(01)   12-7-1990

841 CASTLEQUARTER (Clandonagh By.)
OS 21 NPL
Holy well St Molua's Well was situated in the field next to Lady's Well (No. 865) (Carrigan 1905, vol. 2, 136).
21:47(02)

842 CLONENAGH
OS 17:2:3 (415,564) 'St. Fintan's Well'
OD 400–500   23899,19570
Holy well (site)   No visible surface traces. Reference to a sacred tree opposite the well (O'Hanlon and O'Leary 1907, vol. 1, 209). Church ruins (No. 714) to NNW.
17:3(03)   31-8-1990

843 CLONKEEN (Maryborough West By.)
OS 17:4:3 (863,604) *'Tony Haslem's Well'*
OD 300–400   24372,19617
Holy well (possible)   Marked on the 1841 and 1906–7 eds. OS 6" maps. Now covered over and incorporated into a pump.
17:6   31-8-1990

844 CLONMEEN SOUTH
OS 33:8:4 (721,347) Indicated   OD 400–500
22293,17405
Holy well (site)   Known as Friars' Well (Carrigan 1905, vol. 2, 345). No visible surface traces.
33:8   25-10-1990

845 CLONMEEN SOUTH
OS 33 NPL
Holy well (site)   A deep well, known as the Church Well, lay to S of church (No. 719) and was formerly regarded as holy (Carrigan 1905, vol. 2, 345).
33:25

846 COOLACURRAGH
OS 28 NPL
Holy well (site)   Carrigan (1905, vol. 2, 61–2) refers to a closed-up holy well known as Tubberkierawn or St Kieran's Well. It was situated a few perches from the Erkina River.
28:77

847 COOLANOWLE/GURTEEN
OS 26:13:3 (184,125) 'Shellin's Well'   OD 200–300
26592,18493
Holy well (possible)   Marked only on the 1909 ed. OS 6" map. A shallow pool of water (diam. 2m), to W of a stream, indicates the site.
26:19   5-8-1990

848 COOLE (Maryborough West By.)
OS 23:4:1 (743,569) *'Rahaling Well'*   OD 300–400
24252,18939
Holy well (possible)   Marked on the 1841 and 1909 eds. OS 6" maps. A spring well still in use.
23:9   14-9-1990

849 CORRAUN
OS 22 NPL
Holy well (site)   St Canice's Well, also known as Kenny's Well, was situated 180m SW of Aghaboe Abbey (No. 688). It was infilled almost 100 years ago (Carrigan 1905, vol. 2, 47). No visible surface traces.
22:19(06)   12-8-1991

850 CROMOGE
OS 17:14:6 (446,2) *'St. Fintan's Well'*   OD 300–400
23938,18977
Holy Well   Visited on St Fintan's feast day. Pebbles from it are thought to act as preservatives against shipwreck or accidental death (Comerford 1886, vol. 3, 337). A clear spring is visible.
17:13   28-8-1990

851 DERRYNASEERA
OS 16 NPL
Holy well (site)   Reference to a closed-up holy well known as St Kevin's (O'Flanagan 1933, vol. 1, 141).
16:34

852 DERRYVORRIGAN
OS 22 NPL
Holy well (site)   St Kieran's Well, formerly visited on 5th March, was situated 300–400m N of church (No. 772) (Carrigan 1905, vol. 2, 130). Not located.
22:39

853 DONAGHMORE
OS 28:5:6 (175,343) *'St. Patrick's Well'*
OD 300–400   22686,18045
Holy well   The well was closed *c.* 1845 when a rock was placed over it (Carrigan 1905, vol. 2, 352). It is still visible.
28:23   29-9-1991

854 DURROW TOWNPARKS
OS 29 NPL
Holy well   Reference to St John's Well (Walsh 1972, 19). Not located.
29:57/35:70*

855 DYSART
OS 13 NPL
Holy well   Reference to well in Claxton's quarry known as St Aongus's Well (O'Dooley n.d., 38).
13:76/18:41*

856 ERRILL
OS 27:16:1 (694,126) *'St. Kieran's Well'*
OD 300–400   22261,17812

Holy well This holy well originally flowed out from under St Kieran's tree, but moved a few fields to E after being profaned (Carrigan 1905, vol. 2, 347). Pilgrims came to it on the 5th March, St Kieran's feast day. It is now incorporated into a pump house.
27:26   8-11-1990

857 KILBREEDY
OS 28 NPL

Holy well (site) St Brigid's Well, known as the castle well, lay to SW of church (No. 751), nearly opposite Kilbreedy Castle (No. 959). In summer the well ran dry but in winter it was a powerful stream (Carrigan 1905, vol. 2, 60).
28:92

858 KILFEACLE
OS 25:15:2 (570,99) *'St. Patrick's Well'* OD 600 26024,18460

Holy well Not marked on the 1841 ed. OS 6" map. A shallow pool of water marks the site.
25:32   28-8-1990

859 KILGORY
OS 36:3:4 (484,462) *'St. Longory's Well'* OD 700–800 25943,17562

Holy well This holy well, situated *c.* 40m NW of church (No. 758), has been completely modernised. A pattern day was formerly held here on 24th June (Comerford 1886, vol. 3, 197).
36:2(03)   5-9-1990

860 KILMANMAN
OS 2:7:5 (543,319) *'St. Manman's Well'* OD 300–400 23043,21223

Holy well Situated *c.* 90m SSW of church (No. 767). This well was called after St Manmon, the patron of the parish. The date of the pattern day was forgotten locally by the early nineteenth century (O'Flanagan 1933, vol. 1, 71).
2:2(03)   6-9-1990

861 KNOCKBEG/SLEATY
OS 32:11:0 NPL
Holy well (site) Not marked on the 1841 or 1908 eds. OS 6" map. Known as Tober-Feeg and located near Sleaty church (No. 799) (O'Flanagan 1933, vol. 2, 39). No visible surface traces.
32:18(04)   14-8-1990

862 LEAGH
OS 32:11:2 (607,228) *'Tobernuan'* OD 100–200 27043,17966

Holy well (site) Marked on the 1841 and 1908 eds. OS 6" maps. No visible surface traces.
32:16   15-8-1990

863 MEELICK (Maryborough East By.)
OS 13:14:2 (336,80) *'Tobergaddy'* OD 300–400 24789,19709

Holy well (site) Marked on the 1841 and 1907 eds. OS 6" maps. Reference to a holy well here (O'Hanlon and O'Leary 1907, vol. 1, 192). No visible surface traces.
13:56   8-7-1990

864 MORETT
OS 9:13:4 (7,42) *'St. Brigid's Well'* OD 200–300 25412,20314

Holy Well Recently renovated. Morett church (No. 780) lies *c.* 40m to SSE.
9:21(03)   21-6-1990

865 NEWTOWN OR SKIRK
OS 21 NPL

Holy well (site) A holy well known as Lady's Well was situated to NE of church (No. 783). The original well was destroyed but a spring of pure water rose up in the partially decayed trunk of an old ash tree that grew over it, and it was subsequently venerated (Carrigan 1905, vol. 2, 136). St Molua's Well (No. 841) was situated in the next field.
21:47(01)

866 PARKAHOUGHILL
OS 19:16:4 (763,50) *'Toberneeve'* OD 400–500 26223,19051

Holy well A natural spring given curative properties by St Patrick (Comerford 1886, vol. 3, 126).
19:30(01)   10-9-1990

867 PARKAHOUGHILL
OS 19:16:4 (763,48) *'Tobernasool'* OD 400–500 26222,19048

Holy well Lying *c.* 20m S of holy well (No. 866). A natural spring given curative powers by St Patrick (Comerford 1886, vol. 3, 126).
19:30(02)   10-9-1990

868 RAHEEN (Maryborough West By.)
OS 17:16:5 (791,70) *'Toberkeegaun'* OD 300–400 24301,19053

Holy well Marked on the 1841 and 1910 eds. OS 6" maps. The well is covered and its water is used for local supply.
17:18   28-8-1990

869 RATHNALEUGH
OS 27:4:4 (716,473) OD 300–400 22280,18178

Holy well (possible, site) Reference to a venerable yew tree growing over the Yew Tree Well. The tree had decayed and rotted away by 1838 (Carrigan 1905,

vol. 2, 139–40). A wet area around a whitethorn tree may indicate the site of the well.
27:4(03)   30-9-1991

870 ROSENALLIS
OS 3:15:4 (500,63) '*St. Bridget's Well*'   OD 300–400
23975,20962
Holy well A holy well dedicated to St Bridget whose pattern was formerly held on 1st February. Associated with church (No. 796).
3:16(04)   23-7-1990

871 SHANBALLY
OS 34:8:5 (777,347)   OD 300–400   23328,17415
Holy well (site) Not marked on the 1840 or 1906 eds. OS 6" maps. Reference to St Tierna's Well here (Carrigan 1905, vol. 2, 240). Not visible on the ground.
34:21   25-9-1990

872 TANKARDSTOWN
OS 26:7:2 (603,404) '*St. Thomas's Well*'
OD 200–300   27032,18792
Holy well A shallow pool of water surrounded by a concrete wall. Entrance at N.
26:9(02)   3-8-1990

873 TIMOGUE
OS 19:9:3 (166,264) '*Toberloughra*'   OD 300–400
25590,19270
Holy well Marked on the 1841 and 1909 eds. OS 6" maps. Now covered over and used as a local water supply.
19:10   16-8-1990

874 TOBERBOE or KILLENNY MORE
OS 35:6:1 (279,401) '*St. John's Well*'   OD 300–400
23776,17476
Holy well Dedicated to St John the Baptist, this well was also known as Tubberig and Tubberach (Carrigan 1905, vol. 2, 228). Indicated by a shallow pool of water.
35:29   20-9-1990

875 WHITEFIELD
OS 11 NPL
Holy well (site) Reference to a closed-up holy well known as St Kevin's (O'Flanagan 1933, vol. 1, 141).
11:32

21. Children's Burial Grounds and Graveyards

The custom of setting apart a separate burial place for unbaptized children has a long tradition in Ireland, and was a practise which continued until the mid-1900s. Such burial grounds are known by a variety of names including Lisín, Cillín/Killeen, or simply Children's Burial Grounds. While some are named and indicated on the OS 6-inch maps, others are known only from published references or from oral tradition. They are characterised by the presence of numerous small uninscribed set stones, often arranged in rows.

Also included in this chapter are some isolated burial grounds and graveyards which are not associated with particular church sites; as a result many cannot be closely dated.

876 BALLYLUSK
OS 12:6:5 (367,350)   OD 400–500   23844,19983
Children's burial ground   Uninscribed grave-markers visible in SW quadrant of subcircular enclosure (No. 311).
12:5(01)   9-8-1990

877 BRITTAS (Tinnahinch By.)
OS 2:11:6 (648,166) 'Killyann Burial Gd.'   OD 400
23155,21063
Burial ground   A flat subcircular area enclosed by a hedge and iron railings; no surface evidence of grave-markers, stonework, etc. which might indicate the exact type of site.
2:19   12-9-1990

878 CASTLEFLEMING (STUBBER)
OS 27 NPL
Children's burial ground   To N of the railway line, in a field known as the 'churchyard' field, was a small disused graveyard within which were some rude headstones marking the graves of unbaptized children (Carrigan 1905, vol. 2, 351).
27:7

879 CLONENAGH
OS 17:2:3 (412,553) 'Burial Ground'   OD 400–500
23896,19559
Burial ground   Marked on the 1841 ed. OS 6" map as 'Old Graveyard'. A number of randomly placed, uninscribed grave-markers are visible on top of a natural hill, the summit of which appears to be artifically raised as a result of the burials (pers. comm. E. FitzPatrick).
17:3(08)   17-5-1994

880 GRAIGUEADRISLY
OS 33:12:2 (831,233) 'Burial Gd. (Disused)'
OD 400–500   22410,17286
Graveyard (site)   Marked on the 1841 and 1908 eds. OS 6" maps. Carrigan (1905, vol. 2, 282) notes that there was nothing to indicate a graveyard but that people vaguely remembered one. No visible surface traces.
33:12   16-8-1991

881 KILDELLIG
OS 28:2:3 (392,589)   OD 400–500   22912,18306
Graveyard (site)   Not marked on the 1841 or 1908 eds. OS 6" maps. Reference to a graveyard here (Candon 1986, 22). No visible surface traces.
28:6   11-9-1991

882 KILLEANY
OS 23:6:1 (293,406)   OD 200–300   23778,18762
Graveyard (site)   Not marked on the 1841 or 1909 eds. OS 6" maps. There was a graveyard here but the Grand Jury constructed a road through it before 1839 (OPW file). No visible surface traces. Human bones discovered in 1958 were probably associated with it.
23:12(04)   17-8-1990

883 KILLEEN
OS 21 NPL
Children's burial ground   Reference to many small rude headstones marking the graves of unbaptized children in a field known as the 'Burying Meadow' (Carrigan 1905, vol. 2, 151).
11:21

884 KYLE (Clandonagh By.)
OS 29:7:1 (495,398) 'Burial Ground'   OD 200–300
23998,18115
Burial ground   An earthen mound (dims. 28m E–W, 21.5m N–S, H *c.* 3m) containing one visible uninscribed grave-marker.
29:23   13-8-1990

885 LEAGH
OS 32:11:1 (512,267) 'Burial Ground'   OD 200–300
26943,18006
Burial ground (site)   Reference to a burial ground called Killanure (Comerford 1886, vol. 3, 265). No visible surface traces.
32:15   15-8-1990

886 MORETT
OS 8:16:3 (877,149)   OD 300–400   25354,20426
Graveyard (site)   'Skeaghnakilla Graveyard' marked on the 1841 ed. OS 6" map, as a small almost square area along a field fence, is not indicated on later map eds. No visible surface traces.
8:18   21-6-1990

887 RATHRONSHIN
OS 9:11:2 (558,279)   OD 200–300 'Childrens'
Burial Ground (Disused)'   25991,20570
Children's burial ground   Not marked on the 1841 or
1888 eds. OS 6" maps. Featureless area of scrubland
(diam. *c*. 47m) with no obvious enclosing element.
9:17   24-7-1990

888 SRAHANBOY
OS 10:16:3 (892,105)   OD 700–800   22451,19711
Children's burial ground   Within ecclesiastical
enclosure (No. 800). Burial ground for unbaptized
children. A small number of rough uninscribed upright
grave-markers are visible among a clump of hawthorn
trees. (Carrigan 1905, vol. 2, 150)
10:2(02)   12-9-1991

22. Miscellaneous Burials

This chapter includes burial sites of various ages and types. They can be distinguished from conventional graveyards because they all appear to represent the once-off burial of groups of people or individuals, rather than the location of recurrent burial. The earliest possibly dates to the Iron Age (No. 889) while the most recent may be 'famine graves' (No. 890).

889 BALLINLOUGH (Maryborough East By.)
OS 13:12:3 (904,245)   OD 400–500   25388,19888
Burials (site)   Five skeletons, orientated W–E, and a female skull-burial were discovered 0.25–0.4m below the ground surface during sand-quarrying operations. Possibly dating to the Iron Age (*JKAS* 1974–5, 430–3).
13:50

890 BALLYDAVIS
OS 13:7:3 (669,453) Hachured   OD 300–400   25137,20105
Burials (site)   During levelling operations carried out under a land reclamation scheme in 1953, a number of skeletons, orientated E–W, were found *c.* 1m below ground level. No evidence of wood or stone protection around the burials, and no grave goods were found. Possible famine burials (OPW files).
13:27   22-7-1990

891 BALLYMADDOCK (Stradbally By.)
OS 14 NPL
Burials (site)   Reference to a large quantity of human remains found in a field not far from Ballymaddock Castle (No. 976); thought to represent a battle site (O'Hanlon and O'Leary 1907, vol. 1, 276).
14:51(01)   22-7-1990

892 BALLYMULLEN
OS 30:1:4 (34,520)   OD 400–500   24486,18249
Burials (site)   Two skeletons were discovered while digging for gravel. One was an extended inhumation of a young adult, aligned E–W, found 0.3m below present ground level. The hands were crossed over the left hip-bone and the feet appeared to have been tied together. A possible head-rest existed. No evidence of a burial mound or grave goods (OPW file).
30:5

893 COOLTORAN
OS 13 NPL
Burials (site)   Human bones were discovered when a bank collapsed during work in a sand-pit. No trace of a cist or pottery was noted (OPW file).
13:75

894 CURRAGH (Slievemargy By.)
OS 32 NPL
Burials (site)   Reference to 'ancient inhumed burials'

(OPW file) which were excavated from a sand-pit in the vicinity of a ringfort (No. 187).
32:37

895 FALLOWBEG MIDDLE
OS 25:2:1 (292,592) 'Piper's Pit'   OD 400–500   25726,18977
Burials (site)   Within an oval-shaped pit, human remains and fragments of a bagpipe were found. Possibly a musician of the O'Mores or O'Kellys who died in the battle on the Hill of Vengeance (O'Byrne 1856, 12).
25:3   21-8-1990

896 KILDRINAGH
OS 16:14:2 (374,102)   OD 300–400   22886,19072
Burials (site)   Not marked on the 1841 or 1909 eds. OS 6" map. Reference to burials located outside ringfort (No. 224) (Carrigan 1905, vol. 2, 180). No visible surface traces.
16:23(03)   16-9-1991

897 KILFEACLE
OS 25:15:5 (552,73)   OD 600–700   26005,18432
Burial (site)   While ploughing over 'an old moat' ringfort (No. 225), a number of flat stones, set on edge, were found *c.* 0.3m below the ground surface. Two larger stones which may have been cover-stones were also found; one was inscribed with a Maltese cross (No. 824), the other at E end of the grave was found to cover portions of a human skull. The stone-lined grave suggests that the burial was late medieval, or later, in date (*JRSAI* 1932, 119–20).
25:33(02)   22-8-1990

898 OLDGLASS
OS 28 NPL
Burials (site)   Reference to a twelve acre field called 'Ballina-ghowl' in which large quantities of human remains were found; supposedly a battlefield (Carrigan 1905, vol. 2, 64).
28:108(01)

899 TIMAHOE
OS 18:16:6 (868,27)   OD 300–400   25359,19018
Burials   A large quantity of human remains were discovered within the ruins of Timahoe Castle (No. 967) and beside the round tower (No. 804). In 1598, 1200 people were killed here in the battle between General Harrington and Melaghlen O'Moore (O'Byrne 1856, 39–40).
18:31(04)   13-6-1990

23. Mottes and Baileys

Mottes with or without baileys were first built in Ireland around the time of the Norman incursions of 1169. They appear to have been constructed over a period of about 100 years. Based closely on continental prototypes, they consist of steep-sided, conical, flat-topped earthen mounds, enclosed by a fosse and external bank. The bailey, which is usually either crescent-shaped or rectangular, may be either attached (i.e. not separated from the motte by a fosse) or unattached (i.e. both motte and bailey are enclosed by a fosse which also divides the two). The bailey, is usually slightly raised and enclosed by a bank and fosse. These earthworks were surmounted by wooden structures (palisades, wooden towers or *bretasches* and other dwellings). In some cases stone fortifications were added to them or the motte itself was subsumed into a larger complex at a later date. Where mottes and baileys occur in level terrain, unless badly denuded, they are easily identifiable; however where a natural feature or an existing monument has been adapted, identification is less easy.

900 AGHABOE
OS 22:12:1 (744,253) '*Aghaboe Moat*' OD 300–400 23281,18595
Motte and bailey A slightly squared-off motte (summit diam. *c.* 35m, base diam. *c.* 42m), with a grass-covered stone wall around the edge of the summit, surrounded by a shallow fosse (Wth *c.* 8.6m, D *c.* 1m). Remains of a bailey (diam. *c.* 23.5m N–S), defined by a scarp, to N. (O'Hanlon and O'Leary 1907, vol. 1, 54–5; Orpen 1909, 333–5, Cunningham 1987, 159–61)
22:19(07)   12-8-1991

901 BALLINACLOGH LOWER
OS 24:4:2 (782,570) Hachured OD 552 25268,18950
Motte and bailey An oval-shaped motte (dims. 30m E–W, 15m N–S, H *c.* 2m) separated by a wide shallow fosse (Wth *c.* 7m, D *c.* 1.5m) from a D-shaped bailey (dims. 40m NW–SE, 24m NE–SW) to ESE. The bailey is defined by a low bank (Wth *c.* 4m, int. H *c.* 0.4m) and outer fosse (Wth *c.* 4m, int. D *c.* 0.5m). An outer bank (Wth *c.* 3m) is present from SE–NW. Appears to be constructed within an earlier ringfort (No. 136) (OPW file). (*JKAS* 1992–3, 3–19)
24:15(02)   26-8-1990

902 BALLYROAN (Cullenagh By.)
OS 24:1:6 (210,508) Hachured OD 300–400 24665,18879
Motte A high flat-topped mound (summit diam. *c.* 22m, base diam. *c.* 40m, H *c.* 7m) surrounded by a water-filled fosse (Wth *c.* 4m, D *c.* 1.4m) partly faced with four courses of limestone walling. The mound and fosse are destroyed at NW and N. A raised flat area (H *c.* 1.5m) with scattered stone is visible to S and W of mound. Identified as the castle of Athronny (or Athroynny) which was destroyed by Murtough O'Brien in 1207 (Orpen 1909, 336).
24:6(01)   27-8-1990

903 CASTLETOWN (Slievemargy By.)
OS 26:9:4 (54,176) '*Moat*' OD 200–300 26454,18545
Motte and bailey A flat-topped conical mound (summit diam. 6.5m, base diam. *c.* 30m, H 10–12m) enclosed by a low gapped bank on summit. Steep-sided to W, N and E. Stone steps and a stone-built seat are set into the mound at SE. A cottage to S and farm buildings to SW have caused some disturbance. Slight traces of the fosse and external bank to N. Possible bailey, now landscaped, to SE (Bradley *et al.* 1981, 19–20).
26:11   4-8-1990

904 DONAGHMORE
OS 28:5:6 (179,345) '*Donaghmore Moat*' OD 300–400 22689,18047
Motte A flat-topped steep-sided earthen mound (summit diam. *c.* 8m, H *c.* 7.5m). Slight remains of fosse (Wth *c.* 5.5m, D *c.* 0.97m) visible. No evidence of bailey. (Carrigan 1905, vol. 2, 352; Orpen 1909, 337–8)
28:24(01)   29-9-1991

905 DUNBRIN LOWER
OS 20:11:4 (468,166) Hachured OD 200 26885,19180
Motte A raised oval area (max. dims. *c.* 25m N–S, *c.* 22m E–W, H 4.8m at N) defined by a low bank (Wth *c.* 2.2m, ext. H *c.* 1.8m) at W and N, and a flat-bottomed fosse (Wth *c.* 4.8m) at N and E. Partially destroyed at E and S by quarrying. Reference to a rath here (O'Hanlon and O'Leary 1907, vol. 1, 184).
20:2   8-8-1990

906 GRENAN
OS 35:12:3 (868,299) Hachured OD 200–300 24399,17375
Motte (possible) A large oval-shaped mound (diam. *c.* 60m E–W) rising to a platform (L *c.* 28m, Wth *c.* 6m, H *c.* 5m) at W, and an irregularly shaped platform (dims. *c.* 15m E–W, 9m N–S, H *c.* 7m) at summit. Surrounded by a U-shaped fosse (Wth *c.* 9.5m); entrance at NNW.
35:53   23-9-1990

907 HAYWOOD DEMESNE
OS 30:1:6 (220,466) Hachured OD 500–600 24682,18195

Motte A circular flat-topped earthen mound (summit diam. *c.* 18.6m, base diam. *c.* 40m, H *c.* 3.5–9.5m) with possible fosse at SE and SW.
30:8   5-8-1990

908 KILDELLIG
OS 22:15:1 (520,87)   Hachured   OD 400–500
23046,18418

Motte A square motte (summit dims. *c.* 9m sq., H *c.* 4m) with slight evidence of a fosse at S and W.
22:23   9-8-1991

909 KILLABBAN
OS 26:11:4 (477,187) 'Moat' OD 200–300
26901,18561

Motte (site) A small flat-topped mound (summit diam. *c.* 5m, base diam. *c.* 18m, H *c.* 6m) with slight traces of an enclosing fosse (Bradley *et al.* 1981, 38). Levelled in 1986. Slight traces of the mound visible.
26:13(01)   4-8-1990

910 KILLESHIN
OS 32:14:5 (322,50) *'Killeshin Moat'* OD 300–400
26745,17775

Motte A flat-topped conical earthen mound (summit diam. *c.* 18m, base diam. *c.* 33.8m, H *c.* 8m) (O'Hanlon and O'Leary 1907, vol. 1, 55).
32:20(01)   14-8-1990

911 KILMORONY
OS 26:3:5 (569,518) *'The Mound'* OD 200–300
26994,18912

Motte and bailey A circular earthen flat-topped motte (summit diam. 13m, H *c.* 6m) separated from a bailey at W by an intervening fosse (Wth *c.* 3m, D *c.* 2m). The bailey (Wth *c.* 26m) is surrounded by a fosse (Wth *c.* 4.5m, D *c.* 4m) at SW.
26:6   7-7-1990

912 MIDDLEMOUNT
OS 28:11:5 (558,214) *'Middlemount Moat'* OD 391
23091,17913

Motte and bailey Situated on a gravel ridge. A flat-topped motte (summit diam. *c.* 11.5m, H *c.* 8–9m) encircled by a berm with the remains of a wide stone wall on its outer edge, except at SE. Slight evidence of fosse at base of berm. Ridge to E was utilised as a bailey, and remains of possible outer defences are visible. Known as Monacoghlan or the rath of Laragh (Cunningham 1987 161–2). (Carrigan 1905, vol. 2, 61; Orpen 1909, 335–7)
28:50(01)   29-9-1991

913 MOAT
OS 30:6:3 (429,410)   Hachured   OD 500–600
24903,18137

Motte and bailey A circular flat-topped mound (summit diam. *c.* 12m, base diam. *c.* 46m, H *c.* 6m) defined by a bank (Wth *c.* 3.5m, int. H *c.* 0.7m) on summit. A flat-bottomed fosse (Wth *c.* 7m, D *c.* 2m) at S and W, and an external bank (Wth *c.* 3m, int. H *c.* 1m, ext. H *c.* 0.6m) at S and SW separate the motte from the irregularly shaped bailey (dims. *c.* 62m E–W, 30m N–S) to SW. Castle site (No. 1002) in SW quadrant of bailey.
30:21(02)   21-6-1991

914 MONELLY
OS 11:9:5 (92,182)   Hachured   OD 700–800
22581,19794

Motte A large flat-topped almost oval-shaped mound (summit diam. *c.* 27m N–S, base diam. *c.* 39m N–S, H *c.* 5.5–6m) with a berm. A fosse (Wth *c.* 5.4m, D *c.* 0.75m) is visible at E and S, and an external bank at S. Possible bailey at NNW. (Carrigan 1905, vol. 2, 151)
11:7   25-7-1991

915 NEWTOWN or SKIRK
OS 21:16:1 (731,149) *'Moat of Skirke'* OD 500–600
22293,18476

Motte and bailey A flat-topped mound (diam. *c.* 13m, H 3–3.5m) surrounded by a wide shallow fosse with a substantial bailey (int. dims. *c.* 75m E–W, *c.* 50m N–S) to S, which is defined by a bank (Wth 8–9m, int. H *c.* 1m, ext. H 2.5–3m) and external fosse (Wth *c.* 7m) except at N. Entrance at E. The site appears to have been a henge-type monument (No. 15) before it was adapted as a motte and bailey. Standing stone (No. 16) within the bailey. (Carrigan 1905, vol. 2, 136–7; Orpen 1909, 338–40; Cunningham 1987, 163–4)
21:21(02)   24-6-1990

916 RATHNAMANAGH
OS 13:2:5 (373,474) *'Rathnamanagh'* OD 300–400
24825,20125

Motte and bailey An oval-shaped motte (max. summit diam. 10m, max. basal diam. *c.* 21m, H *c.* 5.4m) in NE section of bailey (dims. *c.* 90m NW–SE, *c.* 50m E–W) and separated from it by a wide shallow fosse (Wth *c.* 5.2m, D *c.* 1m). The bailey, which is probably the remains of an earlier ringfort (No. 264), is defined by a low bank, intervening fosse (Wth *c.* 2.6m) with stone causeway (Wth *c.* 3m), and outer bank (Wth *c.* 5.5m, int. H *c.* 1.3m, ext. H *c.* 1.4m) except at N. Reference to a fort with deep fosses and level interior here (O'Hanlon and O'Leary 1907, vol. 1, 193).
13:4(02)   25-7-1990

917 SRAHANBOY
OS 10:16:6 (879,66)   Hachured   OD 600–700
22437,19670

Motte and bailey A gently sloping flat-topped mound (H *c.* 3.5m), situated in NW section of a D-shaped

Plate 3a—*Newtown or Skirk, standing stone* (**17**)

Plate 3b—*Ballaghmore, tower house* (**940**)

Plate 4a—*Kilmanman, church* (**767**)

Plate 4b—*Aghaboe, friary* (**688**)

raised bailey (max. dims. *c.* 62m E–W, 52m N–S) which is defined by a flat-topped bank (Wth *c.* 10m, int. H *c.* 1.1m, ext. H *c.* 2.4m) except at NE. No evidence now of fosse (Cunningham 1987, 167).
10:5   12-9-1991

24. Moated Sites

Moated sites are rectangular, subrectangular or square in plan and are defined by a bank(s) and a wide external fosse(s) usually containing water. The interior may be raised and would have contained house structures. Palisades were often constructed on the banks for extra protection. Although the moat often appears to have been water-filled, whether due to its location in a low-lying wet area or through its connection with leats to a nearby water source, moated sites also occur on high ground and have dry fosses. They are dated to the end of the thirteenth and the early fourteenth centuries. All rectilinear and subrectilinear enclosures visible as cropmarks on aerial photographs and marked on the current edition of the OS 6-inch maps are categorised as such unless there is more definite evidence to suggest that they are moated sites; they are included in chapter 15.

Fig. 19.—*Raheenduff, moated site* (**929**)

918 ASHFIELD
OS 32:1:4 (61,456) Hachured OD 400–500
26464,18201

Moated site A rectangular-shaped enclosure (dims. *c.* 47.8m N–S, *c.* 32m E–W), situated in a wet low-lying area, defined by an earthen bank (Wth *c.* 3.4m, int. H *c.* 1.2m, ext. H *c.* 2.1m) and external fosse (Wth *c.* 4.5m).
32:3   14-8-1990

919 BALLYROAN (Cullenagh By.)
OS 24:5:2 (126,432) Hachured OD 400
24577,18798

Moated site A rectangular area (dims. *c.* 30m E–W, 19m N–S), situated in gently undulating terrain, enclosed by an inner bank (Wth *c.* 7m, int. H *c.* 0.5m, ext H *c.* 0.9m.), intervening fosse (Wth *c.* 4m), and outer bank (Wth *c.* 4.8m) at W and N. Possible original entrance at E.
24:19   26-8-1990

920 BARROWHOUSE
OS 20:14:6 (449,62) Hachured OD 200–300
26866,19069

Moated site A rectangular enclosure (dims *c.* 56m E–W, 53m N–S), situated in a low-lying area, defined by a bank (Wth *c.* 5.9m, int. H *c.* 0.7m, ext. H *c.* 1.45m) and external fosse (Wth *c.* 3.5m) at W. Slight evidence of bank at S and fosse at N. No other visible surface traces.

20:5   10-7-1990

921 CARRIGEEN (Stradbally By.)
Kilmurry ED
OS 14:5:1 (53,387) Hachured   OD 400–500
25463,20038

Moated site   A rectangular area (dims. *c.* 43m E–W, *c.* 38m N–S), situated on a N–S ridge, defined by a low bank (Wth *c.* 3.5m, int. H *c.* 0.4m, ext. H *c.* 1m) and external fosse (Wth *c.* 4m) at S, W and N.

14:8   22-5-1990

922 COOLDERRY
OS 29:6:3 (404,388) Hachured   OD 200–300
23902,18104

Moated site   A subrectangular enclosure (max. dims. *c.* 80m E–W, *c.* 41m N–S), in low-lying wet land, defined by a scarp with some traces of a bank (Wth *c.* 3.8m, int. H *c.* 0.2m, ext. H *c.* 3.5m), and an external fosse (Wth *c.* 4.8m, D *c.* 1.6m). No visible evidence of original entrance.

29:21   13-5-1990

923 COOLE (Maryborough West By.)
OS 23:4:1 (726,584) Hachured   OD 300–400
24234,18955

Moated site (possible)   A subrectangular enclosure (dims. *c.* 51m N–S, *c.* 45m E–W), situated in a slightly elevated position in a low-lying area, defined by a bank (Wth *c.* 3–5m, ext. H *c.* 1.2m). No evidence of fosse or original entrance.

23:8   17-8-1990

924 COOLOWLEY (MASON)
OS 27:8:5 (845,323)   OD 300–400   22418,18021

Moated site (possible)   Marked on the 1841 ed. OS 6" map. Situated in gently undulating terrain. Traces of a bank at N, NE, SE, S and SW delimit an almost square area (dims. 30m NW–SE, 28.4m NE–SW). No evidence of fosse or original entrance.

27:14   22-10-1990

925 DOOARY
OS 24:2:6 (417,462) Hachured   OD 600–700
24884,18833

Moated site (possible)   A subrectangular enclosure (dims. *c.* 80m E–W *c.* 78m N–S) defined by a bank (Wth *c.* 5.6m, int. H *c.* 1m, ext. H *c.* 1.3m) and external fosse (Wth *c.* 4m, ext. D *c.* 0.5m).

24:14   31-7-1990

926 GARRYDUFF (Clarmallagh By.)
OS 28:3:2 (597,570) Indicated   OD 400–500
23129,18289

Moated site   A subrectangular enclosure (max. dims. *c.* 51m N–S, *c.* 42m E–W), situated in low-lying wet land, defined by an inner bank (int. H *c.* 0.3m), an intervening fosse (Wth *c.* 2.6m, D *c.* 0.8m) with a possible outer bank at NW. Entrance with causeway at N.

28:11   12-9-1991

927 GRANGE MORE
See under rectilinear enclosures.

928 KILMINFOYLE
OS 29:1:4 (17,487)   Hachured   OD 300–400
23492,18204

Moated site (site)   Situated in a low-lying area. Marked on the 1841 and 1906 eds. OS 6" maps, and shown on the 25" map as a square area (dims. 40m sq.) surrounded by a wide fosse and slight external bank (overall dims. *c.* 72m N–S, *c.* 70m E–W). According to local information, the interior of the site was level and covered an area of one and a half Irish acres. It was enclosed by a very deep fosse and high bank. Traditionally known as a flax yard. Site was levelled in late 1950s or early 1960s. No visible surface traces. A series of stone foundations in the area immediately NE of moated site are believed to mark the site of a village associated with the flax yard.

29:1   15-8-1990

929 RAHEENDUFF (Clarmallagh By.)
OS 30:13:1 (30,89)   Hachured   OD 300–400
24485,17794

Moated site   A rectangular area (dims. *c.* 60m N–S, 44m E–W) defined by an inner bank (Wth *c.* 2.8m, int. H *c.* 0.3m, ext. H *c.* 0.5m) from NW–SW and a scarp from SW–NW, an intervening fosse (Wth *c.* 6.8m) and outer bank (Wth *c.* 3.2m, int. H *c.* 0.7m, ext. H *c.* 0.4m) except at W where a stream flows.

30:30   20-6-1991

930 RATHSARAN GLEBE/MOUNTOLIVER
OS 28:9:4 (9,168) Hachured OD 400 22512,17858

Moated site   A raised rectangular area (dims. *c.* 70m N–S, 52m E–W), situated on a ridge, defined by an inner bank (Wth *c.* 6.2m, int. H *c.* 0.6m, ext. H *c.* 1.5m), intervening fosse (Wth *c.* 2.7m), outer bank (Wth *c.* 4.4m, int. H *c.* 0.9m, ext. H *c.* 0.7m), and external fosse (Wth *c.* 4.6m) at S.

28:39   17-9-1991

25. Deserted Settlement

Included in this chapter are deserted settlement sites which date to medieval or early post-medieval times. They are chacterised by distinct house platforms and associated plots, and, more rarely, a sunken trackway or hollow-way.

Fig. 20—*Ballybuggy, deserted settlement* (**931**)

931 BALLYBUGGY
OS 34:1:2 (150,571) Hachured   OD 400–500
22662,17645
Settlement deserted The 'ancient town of Ballybuggy' extended in a SE direction from graveyard (No. 698). Its foundations covered an area of six Irish acres *c.* 1850 but by the early 1900s, as a result of reclamation, it was reduced in size to one and a half acres (Carrigan 1905, vol. 2, 342). The surviving features consist of two adjacent enclosures. The W enclosure (dims. *c.* 35m N–S, *c.* 30m E–W) is defined by a bank (Wth *c.* 3m, int. H *c.* 0.5m, ext. H *c.* 1.6m) except at S, and a shallow fosse at W; the E enclosure (dims. *c.* 60m N–S, *c.* 48m E–W) by a bank (Wth *c.* 1.7m, H *c.* 0.5m) and a fosse (Wth *c.* 2.3m) at N. The interior is divided into three sections by E–W running banks. A house site (dims. *c.* 10m N–S, 7m E–W), with the possible original entrance at W, is visible at NW; at least three house platforms lie in S section, one with a possible central dividing wall.
34:5   27-9-1990

932 CASTLEBRACK
OS 1:15:2 (570,101)   OD 300–400   24043,21643
Settlement deserted   SW and downslope from the ruined tower house (No. 947) appears to have been the site of a deserted medieval village. Slight traces of earthworks visible. Walls *c.* 1m thick discovered some years ago in this area.
1:4(02)   13-8-1990

933 CORRAUN
OS 22:11:6 (693,223)   OD 300–500   23227,18563
Settlement deserted A series of banks visible on aerial

106

photographs (GSI, S 150–1). Possibly the site of secular medieval settlement (Cunningham 1987, 159, 161).

22:19(17)   12-8-1991

934 PARK or DUNAMASE
OS 13:12:4 (760,168) '*Ancient Village* (Site of)'
OD 400–500   25236,19805

Settlement deserted   Reference to an ancient village here (O'Hanlon and O'Leary 1907, vol. 1, 272).

Surviving features consist of a series of low earthen banks, faint traces of a N–S hollow-way (L *c.* 40m, D *c.* 0.3m), and a rectangular-shaped enclosure (dims. 46m E–W, 35m N–S) defined by a bank (Wth *c.* 6.7m, int. H *c.* 0.8m, ext. H *c.* 0.5m) at N, NE and E and elsewhere by a scarp. No evidence of fosse or original entrance. Possible remains of two small rectangular house platforms to NNE of enclosure plus cultivation ridges. Ringfort (No. 245) to NW. These earthworks mark the site of the borough of Dunamase (Bradley *et al.* 1981, 24).

13:51(01)   8-7-1990

26. Medieval Castles

The Anglo-Normans introduced the techniques of stone castle-building into Ireland towards the end of the twelfth century. Stone castles in Ireland can be broadly divided into four groups based on their date and architecture: (1) early fortresses usually of royal or seigneurial castles of the late twelfth or early thirteenth centuries; (2) late thirteenth/early fourteenth-century castles; (3) fourteenth–seventeenth-century tower houses; (4) late sixteenth/early seventeenth-century fortified houses. This chapter includes all castles which are earlier than tower houses (i.e. groups 1 and 2). Dunamase (No. 937) and Lea (No. 936) are good examples of medieval stone fortresses.

Fig. 21—*Dunamase, castle* (**937**)

935 DYSART
OS 13:16:4 (695,66) '*Piggott's Castle* (in Ruins)'
OD 500–600   25169,19697

Medieval castle Marked on the 1563 map of Leix and Offaly (Hore 1863, f.p. 345). Originally belonging to the O'Lalor family (O'Hanlon *et al.* 1914, vol. 2, 524), this castle was granted to John Piggott in 1577 by Queen Elizabeth (Comerford 1886, vol. 3, 276–8). In 1646 Dysart was taken by force, and Pigott was killed by Colonel Farrell and Colonel Roger McGuire's regiments (O'Hanlon *et al. ibid.*, 524–5). Standing remains consist of NE angle tower of curtain wall built of limestone rubble and mortar. No other visible surface traces.
13:61(01)   6-6-1990

936 LEA
OS 5:10:1 (296,276) '*Lea Castle* (in Ruins)'
OD 200–300   25709,21205

Medieval castle Large Anglo-Norman fortress situated on low-lying ground close to S bank of the River Barrow. One of Leask's (1941, 50–1) towered keeps and the only one which has extensive outer defences extant (Leask 1936, Fig. 14). Probably built by the Earl Marshall in the first quarter of the thirteenth century. Its standing remains consist of a keep with large circular angle towers, an inner ward with gateway and a large outer ward with a D-shaped twin-towered gateway which was probably added at the end of thirteenth century. Earthworks of unknown date visible on all but N side of castle. (Fitzgerald

1904, 325–51)
5:6   15-5-1990

937 PARK or DUNAMASE
OS 13:12:5 (820,179) '*Castle* (in Ruins)'
OD 500–600   25300,19818
Medieval castle Large Anglo-Norman fortress
founded on a rock eminence and dominating the
surrounding countryside. Built prior to 1215, this was a
Marshall stronghold *c.* 1216 (O'Leary 1909, 162). It
was enlarged and rebuilt *c.* 1250 by William de Braos
(*ibid.*, 164). In 1650 it was taken by Cromwell's
generals, Hewson and Reynolds, who dismantled it
and blew it up but in the following century it was
partly rebuilt (*ibid.*, 167–8). The castle and its defences
basically consist of a D-shaped bailey to SE, defended
by earthen banks and a fosse, which protects a
gateway, at W, to the outer ward. The outer gatehouse
is at the apex of an almost triangular courtyard which
is enclosed by a badly ruined stone wall. The single
gate-tower is rounded at the front, and is pierced by
the gate-passage. The inner gatehouse, situated on SE
wall of the inner ward, is almost square in plan, two
storeys high, and has a chamber on each side of the
gate-passage. The walls and towers of the inner ward
enclose a large irregularly shaped area of the rock
which has a very uneven surface. In the north central
portion of the ward, at the highest point of the rock,
stands a large rectangular-shaped two-storey high
keep, the S half of which is almost completely
destroyed. The remaining portion has been much-
altered since its erection in the early thirteenth century,
including the insertion of brick vaults in some of the
embrasures. (Leask 1941, 64–5)
13:52   12-8-1991

27. Tower Houses

Tower houses are fortified stone residences built between the fourteenth and seventeenth centuries. They are rectangular in plan, up to five storeys in height, often with two diagonally opposed projecting angle towers and usually containing such features as a barrel vault over the ground floor, mural passages, stairwell, garderobe and murder-hole. Many in County Laois are now destroyed and the majority are in a ruinous state. However, Ballaghmore (No. 940) is a well-preserved example.

938 AGHMACART
OS 34:8:5 (770,361) 'Castle (in Ruins)'
OD 300–400 23320,17430

Tower house Part of N wall and NE angle survive of this two-storey high tower house (dims. 8m E–W, 7.3m N–S) which is built of roughly coursed limestone rubble. It has a N–S barrel vault over ground floor, a large ope with a segmental arch on first floor, and remains of a corbel, to N of this, which carried an attic floor. Evidence of the bawn (dims. 27m E–W, 22m N–S) to N and S defined by a low bank (Wth *c.* 4m) and outer fosse.

34:19(02)   8-10-1990

939 BALLAGHARAHIN
OS 33:3:3 (677,589) 'Ballagh Castle (in Ruins)'
OD 400–500 22244,17661

Tower house A Fitzpatrick castle (Carrigan 1905, vol. 2, 350) (max. ext. dims. 11.25m NE–SW, 9.3m NW–SE, wall T 2.4m) five storeys high with dressed quoins and a slight base-batter. Bartizan on E angle and machicolation on NW and SW walls at third-floor level. Windows consist mainly of simple slits and some two-light ogee-headed opes. The doorway in SW wall has yett holes and a two-centered arch of limestone blocks which are hammer-dressed with fine drafting and chamfered. This doorway leads into an entrance lobby which is protected by a cross loop in NE wall. A further lobby immediately to SE gives access to main ground-floor chamber and stairwell in S angle. Reference to sundials on ten steps of stairs which decreased in size from the upper to the lower stair (*JRSAI* 1867, 4–5). There is no barrel vault. Mural passages in NW wall at first- and second-floor level, and rectangular chambers on each floor level directly above entranceway. Fireplaces on second floor in SE wall, and on third floor in NW wall. Possible bawn SW of tower house.

33:2(01)   26-10-1990

940 BALLAGHMORE LOWER
OS 15:14:6 (433,30) 'Ballaghmore Castle' OD 400
21973,18987

Tower house A rectangular-shaped tower (dims. *c.* 13.65 NE–SW, 11.6m NW–SE), five storeys high, built of rubble limestone with a slight base-batter. Modern entrance in NE wall. Original entrance with murder-hole in NW wall. To N of doorway a mural passage leads to a mural stairs which accesses a spiral stairs in N angle. Access to first floor via two-centered limestone pointed arch doorway. Mural passage in SW wall at first-floor level, and in SE wall at third-floor level which leads to a garderobe in E angle. Wicker-centred mural chamber in W angle. Spiral stairs in N angle leads to fourth-floor chamber, and stairs in SW wall leads to roof level. Windows are mainly narrow slit opes but there is an ogee-headed window in NE wall, and some cross loops in SE wall. On SW wall, between second and third floors, is a sheela-na-gig (No. 1013) carved in relief (Gleeson 1982, 632–6). This tower house has recently been renovated. Remains of a curtain wall (wall T *c.* 0.7m), set close to the tower house wall (i.e. only *c.* 1m out from it), survive. It has a mural tower with a corbelled roof at S angle, and remains of another at W angle.

15:17(01)   31-5-1994

941 BALLINAKILL
OS 30:5:6 (215,336) 'Ballinakill Castle (in Ruins)'
OD 400–500 24678,18056

Tower house A castle was constructed here by Sir Thomas Ridgeway between 1606 and 1612. After the Insurrection of 1641, it was subsequently destroyed. Another castle was built on its site by the Dunne family in 1680 (O'Hanlon and O'Leary 1907, vol. 1, 233–4). Originally five storeys high, remains consist of N gable (L *c.* 5.3m), now three storeys high, constructed of roughly coursed pink shaley stone with dressed limestone quoins, and short returns of E and W sides. Two gun loops visible on ground and first floor; large window on second floor.

30:18(01)   17-6-1991

942 BALLYADAMS
OS 19:16:2 (830,80) 'Ballyadams Castle (in Ruins)'
OD 200–300 26293,19082

Tower house A six-storey high late medieval structure (dim. 10.7m N–S) with rounded towers at SW and NW angles between which is an imposing entranceway. Large rectangular seventeenth-century three-storey house (No. 1021) attached to E side. The entranceway is recessed with a round segmental arch over the recess, while the doorway has a two-centred arch over it. Spanning the area between the towers, flush with their outer faces and just below the uppermost storey, is another segmental arch which forms a machicolation over the entrance below. There is also a murder-hole at first-floor level over the doorway. Garderobe chamber and chute in NE angle and stairwell in NW tower. Most of the window opes are plain but some are ogee-headed with two lights, while the uppermost ones have hood-mouldings.

19:28(01)   30-5-1994

943 BALLYGEEHIN LOWER
OS 23:14:4 (239,7) 'Ballygeehin Castle (in Ruins)'
OD 300–400 23726,18340
Tower house Owned by the Fitzpatricks, Lords of Upper Ossory. The castle was burned down in 1600 to prevent it being converted into an English garrison (Carrigan 1905, vol. 2, 56). Partial remains of NE wall (L c. 16.2m), SW wall (L c. 7.3m) and NE angle tower survive of this uncoursed rubble limestone tower house with a slight base-batter. Evidence of a barrel-vaulted entranceway running NE–SW. Large splayed ope in NE wall at first-floor level. Bawn wall (T c. 1.1m), with a series of gun loops, attached to SE angle encloses an almost circular area.
23:35   30-5-1994

944 BALLYKEALY
OS 35:10:2 (336,244) 'Castle (in Ruins)'
OD 300–400 23838,17312
Tower house References date from 1653, when it was fortified by John McKeallagh Fitzpatrick (Carrigan 1905, vol. 2, 228). The S and W angles of a rubble-built tower house (dims. 9.35m NW–SE, c. 7m NE–SW, wall T 1.25m), at least two storeys high, with a possible entrance at SE survive. Featureless. A piece of masonry 15m out from S angle may represent the remains of a bawn wall.
35:45(01)   27-9-1990

945 BALLYKNOCKAN
OS 18:6:6 (436,323) 'Ballyknockan Castle (in Ruins)'
OD 300–400 24899,19325
Tower house Owned by Sir Thomas Colclough in 1598 (Comerford 1886, vol. 3, 284). Standing remains consist of lower portions of N wall (L c. 7.9m) and E wall (L 8.6m) built of rubble limestone. A N–S barrel vault with wicker-centring survives over ground floor. Entrance in N wall and garderobe in SE angle. Remains of mural passage in N wall and possible evidence of stairway in NE angle.
18:10   11-6-1990

946 BLACKFORD
OS 14:16:4 (695,9) 'Blackford Castle (in Ruins)'
OD 200–300 26145,19646
Tower house Marked on the 1563 map of Leix and Offaly (Hore 1863, f.p. 345). Erected as a defence against the Pale incursions by the O'Moores (O'Hanlon and O'Leary 1907, vol. 1, 223). Built of roughly coursed limestone, remains consist of E wall (L c. 7.4m) and portion of S wall (L c. 2.6m, T c. 1.8m), four storeys high. Featureless, except for slit ope in E wall.
14:45   7-6-1990

947 CASTLEBRACK
OS 1:15:2 (574,102) 'Castle Brack (Site of)'
OD 350–400 24047,21644

Tower house Erected by the Dunne family in 1427 (Crossdaile 1959, 13) and situated c. 25m to SSE of Castlebrack church (No. 707). Reduced to a pile of featureless rubble which probably measured 20m E–W. Remains of bawn wall at S with external fosse at E and S.
1:4(01)   13-8-1990

948 CASTLEFLEMING (STUBBER)/ GARRISON
OS 27:11:3 (649,269) 'Castle (in Ruins)' OD 425 22211,17962
Tower house Marked on the Down Survey map. A rectangular hall-like structure (dims. 17.35m E–W, 16.85m N–S), now two storeys high, with remains of a south projecting tower at SW angle and a later extension off NW angle. A series of opes visible at first- and second-floor level in S wall. Doorway, with remains of an outer doorway, in W end of S wall. Its remaining arch stone is hammer-dressed with fine drafting, dating it to the late sixteenth century. Remains of a murder-hole visible inside the outer doorway; a large fireplace, with an oven to N of it, survives in W gable. No evidence of a stairwell. Possible bawn wall attached to E.
27:16   22-10-1990

949 CASTLETOWN (Clandonagh By.) Donaghmore ED
OS 28:10:1 (288,268) 'Castle (in Ruins)'
OD 300–400 22806,17967
Tower house Known as 'Cody's Castle', this tower house was in almost perfect condition in 1800 (Carrigan 1905, vol. 2, 281). Now only SE gable (Wth c. 8.4m, T c. 1.25m), three storys high, constructed of limestone slabs survives. A slight base-batter is visible. The entrance was towards E end of gable; remains of a segmental pointed arch window visible towards S end on first-floor level. Evidence of a N–S barrel vault over ground floor. Foundations of bawn wall visible to W.
28:42   29-9-1991

950 CLONBURREN
OS 33:8:6 (913,356) 'Clonburren Castle (in Ruins)'
OD 400–500 22496,17417
Tower house In the early seventeenth century, this was the home of Teige Fitzpatrick who was later Lord of Upper Ossory. Shown as a ruin on the Down Survey (Carrigan 1905, vol. 2, 343). A rectangular tower house (12.5m NE–SW, 9.4m NW–SE), five storeys high with a wall-walk and base-batter. The opes are mainly simple slits with two-light ogee-headed windows at the upper level. Remains of doorway in NE wall, directly inside of which is a rectangular-shaped chamber; another lies overhead. Guard chamber in N angle, and stairwell in E angle from which two-centered arched doorways give access to

Left
Fig. 22—*Ballagharahin, tower house* (**939**)

Right Fig. 24— *Ballagharahin, tower house* (**939**)

Below right Fig. 25—*Ballagharahin, tower house, internal details* (**939**)

Below
Fig. 23—*Ballagharahin, tower house* (**939**)

different floor levels. A barrel vault runs NE–SW over fourth floor. Mural passages in SW wall on third and fourth floors. Garderobe chute in NE wall. Cross loops and gun loops visible in E angle.
33:11(01)   22-10-1990

951 CLONREHER
OS 13:5:1 (31,435) *'Clonreher Castle* (in Ruins)'
OD 300–400   24464,20079
Tower house   Probably owned by the O'Dowlings before being granted by the crown to John Dunkirley in 1550. It later belonged to the Hartpoles of Shrule (*JKAS* 1909, 115–6). A four-storey high tower house (dims. 11.75m N–S, 9.45m E–W), built of greywacke, with projecting towers at NE and SW angles which are five storeys high. All the lights are simple slits except for a two-light pointed arch window in E wall and some modern rectangular-shaped ones. There is no dressed stonework or base-batter. The original doorway cannot be identified. There is a N–S barrel vault with a loft over the ground floor, and a mural passage in E wall at loft level, while a spiral stairs in SE angle leads to upper floors which are inaccessible. The SW tower has a barrel-vaulted roof with wicker-centring, and a garderobe in a small chamber at first-floor level. (O'Hanlon and O'Leary 1907, vol. 1, 191–3)
13:19   30-5-1994

952 COOLBANAGHER
OS 8:15:6 (683,61) *'Coolbanagher Castle* (in Ruins)'
OD 300–400   25150,20331
Tower house   NE of Coolbanagher church (No. 721) is the remains of a tower house (max. ext. dims. 11m E–W, 7.5m N–S), three storeys high, built of rubble limestone with a slight base-batter. There is no barrel vault, all floors were wooden. Doorway of heavily punched limestone with fine drafting and yett holes in N wall. Contains some ogee-headed windows of limestone. Possible remains of stairwell in SW angle. (*JKAS* 1904, 301, 310)
8:15   20-6-1990

953 COOLNAMONY LOWER
OS 2:16:6 (874,37) *'Turrets* (in Ruins)'
OD 400–500   23395,20929
Tower house (site)   Reference to the site of a tower house or fortified house, thought to have been built by Teig Oge O'Doyne *c.* 1551 (Crossdaile 1959, 12), situated on slighly elevated ground close to E bank of Glenlahan River. All that remains is W wall of bawn which has three simple splayed gun loops and part of an angle tower at its N end.
2:18(01)   31-10-1990

954 GALESQUARTER
OS 35:5:4 (74,330) *'Castle* (in Ruins)'   OD 300–400

23560,17400
Tower house   Erected by the MacGillapatricks *c.* 1425; damaged by the Cromwellians in the mid-seventeenth century and left uninhabitable (Carrigan 1905, vol. 2, 231–3). Built of roughly coursed limestone, this tower house (dims. 15m x 12.6m, wall T 0.95m) is five storeys high with a wall-walk. Most of N portion is missing, as is the doorway. Mural stairwell in NE angle. There is a N–S barrel vault over the ground floor with evidence of a loft which was accessed from an opening in N wall. Mural passage on first and second floors of S wall, and chambers in SE and SW angles, with remains of wicker-centring in SE ones. Large cut-limestone fireplace on second floor of E wall. The third floor was supported on wall thickness, as was the top floor. Intramural wall-walk and pitched gable on S wall; chimney stack on E wall. Most opes are simple rectangular ones. Carrigan (*ibid.*, 232) refers to a sheela-na-gig (No. 1014) on E wall, and a draw-well in centre of courtyard. No trace of either visible. A large well-preserved seven-sided bawn wall (dims. *c.* 80m N–S, *c.* 60m E–W, wall T *c.* 1.1m), with gun loops at N and E, survives; and an inner defensive wall with angle towers, which is set close to the tower house. It appears to have been destroyed at N and E.
35:22(01)   27-9-1990

955 GARRANMACONLY
OS 21:15:2 (593,92) *'Castle* (in Ruins)'
OD 500–600   22148,18415
Tower house   Built in the sixteenth century by the Lords of Upper Ossory. In 1601 it was occupied by John Fitzpatrick, in 1665 by Peter Buckley, and towards the end of the 1600s by the Vicars family (Carrigan 1905, vol. 2, 138). A five-storey high tower house (dims.10.65m E–W, 8.3m N–S) with an attic overhead, built of randomly coursed limestone blocks. It is founded on bedrock and has a base-batter on N and E walls. Garderobe in projecting tower situated close to NW angle. Bartizan on top of NE angle and machicolation on fourth floor of E wall. Round- and flat-headed single-light windows in N wall and two-light windows visible in E wall. Remains of stairwell survive in NW angle, from which doorways constructed of large hammer-dressed limestone blocks give access to the various floor levels; also mural passage in N wall. The original entrance was probably in W wall, close to NW angle, which has collapsed. Large fireplace in N wall at second-floor level, and a large chimney stack, carried on two corbels, rises from it at wall-walk level. (O'Hanlon and O'Leary 1907, vol. 1, 316–7)
21:13(01)   31-5-1994

956 GASH
OS 16:12:6 (885,219) *'Castle* (in Ruins)'
OD 300–400   23424,19202
Tower house (site)   Gilbert de Clare, Earl of

Gloucester, is recorded as being in possession of the castle of 'Offerclane' (Castletown) in 1290. In 1307 it belonged to his widow Joan, Countess of Gloucester. Thomas de Centewelle was Constable of the castle in 1309 and held it for the crown. In 1600 it was burnt down by Teige Fitzpatrick (Carrigan 1905, vol. 2, 171–2). The SW section of a mural tower, built of roughly coarsed rubble limestone, with the remains of an intramural stairwell, and a late medieval NE angle tower survive. A modern school occupies the site of the tower house.
16:17(01)   16-9-1991

957 GORTNACLEA
OS 23:9:2 (131,275) *'Gortnaclea Castle* (in Ruins)' OD 300–400 23608,18622

Tower house In the ownership of Donal Fitzpatrick in 1566; the Black Earl of Ormond was held prisioner here by Owney O'Moore in April 1600 (Carrigan 1905, vol. 2, 53–4). A five-storey high tower house (dims. *c.* 11.8m E–W, *c.* 9.8m N–S) with base-batter, built of randomly coursed rubble and large limestone quoins. Entrance in N wall; stairwell in NE angle. An E–W barrel vault with wicker-centring is visible over third floor. Mural passage, on first and second floor, in N wall leads to garderobe. Remains of gable at wall-walk level of W wall. Single-light and two-light windows survive. Evidence of bawn to N and W.
23:16   18-8-1990

958 GRANTSTOWN
OS 28:12:2 (777,272) *'Castle* (in Ruins)' OD 300–400 23322,17977

Tower house Originally owned by the Lords of Upper Ossory, it belonged to Gilbert Rawson in 1653, Edmond Morris in 1691 and was granted to Richard and Edward Fitzpatrick in 1696 by William of Orange (Carrigan 1905, vol. 2, 63). A circular tower house (diam. *c.* 11.7m), built of coursed limestone blocks, five storeys high with an attic and wall-walk. The wall has collapsed from NE–SSE. Entrance, now almost completely obscured by rubble, was at E side but its two-centred arch can be seen which leads into a lobby area, which in turn gives access to the main chamber. Intramural stairwell at NE and intramural passages in second-, third- and fourth-floor levels. NE–SW barrel vault with wicker-centring over third floor, while other floors were supported on corbels and the wall thickness. The second-, third- and fourth-floor levels are angular internally with the topmost one being almost square. Most of the opes are simple slits with wide splayed embrasures but there are also a few gun loops. Machicolations on battlement level at NE and S.
28:51   31-5-1994

959 KILBREEDY
OS 28:11:1 (500,292) *'Kilbreedy Castle* (in Ruins)' OD 300–400 23029,17994

Tower house The O'Phelans established a castle here and it remained in their ownership until the mid-seventeenth century (Carrigan 1905, vol. 2, 60–1). A three-storey high rectangular-shaped tower (dims. 16.9m N–S, 10.35m E–W, wall T *c.* 2.05) built of roughly coursed limestone. Broken-out entrance in E end of S wall with murder-hole overhead. Large mural passage in N wall at ground-floor level, and at first-floor level in N and S walls. Intramural stairs in W end of S wall. Large barrel vault over first floor. Three vaulted recesses with opes in E wall and two in W wall at ground-floor level. At first-floor level in E wall are four rectangular-shaped opes.
28:46   29-9-1991

960 KILLEANY
OS 23:6:1 (297,408) *'Killeany Castle* (in Ruins)' OD 200–300 23782,18765

Tower house Marked on the 1563 map of Leix and Offaly (Hore 1863, f.p. 345). Only featureless fragments of masonry remain.
23:12(01)   17-8-1990

961 MILLTOWN
OS 25:8:2 (783,400) *'Castle* (in Ruins)' OD 300–400 26247,18780

Tower house Marked on the Down Survey Barony Map. Known as Milltown or Ballyvuilling castle, it consisted of a square tower with levelled outworks and a modern dwelling-house built against it (O'Hanlon and O'Leary 1907, vol. 1, 302–3). A wall (L *c.* 29m, H *c.* 2.9m, T *c.* 0.9m) built of roughly coursed rubble limestone, running NW–SE, is the only surviving feature.
25:20(01)   23-7-1990

962 MONDREHID
OS 16:13:1 (33,78) *'Mondrehid Castle* (in Ruins)' OD 300–400 22525,19044

Tower house Marked on the Down Survey. Carrigan (1905, vol. 2, 134) refers to a much-ruined castle. Only the fragment of a wall (L 14m, H 5m) built of roughly coursed rubble limestone, running NW–SE, and NW angle survive; also a fragment of the base of SW wall (L 8m). Featureless.
16:19   16-9-1991

963 MORETT
OS 9:13:4 (3,50) *'Morett Castle* (in Ruins)'   OD 300 25407,20323

Tower house A Fitzgerald castle built *c.* 1580 (*JRSAI* 1866 534–5). Rectangular tower house (dims. 15.5m E–W, 11.5m N–S; wall T 2.5m at W, 1.3m at N) built on rock outcrop and constructed with rubble limestone, roughly coursed. It is four storeys high with NE, SE and SW angles extant but most of the connecting walls are levelled. Large central chimney stack and associated fireplaces visible in E gable. Bartizans on NE and SW angles. No evidence of murder-hole, garderobes or doorway. (Comerford 1886, vol. 2, 146–8; Fitzgerald 1904, 285–96)

9:21(01)   21-6-1990

964 SHAEN
OS 8:15:5 (578,44) '*Shaen Castle* (in Ruins)' OD 300–400 25039,20313
Tower house (site) Situated on the summit of a hill is a stone-walled garden, the NW angle of which has a distinct batter and projects forward from the line of the garden. This section of masonry (dims. 3.9m N–S, 3.8m E–W, H 2.8m) is built of roughly coursed limestone blocks and appears to be part of a castle, probably a tower house (*JKAS* 1909, 68) which is said to have been destroyed in 1650 (O'Hanlon and O'Leary 1907, vol. 1, 179). A sheela-na-gig (No. 1016) is thought to have come from here (*JRSAI* 1936, 117).

8:13(01)   21-6-1990

965 SHRULE
OS 32:7:3 (692,395) '*Castle* (in Ruins)' OD 100–200 27132,18143
Tower house Built by Robert Hartpole during the reign of Queen Elizabeth (O'Hanlon and O'Leary 1907, vol. 1, 315–6). A four-storey high tower (dims. *c.* 12.1m E–W, *c.* 11m N–S, wall T 1.8m) built of roughly coursed limestone with a very slight base-batter. The S jamb of the original doorway is visible in N end of E wall. This entranceway accesses a lobby with a murder-hole overhead. Three doorways lead off the lobby; that to S gives access to a mural passage in E wall which in turn leads to a stairwell to first-floor level; from here a spiral stairway rises in SE angle. The doorway to N leads to a guardroom, while that directly opposite the entrance leads to the main ground-floor chamber which is divided E–W by an inserted wall. Each half of the chamber has a barrel vault with wicker-centring. There is a large fireplace at first-floor level in S wall, and at second- and third-floor levels in N wall. Also at this level, a mural passage in N wall leads to a slit ope in NW angle. Garderobe chambers in S wall, to W of stairwell, at first- and second-floor levels. Most windows are single lights, some with ogee heads and hood-mouldings, but in S wall at third-floor level is a two-light transom window. Close to SW angle on S wall, at second-floor level, is a limestone plaque with the date 1640 and the letters RHK. (Craig 1972, 25)

32:12(01)   14-8-1990

966 SRAHANBOY
OS 10:16:6 (914,57) '*Srahan Castle* (in Ruins)' OD 600–700 22475,19661

Tower house Occupied by the O'Connors in 1641 and by the Calcutt family in 1775. Fell into ruin shortly afterwards (Carrigan 1905, vol. 2, 150). Remains consist of S wall (L *c.* 8.2m, Wth *c.* 1.7m) and W wall (L *c.* 9m), two storeys high, built of rubble limestone. Fragment of an ope at NW. Possible evidence of bawn at W.

10:6(01)   12-9-1991

967 TIMAHOE
OS 18:16:6 (868,30) '*Castle* (in Ruins) on Site of Abbey*' OD 300–400 25359,19020
Tower house A sixteenth-century tower house built of roughly coursed sandstone and limestone blocks. Remains consist of E wall (L *c.* 12.45m) and short returns of N and S walls. The E wall incorporates the blocked-up chancel arch (Wth *c.* 3.95m) of an earlier fifteenth-century church (No. 804) (Crawford 1924, 42–5). Large beam holes visible on the inner face of E wall at first-floor level and also a doorway leading to a chamber in SE angle. Evidence of slit opes in remains of N and S walls, now much destroyed and otherwise featureless. Reference to a sheela-na-gig (No. 1017) at the doorway (*JRSAI* 1936, 114), not now visible.

18:31(06)   13-6-1990

968 TINNAKILL (Portnahinch By.)
OS 8:3:2 (563,587) '*Tinnakill Castle* (in Ruins)' OD 256 25018,20885
Tower house Situated in flat countryside on slightly elevated land. A four-storey high tower (max. dims. 11.8m NW–SE, 10m NE–SW, wall T 2.35m) built of roughly coursed limestone. Punch-dressed limestone blocks with finely dressed margins, used as quoins and in windows and doorway, indicate a late sixteenth- or early seventeenth-century date. There is a groin vault over second-floor level, other floors were of wood. Garderobes in NE angle, mural passage in SW wall, and mural stairs in SW and SE walls. Sheela-na-gig (No. 1018) said to have come from here (*JKAS* 1904, 205–15; *JKAS* 1920, 262–3).

8:1(01)   11-6-1990

969 TINTORE
OS 29:5:5 (84,366) '*Tintore House*' OD 300–400 23564,18078
Tower house A Fitzpatrick castle (Carrigan 1905, vol. 2, 66–7) three storeys high with a base-batter; modern N wall, and E wall incorporated with Tintore House. Inward projecting NW angle contains fireplaces. Carrigan (*ibid.*) refers to an inscribed stone dated 1635. Featureless.

29:17   8-11-1990

28. Late Medieval Fort

In the mid-sixteenth century, English attempts to subdue the territories of the O'Mores and O'Conors resulted in the granting of their lands to Lieutenant Francis Bryan, Marshall of Ireland. Bryan built two large 'Campa,' or forts, one in Portlaoise (No. 970) and the other in Dangan, County Offaly. The Laois 'Campa' was known as the 'Fort Protector' or 'The Fort of Leix' but was renamed 'Fort of Maryborough' in 1556 in honour of Queen Mary. The fort attracted settlers and by 1560 a walled town (No. 1019) had developed around it (Bradley, Halpin and King 1986, 49).

970 MARYBOROUGH
OS 13:10:4 (265,213) *'Fort of Maryborough'*
OD 300–400 24713, 19848

Fort Situated on rising ground SW of the Trioge River. Built *c.* 1548 and demolished by the Cromwellians in 1650. Ground plans of the fort preserved on sixteenth-century maps indicate that it was a large rectangular enclosure (1024m x 1015m) with a projecting circular tower at NE corner, a rectangular tower at SW, an entrance in W wall, and a range of two-storey buildings in the interior at S. It was surrounded by an external fosse, partly water-filled.

The N, E and S walls, a short section of N end of W wall, and the circular tower at NE survive. The wall (max. H 6m on N side) has an external batter, visible at NW corner, and it is now incorporated into modern buildings in many places, e.g. a flour mill at NE. Floor ledges in the circular tower (int. diam. 8.2m, wall T 1.5m) indicate that it was originally three storeys high (Bradley *et al.* 1986, 51–2).
13:41(01)   11-6-1990

29. Castle Sites

Monuments shown on the OS maps 6-inch and marked 'Castle' or 'Castle (Site of)', and castles to which documentary references exist but for which no structural evidence survived at the time of inspection are included in this chapter. Where there is evidence to suggest a more specific classification this is indicated at the end of the entry.

971 ABBEYLEIX DEMESNE
OS 29:4:1 (708,582)   OD 200–300   24221,18313
Castle (site)   Not marked on the 1841 or 1907 eds. OS 6" maps. Reference to a castle belonging to Hugh Lacy here (O'Flanagan 1933, vol. 1, 324). No visible surface traces.
29:14   4-7-1990

972 ARCHERSTOWN
OS 35 (NPL)
Castle (possible, site)   The Down Survey shows a high square castle near the S end of the townland, and it is pointed out in Daniel Fitzpatrick's 'Raheens' where there are still traces of ancient mounds and entrenchments (Carrigan 1905, vol. 2, 310). No visible surface traces.
35:60(01)   23-5-1994

973 BALLYBRITTAS
OS 9:6:2 (327,442) *'Glanmalira Castle* (in Ruins)' OD 300–400   25745,20739
Castle (site)   Not marked on the 1841 or 1888 eds. OS 6" maps, only Glenmalire House is shown. No visible surface traces of a castle.
9:10   20-7-1990

974 BALLYFIN DEMESNE
OS 12:6:2 (340,444)   OD 500–600   23815,20083
Castle (site)   Ballyfin Castle was built by the Crosbies during the reign of Elizabeth I (1558–1603). Granted to Piriam Pole in 1666, it was later demolished by his son William who built a house on the site (Comerford 1886, vol. 3, 136–7). The present house was built between 1821 and 1826 (Bence-Jones 1978, 21).
12:4   9-8-1990

975 BALLYLEHANE LOWER
OS 25:12:3 (862,233) *'Ballylehane Castle* (in Ruins)' OD 300–400   26332,18605
Castle (site)   Reference to a castle here in 1346; owned by the Hovendens, an English family, in the sixteenth century (O'Hanlon and O'Leary 1907, vol. 1, 251, 303). An armorial panel of the O'Connors of Offaly, formerly located in the castle, was built into a gate-pier of the field in which the castle was situated (*JKAS* 1910, 241–2). No visible surface traces of it or the castle survive.
25:28   28-8-1990

976 BALLYMADDOCK (Stradbally By.)
OS 14:9:2 (80,251)   OD 300–400 25492,19896
Castle (site)   On the summit of a S-facing slope. According to local information, a castle located here was destroyed, with the aid of dynamite, in the 1950/1960s. A considerable amount of rubble visible at base of field boundary, to E of the site, is probably clearance from the collapsed remains of castle.
14:24(01)   30-5-1994

977 BALLYMADDOCK (Stradbally By.)
OS 14 NPL
Castle (site)   Reference to the foundations and basement cellar of the 'old castle of Kilmartyr' in the middle of an open field; also mentioned in a deed dated 1641. Kilmartyr (listed Killmarten or Kilmarter in the Inquisitions) was an area well known locally but was not marked on the OS maps; apparently it was incorporated with Ballymaddock townland (O'Hanlon and O'Leary 1907, vol. 1, 276). Not located.
14:50*/13:70

978 BALLYNAGALL
OS 32 (NPL)
Castle (possible, site)   Near the cemetery of Arless there was an old castle which was lived in by the Taaffe family (O'Byrne 1856, 35). No visible surface traces.
32:25(01)   23-5-1994

979 BALLYNAHIMMY
OS 2:9:5 (144,181) *'Castle* (Site of)'   OD 500–600 22623,21074
Castle (site)   Situated on an E–W ridge overlooking valley to N. Levelled except for a small stretch of wall which is situated on SW side of a rectangular platform (dims *c.* 20m N–S, *c.* 16m E–W), which in turn is enclosed by a fosse, probably partly of recent origin.
2:3   31-10-1990

980 BAUNAGHRA
OS 33:16:1 (697,136)   OD 400–500   22269,17182
Castle (possible, site)   Reference to 'an old residence or castle' inside enclosure (No. 163); it was 30 ft. x 21 ft., with walls 4 ft. thick (*c.* 10m x 7m, wall T *c.* 1m) (Carrigan 1905, vol. 2, 283). Possible foundations visible.
33:16(02)   25-10-1990

981 CASTLEDURROW DEMESNE

OS 29:15:5 NPL

Castle (possible, site) Not marked on the 1841 or 1906 eds. OS 6" maps. Known as the Old Episcopal Manor-house or castle, it was demolished in the eighteenth century (Carrigan 1905, vol. 2, 220–1). No visible surface traces.

29:44   12-7-1990

982 CASTLEFLEMING (Giles)/ CASTLEFLEMING OR HEATH

OS 27 NPL

Castle (site) Not marked on the 1841 or 1907 eds. OS 6" maps. Associated with the Fitzpatrick family. Still standing in 1657 but only the foundations remained in the early nineteenth century (Carrigan 1905, vol. 2, 71, 92, 96, 351). No visible surface traces.

27:8   7-11-1990

983 CASTLETOWN (Clandonagh By.) Moneymore ED

OS 21:3:3 (683,572) '*Castle* (Site of)'   OD 300 22238,18922

Castle (site) Marked on the 1841 and 1909 eds. OS 6" maps. No known historical references. No visible surface traces.

21:5(02)   24-6-1991

984 CASTLEQUARTER (Clandonagh By.)

OS 21 (NPL)

Castle (possible, site) A little to the E of the church of Skirk (No. 783) there apparently was a castle which was pulled down in the early nineteenth century (Carrigan 1905, vol. 2, 137). No visible surface traces.

21:32   23-5-1994

985 CLARAHILL

OS 2 (NPL)

Castle (possible, site) According to Crossdaile (1959, 13), there was a fortified house at Clarahill which belonged to the Dunne family. However, Coolnamoney tower house (No. 953) which belonged to the Dunne family is close within the vicinity and they may well be one and the same site. Not located.

2:27

986 CLOGRENAN

OS 37:11:1 (539,264) '*Clogrenan Castle* (in Ruins)' OD 154   26978,17363

Castle (site) On the Laois–Carlow border. Sited at a former important crossing point on the River Barrow. Sketch by Thomas Dineley (1680) shows a large house of five floors, with three decorative gables at the front and crenellated parapet at the sides. Sketch dated 1790 shows ruins in remarkably similar condition to a photograph taken in 1870. Derelict buildings were surveyed in 1911, a major part of which collapsed or were demolished in 1931. The original castle was probably substantially rebuilt after Carew's seige of 1569. Present 'Gothic' style arch and windows probably belong to the late eighteenth-century refurbishment. In 1806 work commenced on Clogrenan House and the former 'castle' was transformed into the entranceway to the demesne. Unlikely that much of fifteenth- or sixteenth-century structure survived to 1911. Some overgrown foundations still survive, including a small portion of the entranceway, all of which appear to belong to the eighteenth-century refurbishment. (*JRSAI* 1862–3, 43; *JKAS* 1915–17, 56–62; OPW file)

37:8   15-11-1990

987 CLONIN

OS 16 (NPL)

Castle (possible, site) There was a castle in Clonin with very strong walls about 40 ft high (*c*. 12m) which were taken down almost to the ground in 1850 (Carrigan 1905, vol. 2, 175). Not located.

16:32

988 CLOPOOK

OS 19:14:6 (405,74)   OD 500–600   25844,19072

Castle (possible, site) A possible castle was situated in SE quadrant of hillfort (No. 127). It was built of stone and lime cement and consisted of two chambers, the main one being 4.5m by 4.2m (O'Byrne 1856, 10; O'Hanlon and O'Leary vol. 1, 1907, 342). No visible surface traces.

19:21(04)   16-8-1990

989 COOLKERRY

OS 28:15:1 (480,82) '*Coolkerry Castle* (Site of)' OD 200–300   23010,17773

Castle (site) Reference to castle here (O'Hanlon and O'Leary 1907, vol. 1, 222). No visible surface traces.

28:62   4-9-1991

990 DERRYBROCK

OS 14:12:1 (704,264) '*Ballymanus Castle* (Site of)' OD 200–300   26152,19916

Castle (site) Shown on the 1563 map of Leix and Offaly (Hore 1863, f.p. 345). It was dependent on Dunamase (O'Hanlon and O'Leary 1907, vol. 1, 223). No visible surface traces.

14:36   7-6-1990

991 EMO PARK

OS 8:8:6 (893,362)   '*Castle* (Site of)'   OD 300–400 25369,20651

Castle (site) Marked as 'Site of Castle' on the 1841 ed. OS 6" map. No visible surface traces. (*JKAS* 1904, 196)

8:5   21-6-1990

992 FARNANS
OS 31:4:2 (792,596) *'New Castle (in Ruins)'*
OD 694   26260,18347
Castle (site) Marked on the 1841 and 1906 eds. OS 6"
maps. No visible surface traces.
31:4(01)   12-9-1990

993 GORTNALEE
OS 28:5:1 (6,452) *'Castle (in Ruins)'* OD 400
22506,18158
Castle (site) Marked on the 1841 and 1908 eds. OS 6"
maps. Constructed of green stone, its remains stood to
a height of almost 4ft (1.2m) (Carrigan 1905, vol. 2,
140). No visible surface traces. A ringfort (No. 205)
lies immediately to NW.
28:18(01)   14-9-1991

994 GRANGE (Ballyadams By.)
OS 32:3:3 (683,561) *'Grange Castle on Site of Castle'*
OD 100–200   27120,18318
Castle (site) Built by Robert Hartpole who was
appointed Constable of Carlow Castle and Governor of
the Queen's County during the reign of Elizabeth I
(O'Hanlon and O'Leary 1907, vol. 1, 290). A stone
with the initials RH and gb, carved in relief and dated
1588, was originally located over the entrance
doorway (*JRSAI* 1922, 82–3). According to local
information, the castle was destroyed twenty years
ago. No visible surface traces survive.
32:8(01–02)   14-8-1990

995 GRANGE UPPER
OS 14:13:4 (14,19) *'Castle (Site of)'* OD 400–500
25426,19649
Castle (site) Marked on the 1563 map of Leix and
Offaly (Hore 1863, f.p. 345). No visible surface traces.
14:38   7-6-1990

996 GRENAN
OS 35:12:3 (854,300) *'Castle (in Ruins)'*
OD 200–300   24385,17376
Castle (site) Reference to an old castle in ruins here
on N bank of the River Nore (O'Hanlon and O'Leary
1907, vol. 1, 308). No visible surface traces.
35:52   23-9-1990

997 HARRISTOWN (Clandonagh By.)
OS 34:1:1 (76,591)   OD 364   22584,17666
Castle (site) Reference to a Fitzpatrick castle here in
the 'Old Meadow' (Carrigan 1905, vol. 2, 342). No
other known reference. No visible surface traces
34:3   17-10-1990

998 KILLASMEESTIA
OS 21:16:6 (850,11)   OD 400–500   22420,18332

Castle (possible, site) Carrigan (1905, vol. 2, 141)
refers to ringfort (No. 227) which may be the site of a
castle marked on the Down Survey map. No visible
surface traces.
21:30(02)   26-6-1991

999 KILLESHIN
OS 32:14:5 (322,50)   OD 300–400   26745,17776
Castle (possible, site) Reference to possible castle
here (O'Hanlon and O'Leary 1907, vol. 1, 262). No
visible surface traces.
32:20(06)   14-8-1990

1000 KILMINCHY
OS 13:7:0 NPL
Castle (site) Reference to the last remains of a castle
represented by a gate entrance which faces onto the
road (O'Hanlon *et al.* 1914, vol. 2, 521). However, the
gateway appears to date to the eighteenth century. No
surface traces of the castle survive but it is possible
that the masonry of walls and outbuildings associated
with nineteenth-century Kilminchy House were built
from rubble of an earlier structure. Of particular
interest is small single-storey outbuilding, to NW,
which has a pronounced base-batter, large quoin stones
and small cut-limestone rectangular opes.
13:88   30-5-1994

1001 LOUGHTEEOG
OS 18:8:3 (901,448)   OD 300–400   25389,19462
Castle (possible, site) According to present occupant
of Prospect House, it is traditionally believed that the
house, which was built in the 1950s when old Prospect
House was knocked down, occupies the site of a castle,
no trace of which survives.
18:49(01)   30-5-1994

1002 MOAT
OS 30:6:3 (425,406) *'Moat Castle (Site of)'*
OD 500–600   24899,18133
Castle (site) Marked in SW quadrant of motte and
bailey (No. 913) on 1908 ed. OS 6" map. Reference to
castle here (O'Flanagan 1933, vol. 2, 274). No visible
surface traces.
30:21(01)   21-6-1991

1003 RAHANAVANNAGH
OS 24:6:5 (355,317)   OD 500–600   24820,18679
Castle (possible, site) Reference to an eighteenth-
century house built on the ruins of an O'Moore fortress
(Bence-Jones 1978, 43). No other information. No
visible surface traces.
24:24   29-8-1990

1004 RATHPIPER SOUTH
OS 28:14:6 (436,34) '*Castle* (Site of)' OD 300–400
22964,17721
Castle (site) Marked within N half of enclosure (No. 520) on the 1908 ed. OS 6" map. This castle, which was associated with Pipard a descendant of Adam de Hereford, stood until about 1836 (Carrigan 1905, vol. 2, 6, 71). No visible surface traces.
28:60(01)   6-9-1991

1005 REDCASTLE
OS 17:2:1 (251,587) '*Castle* (Site of)' OD 473
23725,19592
Castle (site) A Fitzpatrick castle, possibly a tower house, built in the sixteenth century (O'Byrne 1856, 73; O'Hanlon and O'Leary 1907, vol. 1, 210) in ringfort (No. 266). No visible surface traces.
17:2(01)   31-8-1990

1006 ROSKEEN
OS 1:12:4 (728,210) '*Roskeen Castle* (in Ruins)'
OD 387 24209,21760
Castle (site) Marked on the 1841 ed. OS 6" map. The castle has been levelled; only grass-covered foundations survive.
1:2   13-8-1990

1007 STRADBALLY
OS 14:14:4 (303,8) OD 200–300 25731,19641
Castle (site) An O'Moore castle situated here was known as the Castle of Palace. It was destroyed by the Cosbies who built a fortified house (No. 1031) on its site (O'Hanlon and O'Leary 1907, vol. 1, 327–9). No visible surface traces.
14:39(02)   7-6-1990

1008 TANKARDSTOWN
OS 26:7:2 (597,412) '*Castle* (Site of)' OD 200–300
27025,18801
Castle (site) Marked as a ruined castle on the Down Survey. No visible surface traces.
26:9(01)   3-8-1990

1009 TANKARDSTOWN
OS 26:7:6 (623,351) '*Castle* (Site of)' OD 200–300
27053,18736
Castle (site) Marked on the 1841 and 1909 eds. OS 6" maps. No visible surface traces.
26:10   5-8-1990

1010 TIMOGUE
OS 19:5:5 (124,354) '*Castle* (in Ruins)'
OD 300–400 25544,19364
Castle (site) Reference to site of castle here (O'Hanlon and O'Leary 1907, vol. 1, 338). No visible surface traces.
19:6   2-5-1990

1011 TOWNPARKS (Clarmallagh By.)
OS 22:5:1 (28,423) '*Castle* (in Ruins)' OD 300–400
22523,18768
Castle (site) The earliest reference to the castle or 'house of Borreidge' is dated 1581. It was built of rough unhewn stone, and only the first storey and fragments of the second remained in the early 1900s. There was a barrel vault over the ground floor, an entrance doorway in E half of N wall, and a straight stairway in E wall. The structure appears to have been a fifteenth-century tower house. Borris House was built over the foundations of a demolished part of the castle (Carrigan 1905, vol. 2, 127–8). No visible surface traces survive.
22:11   6-8-1991

1012 WATERCASTLE
OS 29:8:4 (737,332) '*Water Castle*' OD 300–400
24254,18049
Castle (site) Marked on the 1841 and 1906 eds. OS 6" maps and on the Down Survey Barony map. Reference to an old castle which, in the early eighteenth century, had undergone repairs, had been enlarged, and converted into a dwelling called Watercastle House (O'Hanlon and O'Leary 1907, vol. I, 156). No visible surface traces.
29:24   13-8-1990

30. Sheela-na-gigs

Sheela-na-gigs are female exhibionist figures noted for their ugly repellent features including a large disproportionate head, big ears and shoulders, staring eyes, wedge-shaped nose, gaping mouth and, in particular, their flagrant display of the genitalia. They are Christian carvings, dating not earlier than the eleventh century, and are often found on archways in medieval churches where they formed part of an iconography aimed at castigating the sins of the flesh. They are also found high on the walls of tower houses, and here their function appears to have been apotropaic, that is, acting as guardians against evil (Weir and Jerman, 1986). Apart from one sheela-na-gig (No. 1015) which was found in a graveyard, all the other examples noted in Laois are associated with tower houses.

1013 BALLAGHMORE LOWER
OS 15:14:6 (433,30)   OD 400   21973,18987
Sheela-na-gig Situated on an L-shaped quoin on SW wall of Ballaghmore Castle (No. 940) at a height of *c.* 10m above ground level. An asymmetrical female figure carved in bold relief in soft white sandstone of local origin (*JRSAI* 1975, 117–8).
15:17(02)   5-9-1991

1014 GALESQUARTER
OS 35:5:4 (74,330)   OD 300–400   23560,17400
Sheela-na-gig A rude carving in relief of a female figure was visible, at a height of 13m, on S end of E wall of Cullahill Castle (No. 954) (Carrigan 1905, vol. 2, 232). Not visible due to ivy growth.
35:22(02)   27-9-1990

1015 ROSENALLIS
OS 3:15:4 (499,60)   OD 400–500   23974,20960
Sheela-na-gig Found in Rosenallis graveyard (No. 796) among rows of inscribed tombstones during graveyard clean-up in October 1991. Subrectangular slab with figure of sheela-na-gig carved in relief. Now in the National Museum of Ireland.
3:16(08)   1-8-1994

1016 SHAEN
OS 8:15:5 (578,44)   OD 300–400   25039,20313

Sheela-na-gig Reference to a figure of hideous character in Shaen Castle (No. 964) (*JRSAI* 1936, 117).
8:13(02)   21-6-1990

1017 TIMAHOE
OS 18:16:6 (869,30)   OD 300–400   25359,19021
Sheela-na-gig Reference to a strange figure in stone at the doorway of Timahoe tower house (No. 967) (*JRSAI* 1894, 80) and a grotesque figure (*ibid*, 393). Not clear whether this is referring to the same or a second figure. According to local information, there was a figure on the part of N wall which has fallen; it may be buried beneath debris (*JRSAI* 1936, 114).
18:31(07)   13-6-1990

1018 TINNAKILL (Portnahinch By.)
OS 8:3:2 (563,587)   OD 200–300   25018,20885
Sheela-na-gig Two grotesque female figures were to be seen in 1918 built into the farmyard wall to SSW of Tinnakill Castle (No. 968). According to the present owner of the castle and farmyard, they were broken up by a person or persons unknown and buried. One was said to have come from a window jamb of the castle; the other from somewhere in Portnahinch (*JKAS* 1920, 262–3). Photographs of them, taken by Helen Roe, can be seen in the Laois County Library.
8:1(02)   8-12-1990

31. Town Defences

This chapter includes town defences of the medieval period (1200–1500). Six medieval centres have been identified, only two of which have either standing remains (Portarlington) or documentary evidence (Portlaois) for town defences. Information in this chapter is based on the Office of Public Works Urban Survey which was carried out in County Laois in 1986. Other sites within these medieval towns and boroughs are included under their separate headings.

1019 BORRIS LITTLE/CLONMINAM/ KYLEKIPROE/MARYBOROUGH/ MONEYBALLYTYRRELL (Portlaise Town)

OS 13:10:4 (265,213)   OD 300–400   24713,19848

Town defences   A map of Maryborough dated *c.* 1560 shows a small township around the fort (No. 970) enclosed by a wall delimiting a rectangular area. No mural towers or gatehouse are indicated but two openings are shown in W wall, immediately to N and S of the fort, and also a probable opening in E wall. An unusual feature is the presence of an intra-mural walled enclosure in SE angle, its function is unknown. There are no surviving traces of the defences (Bradley *et al.* 1986, 52–3).

13:41   11-6-1990

1020 COOLTEDERY (Portarlington Town)

OS 5:5:4 (29,336)   OD 200–300   25425,21264

Town defences   The town dates from about 1666 when the borough was created. A plan dated 1678 shows that it lay in a bend of the River Barrow which acted as a natural moat on W, N and E sides. A canal dug on S side completed the encirclement of the town. The roughly rectangular area thus enclosed (*c.* 20 acres) was fortified with earthworks with large bastions at each corner. In the town centre was a large square with a market house, from which the four main streets radiated in a cruciform pattern. No positively identified remains survive. Some irregular features on NW side may have formed part of the defences (Bradley *et al.* 1986, 42–3).

5:31*/4:1   15-5-1990

32. Fortified Houses

Towards the end of the sixteenth century and in the early seventeenth century, a new type of castle evolved, the semi-fortified house (Bence-Jones 1978, xii). Features of these houses, which were usually symmetrical, include gables with massive lozenge/diamond-shaped chimney stacks and mullioned windows. The presence of defensive loops, as well as a surrounding bawn wall are indicative of their design to repel an attack.

Fig. 26—*Castlecuffe, fortified house* (**1024**)

1021 BALLYADAMS
OS 19:16:2 (830,80)   OD 200–300   26293,19082
Fortified house   Large rectangular seventeenth-century three-storey house (ext. dims. 19.95m N–S, 11.42 E–W), built of roughly coursed limestone, attached to E side of tower house (No. 942). Parts of the house are possible contemporary with the tower house, while others are definitely of a later period. Features include splayed opes, rectangular windows in N wall and possible fireplaces in N and S walls. The only access to the various floors of the house appears to have been from NW tower of tower house. Possible evidence of bawn wall at SE.
19:28(02)   2-5-1990

1022 BALLYMADDOCK (Stradbally By.)
OS 14:9:2 (111,252) *'Cahernagapol's House* (in Ruins)'   OD 300–400   25526,19897
Strong house   A seventeenth-century T-shaped house,

the N half (ext. dims. 13m N–S, 12.2m E–W) of which has been modernised and is inhabited. Its SW corner is rounded and cut back. Main features of the almost totally ruined S half (int. dims. 10.5m N–S, 6m E–W) include a ruined rubble-built fireplace in SE corner, a single-light ope at S end of E wall and a tall ivy-clad chimney stack at SE. The N gables of two outbuildings with pronounced base-batters, a possible gun loop and a large rectangular window survive at NW. A ruined rectangular building at SW appears nineteenth century in date. Remains of S wall of bawn, running E–W, extend from SE corner of house. Possible N bawn wall visible to E of gabled outbuildings. (O'Hanlon and O'Leary 1907, vol. 1, 273–6)
14:26   30-5-1994

1023 BALLYNAKILL (Tinnahinch By.)
OS 2:12:4 (709,223) *'Ballynakill Castle* (in Ruins)'
OD 300–400   23219,21124

Fortified house Ivy-covered roughly coursed rubble and limestone building (*c.* 22m N–S, 17.9m E–W, wall T 0.73m), L-shaped with projections at three of its angles; Jacobean chimney stacks similar to Castlecuffe (No. 1024) survive; no doorways or windows visible. Probably an early seventeenth-century fortified house.
2:11   6-9-1990

1024 CASTLECUFFE
OS 2:10:5 (325,226) '*Castle Cuffe* (in Ruins)'
OD 400   22814,21123
Fortified house Situated in flat low-lying land. A large limestone-built house (max. dims. 30.25m E–W, 20.5m N–S, wall T 1.3m but 0.9m at N), rectangular in plan with projecting angles at SE and SW, in very poor condition. Jacobean-type chimney stacks and associated fireplaces, similar to those at Ballynakill Castle (No. 1023), visible. No evidence of outer defences. Would appear to be mid/late seventeenth-century building.
2:8   6-9-1990

1025 CLONCOURSE (Clandonagh By.)
OS 15:15:6 (632,73) '*Cloncourse Castle*' (in Ruins)
OD 400–500   22183,19035
Fortified house A four-storey high house, built of roughly coursed rubble, with projecting tower in centre of S wall. Chimney stacks survive on E and W gables. N wall destroyed. Fireplaces in E gable on first, second and third floor. Other features include rectangular chamfered limestone windows, a machicolation on top level over the doorway, and three spouts projecting from top of S wall. Remains of a rectangular-shaped bawn with splayed gun loops and outbuildings in NE angle survive, and also a gatehouse in centre of S wall.
15:21   15-9-1991

1026 CULLENAGH (Cullenagh By.)
OS 18:15:2 (574,98)   OD 600–700   25048,19089
Fortified house On a gentle E-facing slope. An early/mid-seventeenth-century, four-storey fortified house built of randomly coursed limestone rubble with larger quoin stones. Standing remains include the ivy-clad N gable (int. L 6.15m, wall T 0.95m) with an external chimney projection, and N end of E and W walls. Two rectangular cut-limestone single-light windows with glazing-bar-holes visible at first-floor level, beneath which lie two possible gun loops, now blocked up. Slopstone on ground-floor level, and three staggered fireplaces at first, second and third floors. Modified portions of the bawn wall to S, with E half of circular corner turret at SE and two rectangular towers, later in date, to SW.
18:39   30-5-1994

1027 FERMOYLE
OS 29:16:2 (788,138)   OD 300–400   24310,17845
Fortified house Marked on the Down Survey and as

'Castle (in Ruins)' on the 1841 ed. OS 6" map. A three-storey high house built of roughly cut limestone. Remains include E gable with a central fireplace, and part of S wall with simple slit opes at ground-floor level and narrow windows on first and second floors. Remains of the bawn wall project southwards from SW angle. No other visible surface traces.
29:48   8-7-1990

1028 GRANGE MORE
OS 22:10:4 NPL
Fortified house (site) Ruined castle shown on the Down Survey Barony map. Carrigan (1905, vol. 2, 132) refers to it as an early seventeenth-century castellated house, four storeys high, with lozenge-shaped chimney stacks. It belonged to the Phelans. No visible surface traces.
22:17(02)   4-8-1991

1029 RUSH HALL
OS 16:15:5 (578,25) '*Rush Hall Court* (in Ruins)'
OD 400–500   23102,18993
Fortified house Plain limestone L-shaped seventeenth-century house, four storeys high, comprising the main rectangular block (int. dims. 28.7m E–W, 7.2m N–S) with a much-ruined annexe (int. dim. 14m E–W) to N. The N wall and gables survive of the main block; the upper floors are ivy-covered. Features include a rectangular recess at E end of N wall on ground floor; joist holes, three plain fireplaces in N wall and a rectangular window in E and W gables on first floor. An ope at W end of N wall on second floor may have accessed the annexe. Large ivy-clad chimney stack on W gable. Only portions of the annexe gables survive; rectangular window visible in W gable on first floor and fireplace in SW corner. Most of the annexe was destroyed in 1977 as well as an adjoining enclosed cobbled courtyard with outbuildings at NW. Impressive bawn (64.85m sq., H 3.7m), with extension to S end of W wall, lies to E of house, and has three five-sided corner towers (int. dims. 3.85m x 3.5m, wall T 0.62m) with gun loops at NE, SE and SW, and remains of a possible fourth at NW. (Carrigan 1905, vol. 2, 182–3)
16:26   23-5-1994

1030 SCOTCHRATH
OS 23:9:3 (175,236)   Indicated   OD 300–400
23655,18581
Fortified house Marked on the 1841 and 1909 eds. OS 6" maps. No known historical references. Ruins of possible late medieval house (dims. 8.7m NE–SW, 5.6m NE–SE), rectangular in plan, constructed with limestone rubble. Entrance at NE. Enclosed by a bawn wall (L *c.* 40m, H *c.* 3.5m) built of limestone rubble with a slight base-batter.
23:17(01)   18-8-1990

1031 STRADBALLY
OS 14:14:4 (303,7)   OD 200–300   25731,19641
Fortified house (site)   A fortified house was built by the Cosbies on the site of O'Moore's castle (No. 1007). Now demolished (O'Hanlon and O'Leary 1907, vol. 1, 328). No visible surface traces.
14:39(04)   7-6-1990

1032 TULLOMOY
OS 19:15:2 (584,92) *'Tullomoy Castle* (in Ruins)'
OD 400–500   .26033,19093
Fortified house   Known as 'the castle of Tulla', constructed by Billy George, an ancestor of the Georges of Mullaghmore (O'Byrne 1856, 70). An early seventeenth-century house (L *c.* 19.6m, Wth *c.* 9.25m, wall T 1.45m), now two storeys high but with evidence of a third storey at E end, built of roughly coursed limestone. It has a series of large triple-light cut-limestone windows with hood-mouldings on first, second and third floors. Small rectangular windows (0.6 x 0.5m) with glazing-bar-holes at ground-floor level. Three fireplaces in both S and W walls. Remains of a wall, running E–W, to E of house, and a rectangular-shaped platform to N.
19:27   2-11-1990

33. Houses

Most of the houses of County Laois have not been recorded since they fall outside the scope of this archaeological survey. However, a small number of houses which are known to pre-date 1700 are included here, and probably represent a sample rather than a full survey.

1033 BALLYTHOMAS
OS 14:5:6 (218,364) 'Ballythomas House'
OD 300–400   25638,20016
House   Reference to an old seventeenth-century mansion, originally three storeys high but reduced to two following alterations which removed the upper castellated storey (Comerford 1886, vol. 3, 282). The house (L *c.* 15.5m, Wth *c.* 6.1m) is rendered with peppledash and has a dressed cut-stone doorway with keystone. Still occupied.
14:12   12-7-1990

1034 DERRIN
OS 22:1:5 (104,489) *'Derrin Castle'* (in Ruins)
OD 300–400   22602,18839
House   Constructed in the early seventeenth-century, its last occupant was traditionally believed to have been Dorothy Hedges who died in 1675 (Carrigan 1905, vol. 2, 129). A T-shaped building (L 11.2m N–S) built of roughly coursed rubble limestone, three storeys high, with projecting massive diagonal chimney stacks on N and S gables. Entrance in projecting W tower. Fireplaces visible on first, second and third floors of N gable, and on first and second floors of S gable. Large splayed windows visible. (Craig 1982, 134–5)
22:3(01)   5-8-1991

1035 GRANGE BEG
OS 22:9:6 (183,194)   OD 400–500   22689,18528
House   Marked 'Grange Ho. (in Ruins)' on the 1841 ed. OS 6" map. A rectangular house (dims. *c.* 9.9m NW–SE, *c.* 6.3m NE–SE) constructed of rubble limestone, two storeys high with a third storey or attic in SE gable. Entrance, now blocked, in SW wall.

Projecting chimneybreast and tall chimney stack in NW wall and also the remains of a cornice. Internal dividing wall running NW–SE.
22:14   8-8-1991

1036 KNAPTON
OS 29:3:2 (601,577)   OD 300–400   24108,18306
House (site)   Reference to a small house dated *c.* 1773 which was built onto an older structure now demolished (Bence-Jones 1978, 178).
29:10   5-7-1990

1037 PASS
OS 18:10:3 (417,254)   *'Pass House'*   OD 300–400
24880,19252
House   Not marked as an antiquity on the 1841 or 1909 eds. OS 6" maps. The house was built in Cromwellian times (O'Dooley n.d., 61). A two-storey high rectangular-shaped house with attic (L *c.* 21.2m, Wth *c.* 10m, T *c.* 1.4m). Still occupied.
18:16   12-6-1990

1038 RUSH HALL
OS 16:15:5 (564,8)   OD 400–500   23087,18975
Inn (site)   Marked on the 1841 ed. OS 6" map only. Described as a building with projecting chimneys and lozenge-shaped chimney stacks. Traditionally said to have been built to accommodate the men employed in building Rush Hall Court (No. 1029). It was used as a public inn until *c.* 1860 (Carrigan 1905, vol. 2, 183). Site occupied by post-1700 house.
16:25   18-9-1991

34. Bridges

Prior to the development of bridges, fords and causeways were among the more hazardous means of crossing Irish rivers. Given that the art of togher construction had been mastered as early as Prehistoric times, it is reasonable to assume that this technology was easily transfered to bridge-building. The early medieval Brehon Laws required the 'ollamh saor' to be proficient in the craft of erecting bridges, and the Irish annals provide us with a reference to the construction of a plank bridge at Killaloe, County Clare as early as the eleventh century, and several allusions to a wicker bridge over the Shannon at Athlone between 1120 and 1159. In County Laois the finest examples of medieval masonry bridges are Monks Bridge (No. 1039) on the Abbeyleix estate and that at Watercastle (No. 1042). Monks Bridge is one of the oldest surviving, if not the oldest, masonry arch bridge in Ireland and dates to the thirteenth century (O'Keeffe and Simington 1991, 122).

1039 ABBEYLEIX DEMESNE
OS 29:3:6 (689,512) 'Wooden Bridge' OD 200–300 24201,18238

Bridge   Spanning the River Nore. An eight-arch bridge with a larger central navigation arch and pier, triangular hammer-dressed ashlar-coursed cutwaters on the upriver side, and a carriageway flanked by stone parapet walls. The first arch and pier from left hand bank downriver are part of the original bridge and date to the thirteenth century. The arch is of rubble stone partly corbelled with two heart-shaped keystones separated by an inverted third; similar masonry visible in the adjoining pier and cutwater. Most of the other arches, piers and cutwaters were rebuilt between 1670 and 1800. Also known as Monks Bridge in association with the nearby site of the Cistercian abbey (No. 685) (O'Keeffe and Simington 1991, 122–4). Not visited.
29:73

1040 BALLYGARVAN GLEBE/RATHMAKELLY GLEBE
OS 29:9:2 (151,243) 'Old Bridge' OD 275 23637,17949

Bridge (site)   The 'old bridge' marked on the 1841 and 1909 eds. OS 6" maps may have been built on the site of an earlier bridge which is marked on the Down Survey map; no trace survives.
29:29   13-8-1990

1041 COOLNAMONY LOWER
OS 2:16:6 (865,37) OD 400–500 23386,20929

Bridge   Small narrow single-eyed bridge which gives access to tower house (No. 953). Built of rubble stone and founded on bedrock. No evidence of plank- or wattle-centring in the barrel vault. The size and shape of this bridge and its position in relation to the castle would suggest a late medieval date.
2:18(02)   31-10-1990

1042 KILDRINAGH/PEAFIELD/ SHANGOWNAGH
OS 16:14:0 NPL

Bridge (site)   When the bed of the Nore was being deepened by the OPW in 1847, foundations of an oak bridge were found (Carrigan 1905, vol. 2, 180). No visible traces survive.
16:24(01)   16-9-1991

1043 WATERCASTLE/GRANAFALLOW
OS 29:8:4 (739,314) 'Watercastle Bridge' OD 200–300 24256,18029

Bridge   Originally spanning the River Nore, now on dry land on W bank as a result of diverting the course of the river. The 1841 ed. OS 6" map depicts three cutwaters on each side of the bridge, indicating four arch-spans. Four overgrown arches survive, a central pair with two others, one on each side, some distance away. The arch rings on the upriver side appear to be original, those downriver indicate the bridge was widened. One arch with evidence of punching on some stones indicates a pre-1563 date (O'Keeffe and Simington 1991, 175–6). Not visited.
29:74

35. Mills

This chapter includes horizontal mills which have been dated by means of dendrochronology (the dating of tree-rings) to between the early seventh and late tenth centuries. They functioned by employing horizontal waterwheels driven by water directed by a wooden flume. Also included is a possible fulling mill which would have been used in connection with the woollen or cotton industry.

1044 AGHMACART
OS 34 NPL
Mill (site) Not marked on the 1841 or 1906 eds. OS 6" maps. Reference to a water-mill here in 1601 (Carrigan 1905, vol. 2, 90). No visible surface traces.
34:19(09)   8-10-1990

1045 ARDLEA
OS 17:11:6 (645,188) OD 300–400 24146,19176
Watermill - horizontal (site) Reference to a horizontal watermill (NMI files). No visible traces.
17:10   14-9-1990

1046 BALLYGORMILL SOUTH
OS 18:8:4 (754,326) OD 400–500 25235,19332
Watermill - horizontal (site) Reference to a horizontal watermill (NMI files). No visible traces.
18:14   12-6-1990

1047 CRANNAGH (Upperwoods By.)
OS 16:7:6 (634,335) OD 300–400 23158,19321

Watermill - horizontal (possible) Not marked on the 1841 or 1909 eds. OS 6" maps. Wooden uprights visible in the stream.
16:41(02)

1048 MILL LAND
OS 14:15:2 (548,87) OD 200–300 25989,19727
Fulling mill (site) Reference to a fulling mill site here in 1641 (Feehan 1983, 353). No visible surface traces.
14:42   12-6-1990

1049 MORETT
OS 9:13:4 (62,51) OD 200–300 25470,20324
Watermill - horizontal (site) Discovered in 1952. The understructure of the mill, comprising the dam, a large wooden trough and the wheelhouse, was uncovered (Lucas 1953, 15–27). Site now levelled and covered over. No visible surface traces.
9:22   20-7-1990

36. Addenda

1050 BALLAGHMORE LOWER
OS 15:15:5 (548,5) Indicated OD 400–500
22094,18963
House Situated on the brow of a low hill. A ruined rectangular two-storey four-bay early eighteenth-century house (ext. dims. 10.5m N–S x 6.75m E–W, wall T *c.* 0.68m) with attic, built of randomly coursed limestone and sandstone rubble; formerly rendered. A contemporary single-storey extension (ext. dims. *c.* 10m N–S x 6.75m E–W) adjoined N wall. A moulded cornice skirts top of E and W side-walls. Most windows have brick fill around reveals and relatively modern sills in place. Small round-headed niche visible at first-floor level at N end of W wall. The house was probably a hunting lodge. Its E wall incorporates possible seventeenth-features, most notably a broad chimney projection, surmounted by a stout chimney stack with a string course. The house is presently used as a hayshed. Traces of outbuildings survive to W (information from R. Loeber).
15:35   23-12-1994

1051 MOUNTRATH (Maryborough West By.)
OS 17: 1:4 (68,461) OD 300–400 23533,19458
Plantation town Situated on E side of the Mountrath River. The earliest known settlement dates to 1620, when the town was established by Emanuel Dowling and others mainly from Suffolk in England. In 1628 Sir Charles Coote obtained a license for a market and before 1641 the town had a cloth and iron-manufacturing industry. By 1659 it was the largest and most important settlement in the county. Several buildings are marked on the Down Survey map, and the outline of possible town defences are visible on E side of the town on a map dated 1730. On the W side of Shannon Street, a two-storey house with a massive chimney stack crowned by diagonally placed flues probably dates to the seventeenth century. The foundry house, formerly a Quaker's Meeting House, on W side of Coote Street possibly incorporates an earlier seventeenth-century house (information from R. Loeber).
17:37   17-3-1995

1052 PASS
OS 18:10:6 (436, 216) OD 400–500 24901, 19213
Architectural fragment In low-lying marshy land beside a stream. Masonry from Kilvahan church (No. 771) was used in the construction of a nearby tuck mill (O'Hanlon and O'Leary 1907, vol. 1, 189). Six cut and roughly dressed stones and a number of large undressed stones are visible in S wall of mill; also a cut stone in NW corner.
18:18   12-6-1990

Bibliography

Abbreviations

ACAP	Air Corps Aerial Photographs
BKS	Aerial photographs, Consultative Technical Services Ltd.
CUCAP	Cambridge University Collection of Aerial Photographs
GSI	Geological Survey of Ireland Aerial Photographs
JIA	*Journal of Irish Archaeology*
JKAS	*Journal of the Kildare Archaeological Society*
JRSAI	*Journal of the Royal Society of Antiquaries of Ireland*
NMI file	National Museum of Ireland, Topographical File
OPW file	Office of Public Works, Topographical File
PRIA	*Proceedings of the Royal Irish Academy*

BARROW, G.L. (1979) *The round towers of Ireland*. The Academy Press, Dublin.

BENCE-JONES, M. (1978) *Burke's guide to country houses vol. 1: Ireland*. Burke's Peerage Ltd., London.

BRADLEY, J., HALPIN, A. and KING, H.A. (1986) *Urban archaeological survey — Co. Laois*. (limited distribution) Office of Public Works, Dublin.

BRINDLEY, A.L., LANTING, J.N. and MOOK, W.G. (1983) 'Radiocarbon dates from the Neolithic burials at Ballintruer More, Co. Wicklow and Ardcony, Co. Tipperary', *JIA* **1**, 1–9.

CANDON, A. (1986) Archaeological survey of the barony of Clandonagh, Co. Laois. Unpublished AnCo/Roscrea Heritage Society report.

CANDON, A. (1987) Archaeological survey of Upper Ossory, phase 2. The barony of Clarmallagh. AnCo/Roscrea Heritage Society report.

CARRIGAN, REV. W. (1905) (Reprint 1981) *The history and antiquities of the diocese of Ossory*, 4 vols. Roberts Books and Wellbrook Press, Kilkenny.

COMERFORD, REV. M. (1886) *Collections relating to the dioceses of Kildare and Leighlin*, 3 vols. James Duffy & Sons, Dublin.

CRAIG, M. (1982) *The architecture of Ireland from the earliest times to 1880*. Eason and Son Ltd., Dublin.

CRAWFORD, H. (1924) 'The round tower and castle of Timahoe', *JRSAI* **54**, 31–45.

CRAWFORD, H.S. and LEASK, H.G. (1925) 'Killeshin church and its Romanesque ornament', *JRSAI* **55**, 83–94.

CROSSDAILE, REV. L.H. (1959) Notes on the parish of Rosenallis. Typescript, Offaly Historical Society.

CUNNINGHAM, G. (1987) *The Anglo-Norman advance into the south-west midlands of Ireland 1185–1221*. Parkmore Press, Roscrea.

DE VALERA, R. and Ó NUALLÁIN, S. (1972) *Survey of the megalithic tombs of Ireland, vol. 3, Counties Galway, Roscommon, Leitrim, Longford, Westmeath, Laoighis, Offaly, Kildare, Cavan*. Stationery Office, Dublin.

DOWLING, A. (1981) *Ancient parish of Aghaboe now Clough-Ballacolla*.

FEEHAN J. (1979) *The landscape of Slieve Bloom*. Blackwater, Dublin.

FEEHAN J. (1983) *Laois an environmental history*. Ballykilcavan Press, Stradbally.

FITZGERALD, Lord W. (1904) 'The history and antiquities of the Queen's county barony of Portnahinch', *JKAS* **4**, 184–204, 285–311, 325–51.

FITZPATRICK, E. (1991) 'An Early Christian site at Curraclone, Co. Laois', *JKAS* **18**, 213–5.

FITZPATRICK, E. (1993) St. Molua's medieval church and graveyard, Kyle, Co. Laois. Unpublished report.

GRAVES, J. (1852) 'Proceedings', *JRSAI* **2**, 358.

GWYNN, A. and HADCOCK, R.N. (1970) *Medieval religious houses, Ireland*. Longman Group Ltd., Dublin.

HARBISON, P. (1970) *Guide to the national monuments in the Republic of Ireland*. Gill and Macmillan Ltd., Dublin.

HORE, H.F. (1863) 'Notes on a fac simile of an ancient map of Leix, Ofaly, Irry, Clanmalier, Iregan and Slievemargy, preserved in the British Museum', *JRSAI* **7**, 345–72.

LEASK, H.G. (1936) 'Irish castles: 1180 to 1310', *Archaeological Journal* **93**, 143–98.

LEASK, H.G. (1941) *Irish castles and castellated houses*. Dundalgan Press, Dundalk.

LEDWICH, E. (1803) *Antiquities of Ireland*. (2nd edition) Jones, Dublin.

LUCAS, A.T. (1953) 'The horizontal mill in Ireland', *JRSAI* **23**, 15–36.

O'BYRNE, D. (1849–51) 'Proceedings', *JRSAI* **1**, 131–2.

O'BYRNE, D. (1856) *The history of the Queen's county*. John O'Daly, Dublin.

O'DOOLEY, J. (n.d.) Ancient parishes of Portlaoise. Typescript of articles in the Leinster Express (Newspaper), Laois County Library.

O'FLANAGAN, M. (compiler) (1933) Letters containing information relative to the antiquities of the Queen's County collected during the progress of the Ordnance Survey in 1838. Typescript in 2 vols. Bray.

O'HANLON, REV. J. and O'LEARY, REV. E. (1907) (Reprint 1981) *History of the Queen's county*, vol. 1. Roberts Books Ltd., Kilkenny.

O'HANLON, REV. J., O'LEARY, REV. E. and LALOR, REV. M. (1914) (Reprint 1981) *History of the Queen's county*, vol. 2. Roberts Books Ltd., Kilkenny.

O'KEEFFE, P. and SIMINGTON, T. (1991) *Irish stone bridges: history and heritage*. Irish Academic Press, Dublin.

O'LEARY, REV. E. (1909) 'The rock of Dunamase', *JKAS* **6**, 161–71.

ORPEN, G.H. (1909) 'Mottes and Norman castles in Ossory', *JRSAI* **39**, 313–42.

PETRIE, G. (1845) *The ecclesiastical architecture of Ireland... the round towers of Ireland*, 234–43. Hodges and Smith, Dublin.

ROE, H.M. (*c.* 1940) Uncatalogued papers, Laois County Library.

ROE, H.M. (1947) 'Two baptismal fonts in county Laoighis', *JRSAI* **77**, 81–3.

RYAN, M. (1981) 'Poulawack, Co. Clare: the affinities of the central burial structure', in Ó Corráin, D. (ed.), *Irish Antiquity, essays and studies presented to M.J. O'Kelly*, 134–46. Cork.

RYAN, M. (1991) 'Early Irish monasteries', in Ryan, M. (ed.), *The illustrated archaeology of Ireland*, 136–7. Country House, Dublin.

STALLEY, R. (1987) *The Cistercian monasteries of Ireland*. Yale University Press, London and New Haven.

SWEETMAN, H.S. 1875–86 *Calendar of documents relating to Ireland, 1171–1307*, 5 vols. London.

WADDELL, J. (1990) *The Bronze Age burials of Ireland*. Galway University Press.

WALSH, A. (1972) A preliminary report on monuments of archaeological interest in county Laois. An Foras Forbartha Teoranta, Dublin.

WEIR, A. and JERMAN, J. (1986) *Images of lust: sexual carvings on medieval churches*. B.T. Batsford Ltd., London.

WOOD-MARTIN, W.G. (1886) *The lake dwellings of Ireland*. Hodges, Figgis and Co., Dublin.

Index

Brittas (Tinnahinch By.)
  burial ground 877
Bunlacken
  enclosures (site) 343
  field banks (site) 104

Capard
  enclosure 344
  hillfort (possible) 126
Cappagh North
  holy well (site) 839
Cappakeel
  earthwork (site) 604
Cappalinnan
  enclosure 345
Cappaloughlin or Clonard
  enclosure (possible) 356
Cappanacloghy
  earthwork (site) 605
Cappanafeacle
  ringfort 169
Cappanarrow/Killeen (Upperwoods By.)
  enclosure (site) 346
Cappanashannagh
  earthwork (site) 606
Capponellan/Clonageera
  earthwork (site) 610
Cardtown
  enclosure (site) 347
Carricksallagh
  church 705
Carrigeen (Stradbally By.) Kilmurry ED
  enclosure 348
  moated site 921
Carrowreagh (Upperwoods By.)
  barrow (possible, site) 44
  bowl-barrow 45
  fulacht fiadh (possible) 85
  ring-barrow 46
  ringfort 170–71
Carrowreagh and Derreen
  ringfort 188
Cashel (Cullenagh By.)
  enclosure (site) 349
Cashel (Upperwoods By.)
  church (site) 706
  ringfort 172
  road (site) 117
Castlebrack
  church 707
  settlement deserted 932
  tower house 947
Castlecuffe
  enclosure 350
  enclosure (possible, site) 351

fortified house 1024
Castledurrow Demesne
  castle (possible, site) 981
  cross (base, site) 817
  enclosure (site) 352
  holy well 840
Castledurrow Demesne/Durrow Townparks
  monastery (possible, site) 708
Castlefleming (Giles)/Castlefleming or Heath
  castle (site) 982
Castlefleming (Stubber)
  children's burial ground 878
Castlefleming (Stubber)/Garrison
  tower house 948
Castlefleming or Heath
  earthwork (site) 607
Castlefleming or Heath/Castlefleming (Giles)
  castle (site) 982
Castlequarter (Clandonagh By.)
  castle (possible, site) 984
  holy well 841
Castlequarter (Clarmallagh By.)
  church 709
Castletown (Clandonagh By.) Donaghmore ED
  enclosure (site) 353
  tower house 949
Castletown (Clandonagh By.) Moneymore ED
  castle (site) 983
  earthwork (site) 608
Castletown (Slievemargy By.)
  motte and bailey 903
Churchtown
  church 710
Clarahill
  castle (possible, site) 985
Clashboy
  enclosure (site) 354
Cleanagh
  standing stone (site) 10
Cloghoge
  enclosure (site) 355
  ringfort 173
Clogrenan
  castle (site) 986
  earthwork (site) 609
  ringfort 174
Clonaddadoran
  ringfort 175
Clonageera/Capponellan
  earthwork (site) 610
Clonagh (Slievemargy By.)
  monastery 711
Clonanny
  earthwork (site) 611
Clonard or Cappaloughlin
  enclosure (possible) 356
Clonaslee

Cooperhill Demesne
  earthwork (site) 622
Coorlaghan
  ringfort 181
Corbally (Ballyadams By.)
  church 724
  ringfort 182–3
Corbally (Tinnahinch By.) Meelick ED
  enclosure 375
Corraun
  enclosure (site) 376
  holy well (site) 849
  settlement deserted 933
Course
  monastery (site) 725
  subrectilinear enclosure (site) 726
Crannagh (Upperwoods By.)
  ringfort 184
  watermill - horizontal (possible) 1047
Creelagh
  enclosures (site) 377
Cremorgan
  church 727
  enclosure 378
Cromoge
  church 728
  holy well 850
Cross
  cross-shaped depression 820
Crossneen
  ringfort 185
Crubeen
  enclosure (possible, site) 382
  enclosure (site) 379–81
Cuddagh
  earthwork (site) 623
  enclosure 383
Cuffsborough
  church (site) 729
  cist (site) 25
  megalithic tomb (possible, site) 1
Cullahill Mountain
  earthwork (site) 624
  ringfort 186
Cullenagh (Cullenagh By.)
  church 730
  enclosure (site) 384–5
  fortified house 1026
Cummer
  barrow 47
Curraclone
  early ecclesiastical remains 731
Curragh (Slievemargy By.)
  burials (site) 894
  ringfort (site) 187

Dairyhill
  church (possible, site) 732
  enclosure 386
  enclosure (site) 387
Dangans
  church (site) 733
Derreen and Carrowreagh
  ringfort 188
Derrin
  earthworks (site) 625
  house 1034
Derrinduff
  earthwork (site) 626
Derrinsallagh/Doon (Clandonagh By.)
  earthwork (site) 627
Derry (Maryborough East By.)/
Kilcolmanbane/Rathleague
  enclosure 388
Derry (Tinnahinch By.) Meelick ED
  enclosure (site) 389
Derrybrock
  castle (site) 990
Derrycarrow
  ring-barrow 48
Derrygarran
  enclosure 390
  enclosure (site) 391
Derrykearn
  church 734
  earthworks (site) 628
  enclosure 393
  enclosure (site) 392, 394
  ringfort 189
Derrynaseera
  enclosure (possible, site) 395
  holy well (site) 851
Derryvorrigan
  holy well (site) 852
Donaghmore
  church (site) 735
  enclosure (site) 396
  holy well 853
  motte 904
  ringfort 191
Dooary
  enclosure 397–8
  moated site (possible) 925
  rectilinear enclosure (site) 578
  ringfort 192–3
Doon (Clandonagh By.)/Derrinsallagh
  earthwork (site) 627
Doon (Maryborough West By.)
  enclosure (site) 399
Drimaterril
  ringfort 194
Droughill
  enclosure 400

Glenbower
  ringfort 203
Glenmacolla and Scrub
  enclosure (possible) 529
  enclosure (site) 530–2
Gortaroata
  enclosure (site) 412
Gorteennahilla
  enclosure (site) 413
Gorteennameale
  field system (possible) 106
Gorteennameale/Moher East
  enclosure 414
Gortnaclea
  mound 78
  tower house 957
Gortnaglogh
  standing stone (site) 11
Gortnalee
  castle (site) 993
  enclosure (site) 415
  ringfort 204–5
Graigueadrisly
  church 748
  earthwork (site) 634
  enclosure 416
  graveyard (site) 880
  ringfort 206–10
Graigueanossy
  ringfort 211
Graigueard
  enclosure (site) 417
  ringfort 212
Graigueavallagh
  rectilinear enclosure (site) 580
Graigueavoice
  earthwork (site) 635
  enclosure 418
  enclosure (site) 419–20
  ringfort 213–14
Granafallow/Watercastle
  bridge 1043
Grange (Ballyadams By.)
  castle (site) 994
  church (site) 749
  enclosure (site) 421–2
Grange Beg
  house 1035
Grange More
  enclosure 423
  enclosure (site) 424
  fortified house (site) 1028
  rectilinear enclosure (site) 927
Grange Upper
  castle (site) 995
  enclosure 425
  field system 107

Grantstown
  crannóg 102
  tower house 958
Greatheath (Maryborough East By.)
  chapel (site) 750
  earthwork (site) 636–7
  enclosure (site) 426–7
  ring-barrow 51–9
Greatheath (Maryborough East By.)/
Greatheath (Portnahinch By.)
  ringfort 215
Grenan
  castle (site) 996
  enclosure (possible, site) 429
  enclosure (site) 428, 430–2
  motte (possible) 906
  subrectilinear enclosure (site) 581
Grenan/Glebe (Clarmallagh By.) Durrow ED
  church (site) 747
Guileen (Stradbally By.) Luggacurren ED
  enclosure (site) 433
  field systems 108
Guileen (Stradbally By.) Luggacurren ED /Ballycoolan
  field bank 103
Gurteen
  earthwork (site) 638
Gurteen/Coolanowle
  holy well (possible) 847

Harristown (Clandonagh By.)
  castle (site) 997
  enclosure (site) 434
  ringfort (site) 216
Harristown (Slievemargy By.)
  enclosure (site) 435
  ringfort (possible, site) 217
Haywood Demesne
  cist (site) 28
  enclosure (site) 436
  font 822
  motte 907
Heath or Castlefleming
  earthwork (site) 607
Heath or Castlefleming /Castlefleming (Giles)
  castle (site) 982

Inch (Ballyadams By.)
  enclosure 437
Inchacooly
  enclosure 438
  mound 79–80
Inchanisky
  earthwork (site) 639

140

megalithic tomb (possible) 2
Killinure
  church (site) 760
Killinure (Upperwoods By.)/Mountainfarm
  font 826
Kilmainham
  church 767
  friary 766
Kilmanman
  enclosure (site) 452
  holy well 860
Kilminchy
  castle (site) 1000
Kilminfoyle
  church (possible, site) 768
  fulacht fiadh (site) 87
  moated site (site) 928
Kilmorony
  motte and bailey 911
Kilmurry
  church 769
  enclosure (site) 453
Kilnashane
  earthwork (site) 643
Kilpurcel
  field system 109
  trackway (site) 121
Kilrory
  earthwork (site) 644–7
  enclosures (site) 454
Kilteale
  church 770
Kilvahan
  church (site) 771
  road 122
Knapton
  house (site) 1036
Knockahaw
  enclosure (site) 455
Knockardagannon North
  enclosure 456
Knockardagannon South
  enclosure (site) 457
Knockardagur
  cist (site) 30
  enclosure (site) 458
Knockbaun
  enclosure 460
  enclosure (site) 459
  megalithic structure 3
  megalithic structure (site) 4
  standing stone 12–13
Knockbeg/Sleaty
  holy well (site) 861
  tumulus 68
Knockfin
  earthwork (site) 648

ringfort 230
Knocknagrally or Killenny Beg
  enclosure (site) 461
Knockphilip
  earthwork (site) 649
Knockseera
  church (site) 772
Kyle (Clandonagh By.)
  burial ground 884
  early ecclesiastical remains 773
  enclosure 462
  megalithic structure (site) 5
  standing stone 14
Kyle (Tinnahinch By.)
  church (site) 774
Kylebeg (Clarmallagh By.)
  ringfort 231
Kyleclonhobert
  church (site) 775
Kylekiproe/Borris Little/Clonminam/
Maryborough/ Moneyballytyrrell
  town defences 1019
Kyletalesha
  enclosure (site) 463
Kyletilloge/Oldglass
  enclosure (possible, site) 464

Lackey
  enclosure 465
Lamberton Demesne
  ringfort 232–3
Larragan
  enclosure 466
Lea
  medieval castle 936
Leagh
  burial ground (site) 885
  holy well (site) 862
Lisbigney
  enclosure 468
  enclosure (site) 467
Lisduff
  enclosure (site) 469
Lismore
  church 776
Lismurragha
  enclosure 470
Lisnagommon
  enclosure (site) 471
Longford
  enclosure (site) 472
  ringfort 234
Lough/Emo Park
  mound (site) 76
Loughakeo

fulacht fiadh (site) 92–5
henge 15
holy well (site) 865
megalithic structure 8
motte and bailey 915
mound 82
ringfort 241
standing stone 16–17
urn burials 34
Slatt Lower
  enclosure 535
  fulacht fiadh 100
  fulacht fiadh (site) 96–9, 101
  ring-barrow 67
  standing stone 19
  stone circle 18
Slatt Upper
  earthwork (site) 668
Sleaty
  early ecclesiastical remains 799
Sleaty/Knockbeg
  holy well (site) 861
  tumulus 68
Spaquarter
  enclosure 536
Srah
  enclosure 538
  enclosure (site) 537
  ringfort 270–71
Srahanboy
  children's burial ground 888
  early ecclesiastical remains 800
  motte and bailey 917
  tower house 966
Stooagh
  ringfort 272–3
  souterrain (possible) 284
Straboe
  church 801
Stradbally
  abbey (site) 802
  castle (site) 1007
  enclosure (possible, site) 539
  fortified house (site) 1031

Tankardstown
  castle (site) 1008–9
  church 803
  enclosure (possible, site) 540–1
  holy well 872
Timahoe
  abbey 967
  burials 899
  early ecclesiastical remains 804
  enclosure 542

sheela-na-gig 1017
urn burial (site) 36
Timogue
  castle (site) 1010
  church (site) 805
  cist (site) 37
  enclosure (site) 543
  holy well 873
  ringfort 274
Tinnaclohy
  ringfort 275–6
Tinnaclohy/Beckfield
  enclosure (site) 332
Tinnahinch
  earthwork (possible, site) 669
  enclosure 544–6
  ringfort 277
Tinnakill (Portnahinch By.)
  sheela-na-gig 1018
  tower house 968
Tinnaragh
  enclosure (site) 547
  ringfort 278
Tintore
  church (site) 806
  ringfort 279
  tower house 969
Tinwear
  enclosure (site) 548–9
Tirhogar
  church 807
Toberboe or Killenny More
  early ecclesiastical remains 808
  earthwork 670
  enclosure 553
  enclosure (possible, site) 554
  enclosure (site) 550–2
  holy well 874
Tomoclavin
  earthwork (site) 671
Toortaun
  tumulus 69
Towlerton
  enclosure 555
Townparks (Clandonagh By.)
  barrow (possible) 70
  castle (site) 1011
Tullacommon
  ringfort 280
Tullomoy
  fortified house 1032
  church (site) 809
  standing stone 20
Tullore
  tumulus 71
Tullyroe
  enclosure (site) 556

Subject Index

This index lists various monuments and sites which are referred to within other entries, but which are not listed separately.

Altar-tomb

695   Ballyadams church

Armorial panel

975   Ballylehane Lower castle (site)

Battlefields/battle sites

71   Tullore tumulus
891   Ballymaddock (Stradbally By.) burials (site)
895   Fallowbeg Middle burials (site)
898   Oldglass burials (site)
899   Timahoe burials

Bullauns

698   Ballybuggy church (site)
706   Cashel (Upperwoods By.) church (site)
745   Garryduff (Clandonagh By.) church (possible, site)
773   Kyle (Clandonagh By.) early ecclesiastical remains
800   Srahanboy early ecclesiastical remains

Burials

81   Kilcoran mound (site)
215   Greatheath (Maryborough East By.) ringfort
515   Rathdowney enclosure (site)

Burial vault

689   Aghamacart priory

Castle possible, site

525   Rossdarragh enclosure (site)

Cists

39   Ballycoolan cairn

Church, tradition of

392   Derrykearn

Crosses and cross-base

690   Aghnacross church
799   Sleaty early ecclesiastical remains

Cross-slabs

686   Acragar church (site)
714   Clonenagh graveyard
731   Curraclone early ecclesiastical remains
774   Fossy Lower church
773   Kyle (Clandonagh By.) early ecclesiastical remains

Sacred trees/bush

772	Knockseera church (site)
842	Clonenagh holy well (site)
856	Errill holy well
869	Rathnaleugh holy well (possible, site)

Saint's grave

773	Kyle (Clandonagh By.) early ecclesiastical remains

Quernstones

693	Anatrim church and graveyard
700	Ballynahown church

Urns

68	Sleaty/Knockbeg tumulus

Location Maps

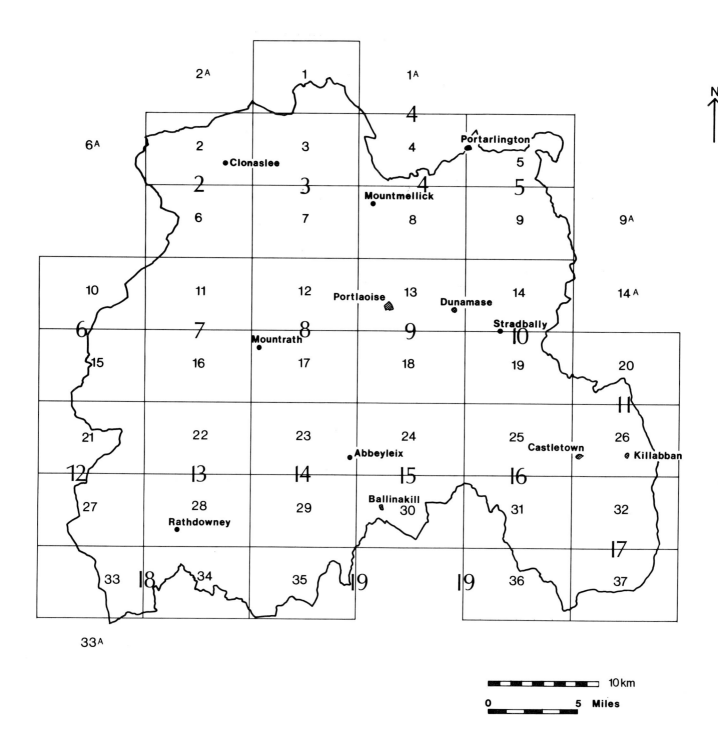

Based on O.S. 6" Sheet Index

—*Key to location maps*

Map 1

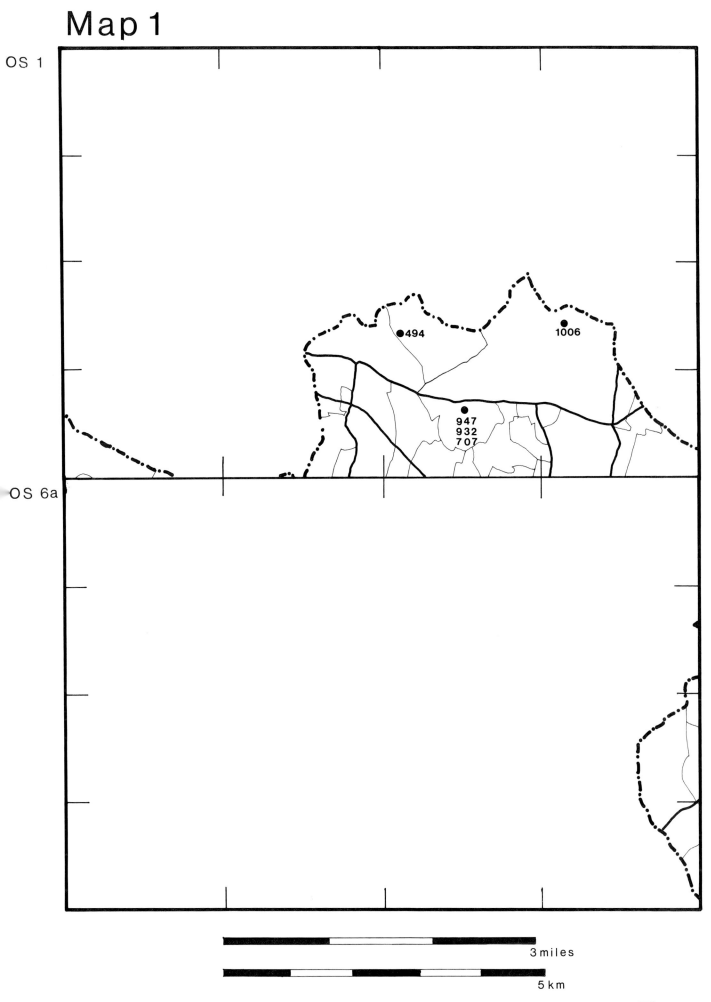

OS 1

OS 6a

●494

1006

● 947
932
707

3 miles

5 km

153

Map 2

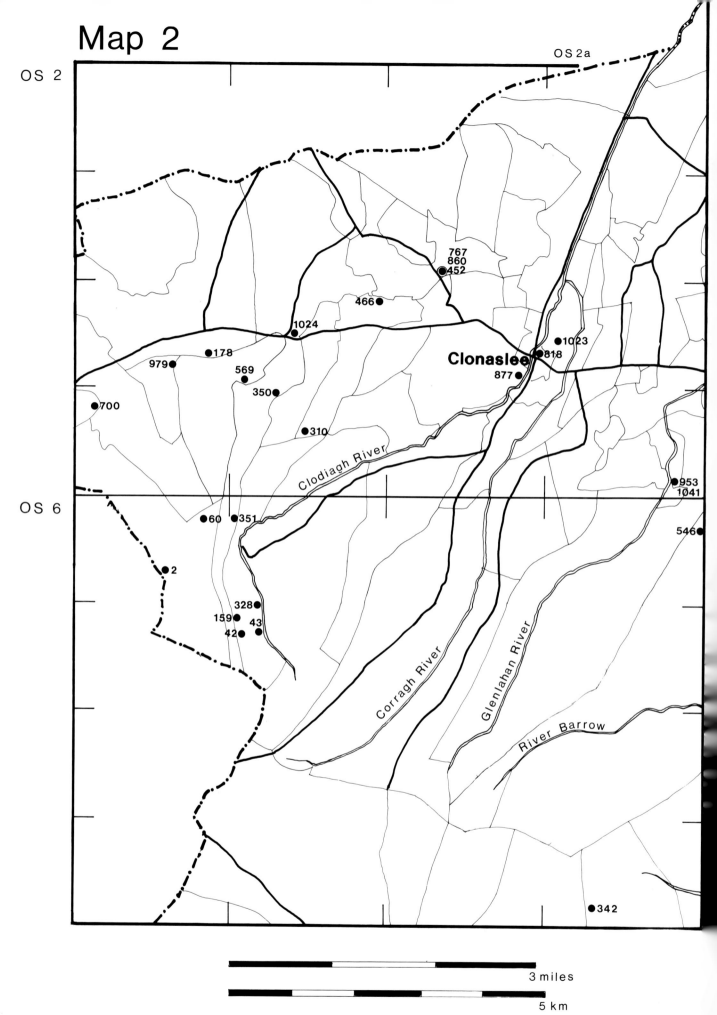

OS 2

OS 2a

OS 6

767
860
452

466

1024

●178
979●

569

350

●700

310

Clodiagh River

●953
1041

●60 ●351

546●

●2

328●
159● 43
42●

Corragh River

Glenlahan River

River Barrow

Clonaslee

●1023
818

877●

●342

3 miles

5 km

154

Map 3

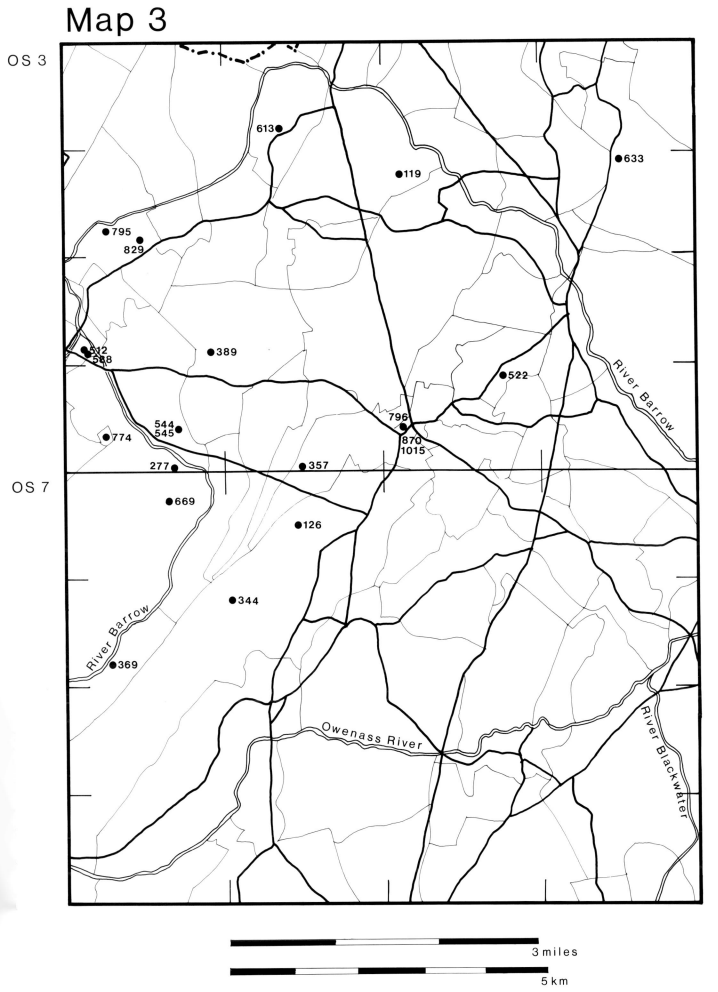

OS 3

OS 7

613

119

633

795
829

512
588

389

522

544
545

796
870
1015

774

277

357

669

126

344

369

River Barrow

River Barrow

Owenass River

River Blackwater

3 miles

5 km

155

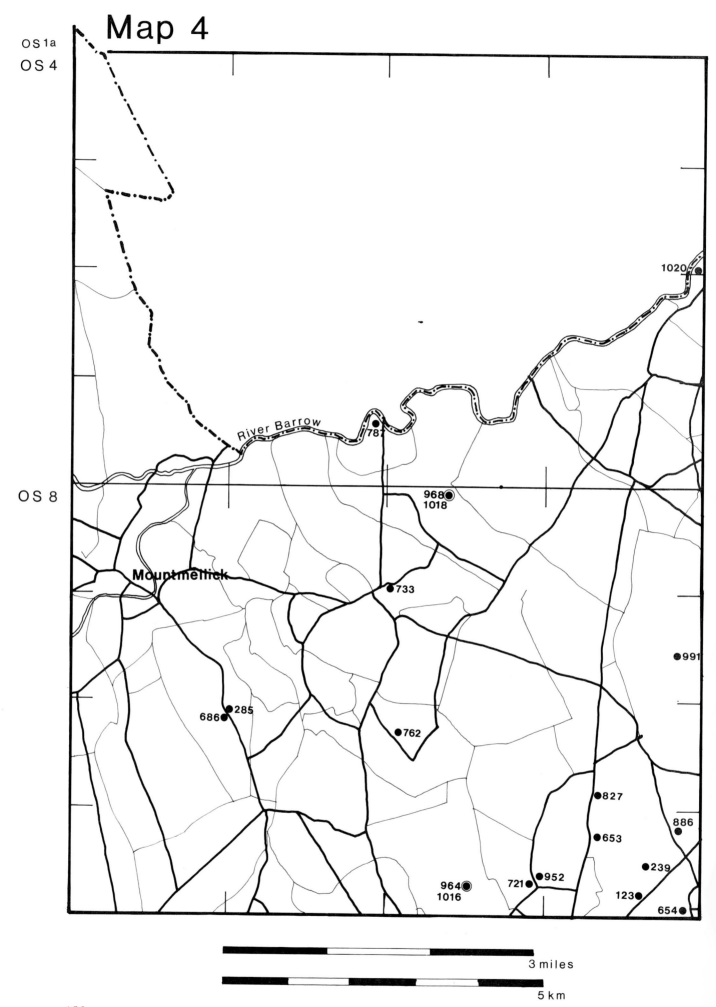

Map 4

OS 1a
OS 4

OS 8

1020

River Barrow
787

968
1018

Mountmellick

733

991

285
686

762

827

886

653

239

964
1016

721 952

123

654

3 miles

5 km

156

Map 5

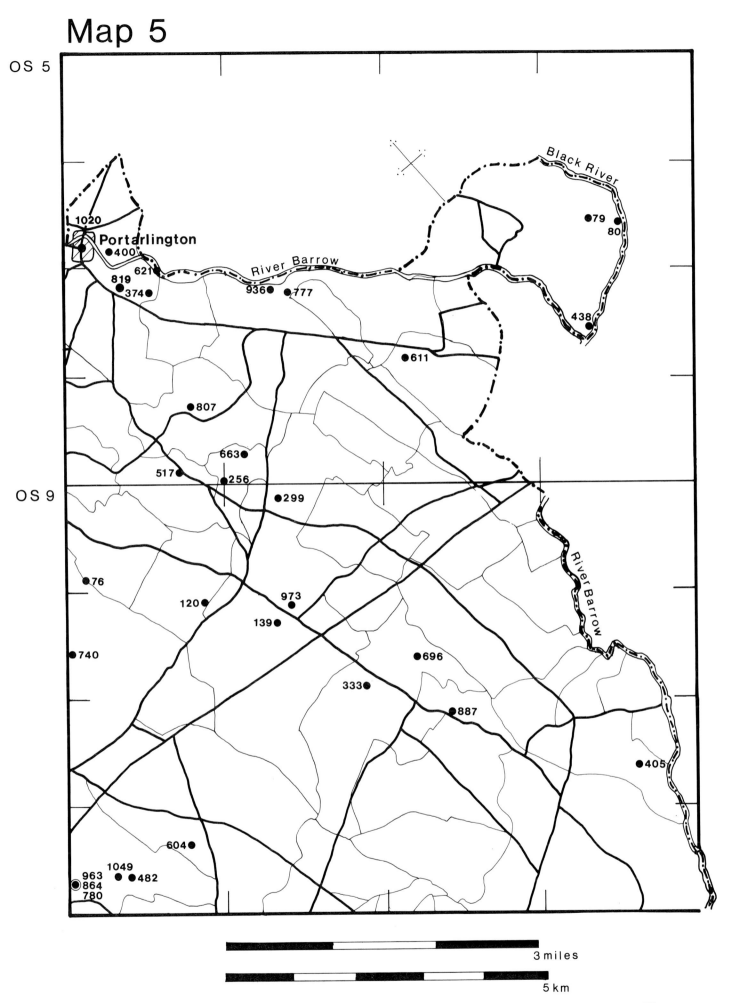

OS 5

Black River

●79
80 ●

●1020
Portarlington
●400

River Barrow
621●
819●
374●   936● ●777

438●

●611

●807

663●
517● ●256

OS 9

●299

●76

●973
120●
139●

●740

●696

333●

●887

●405

604●

1049
963 ● ●482
864
780

River Barrow

3 miles

5 km

157

Map 6

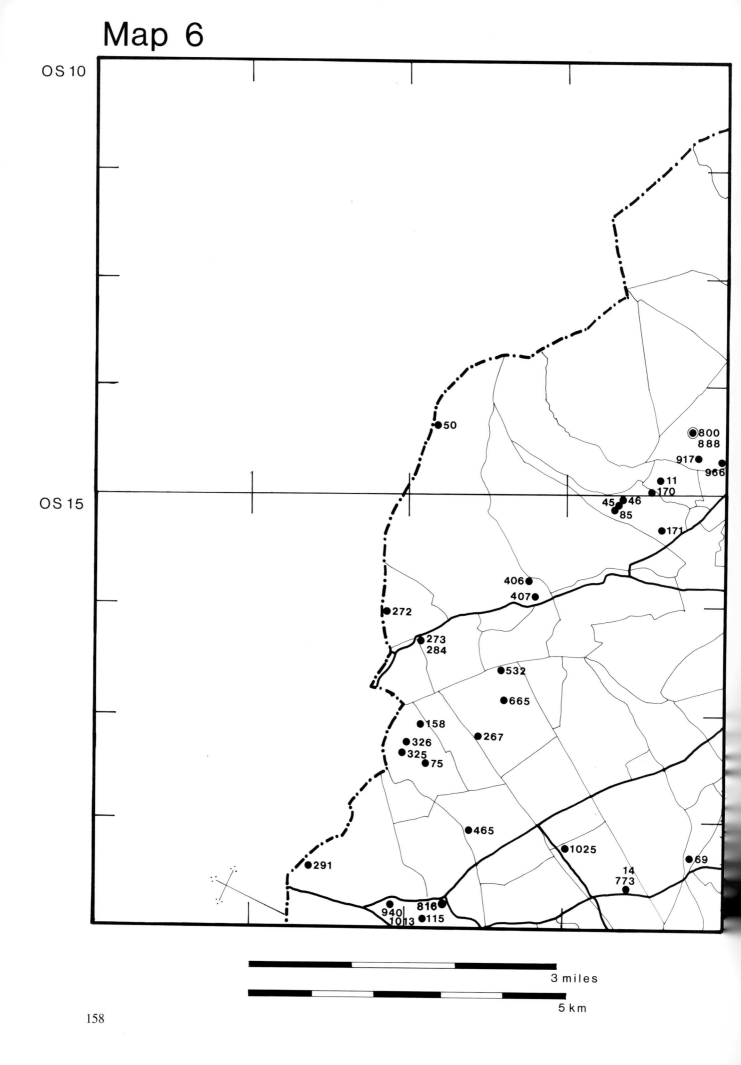

OS 10

OS 15

●50

⊚800
888

917● ●966

●11
●170

45●●46
●85

●171

406●
407●

●272

●273
284

●532

●665

●158
●267

●326
●325
●75

●465

●1025 ●69

14
773●

●291

816●
940●
1013 ●115

3 miles

5 km

158

Map 7

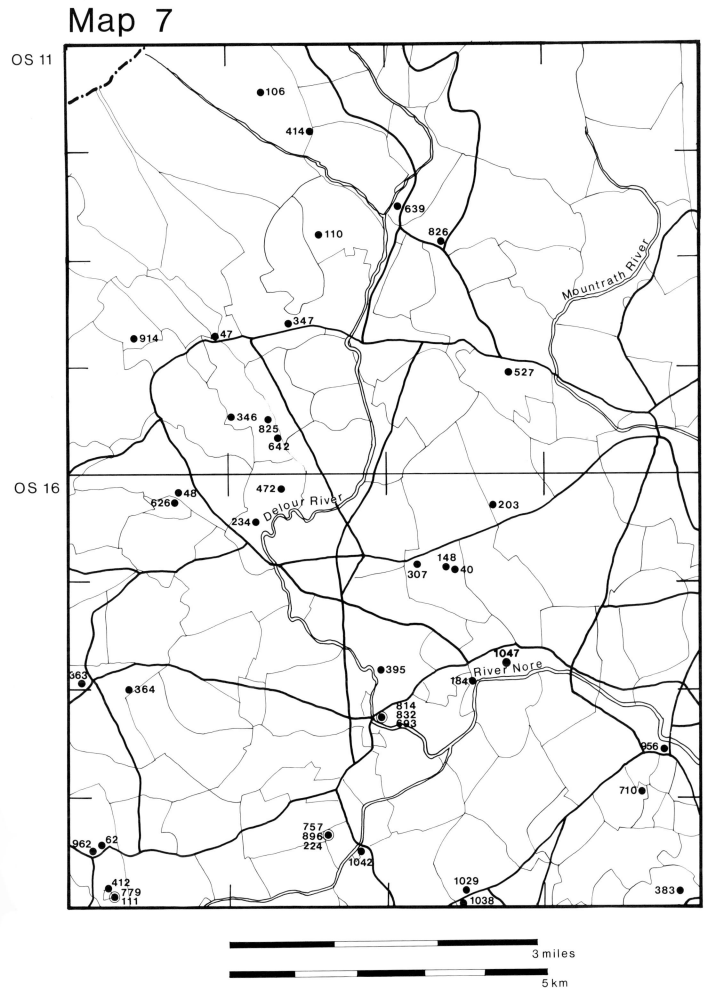

OS 11

● 106

414 ●

● 639

826 ●

● 110

Mountrath River

● 347

● 914 ● 47

● 527

● 346
● 825
642 ●

OS 16

● 48
626 ●   472 ●

234 ●   Delour River

● 203

148 ●
307 ● 40

1047 ●
● 395   River Nore
363 ●   184 ●
● 364

814
832
693

956 ●

710 ●

757
896
224

1042 ●

1029 ●
1038 ●
383 ●

962 ● ● 62

412
779
111

3 miles

5 km

159

Map 8

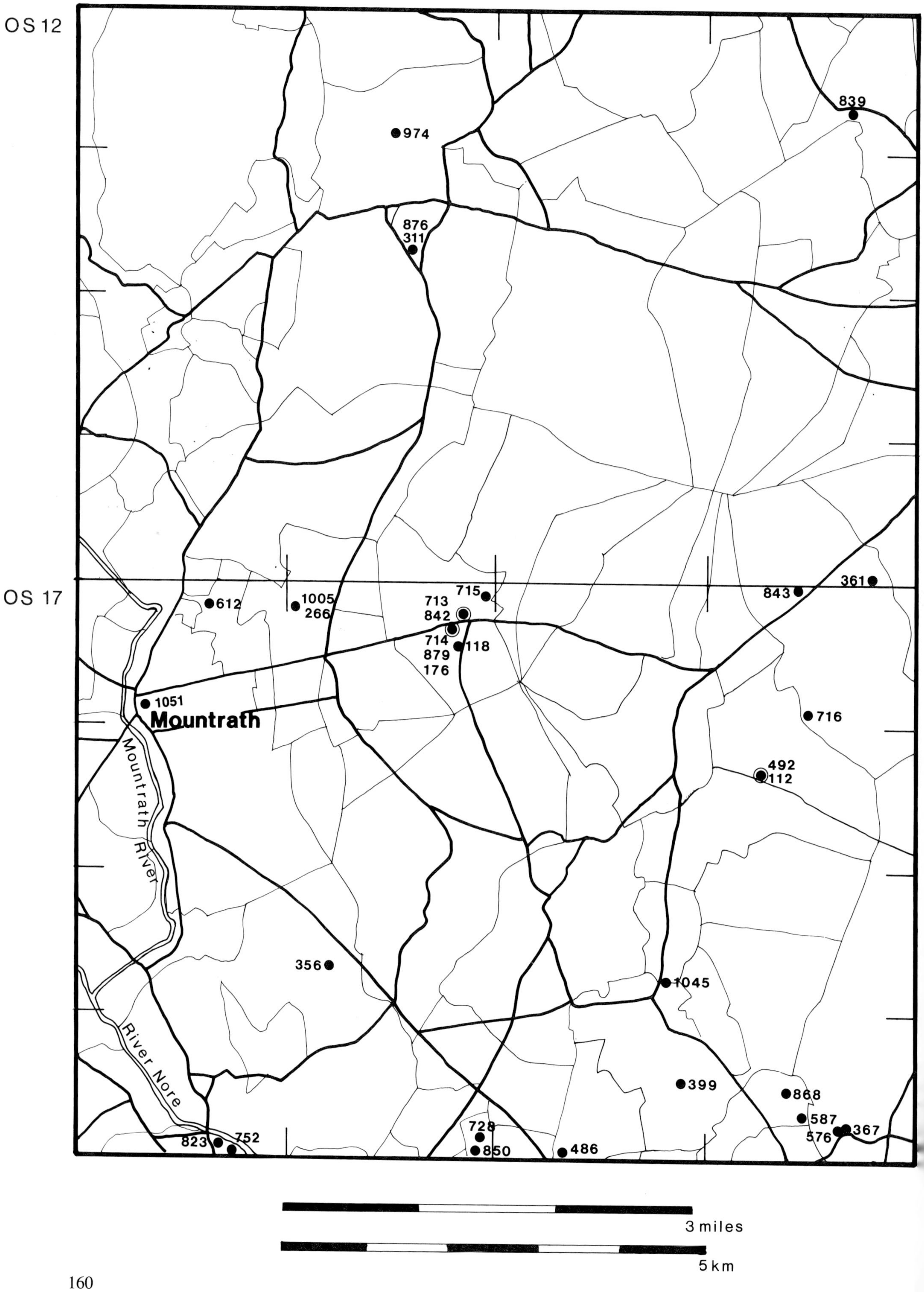

● 974

● 839

876
311 ●

715
● 612   ● 1005   ● ●
                  266   713
                              842 ◉
                              714 ● ●118
                              879
                              176

843 ●   361 ●

● 1051
Mountrath

● 716

492
◉ 112

Mountrath River

356 ●

● 1045

River Nore

● 399

● 868

728
823 ● ● 752   ● 850   ● 486   ● 587
                                                    576 ● ●367

3 miles

5 km

Map 9

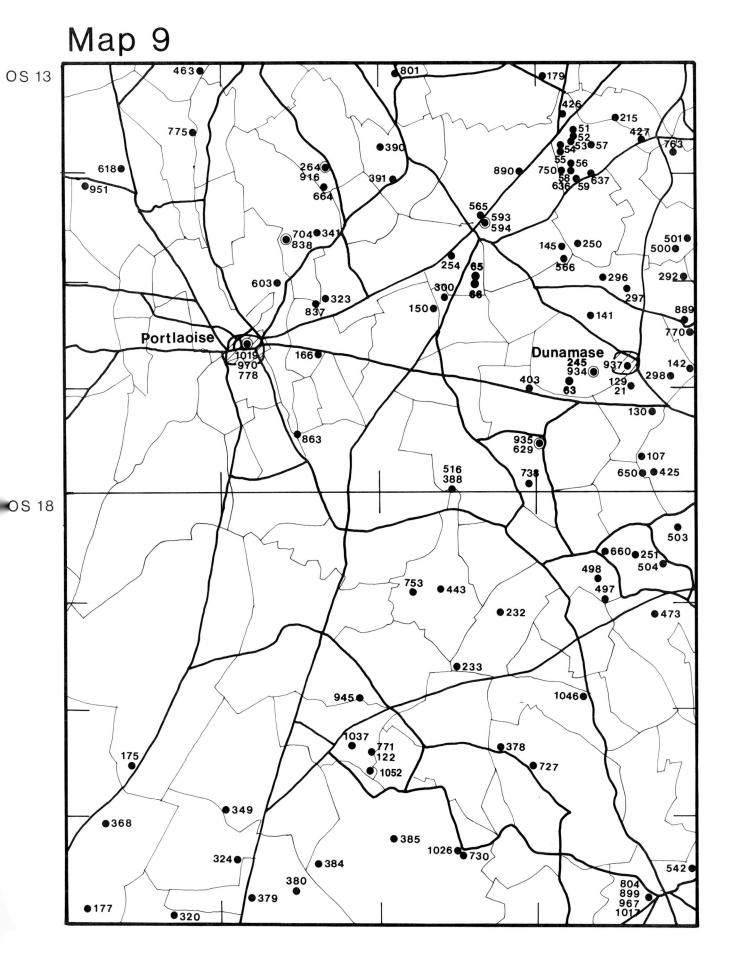

OS 13

OS 18

463

801

179

426

775

215

51
52
53 57
54
55 56
750
58
636 59 637

427

763

618

390

951

264
916

391

890

565
593
594

145 250

501
500

292

664

704 341
838

254 65

296

889

297

603

300

66

141

770

323
837

150

Portlaoise

166

Dunamase

245
934 937

142

1019
970
778

403

63

129
21

298

130

863

935
629

107

650 425

516
388

738

503

660 251
504

498
497

473

753 443

232

233

1046

945

1037
771
122
1052

378
727

175

349

368

385

324

384

1026 730

542

380

804
899
967
1017

177

379

320

3 miles

5 km

161

Map 10

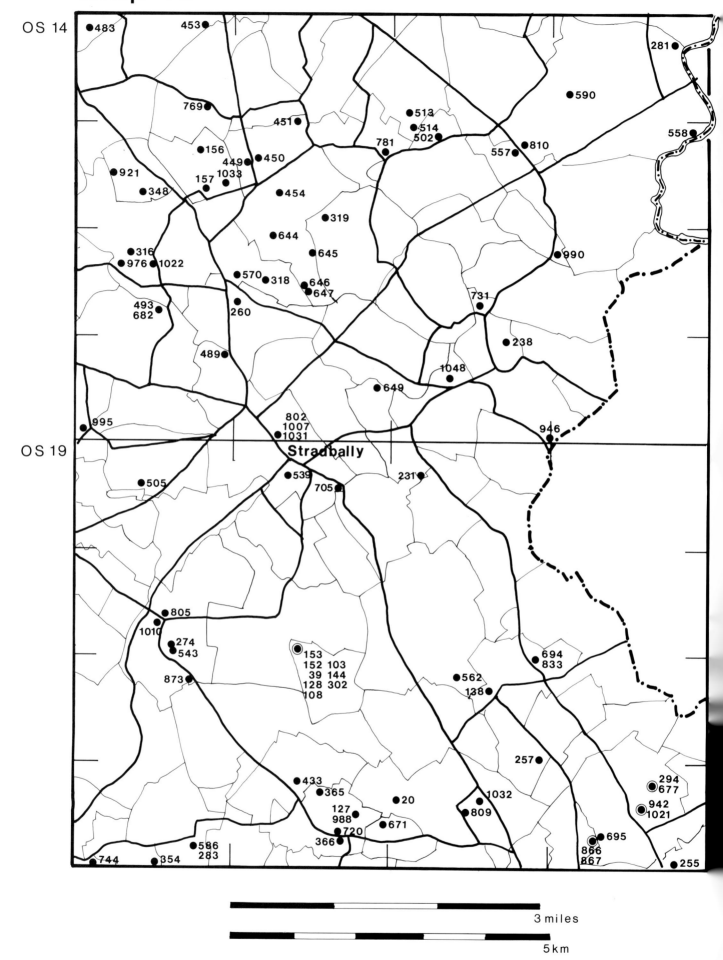

OS 14

●483　　　453●

281●

●590

769●

451●

●513
514●
502●

558●

781●

557●810●

●156　450●
449●　　1033
921●　157●
●348　●454

●319

●644

●316
976●1022
●570　318●
●646
647●

●645

990●

731●

493
682●

260●

238●

489●

1048●

●649

946●

995●

OS 19

Stradbally

802
1007
1031●

●505

●539
705●

231●

805●
1010●

274
543●

●153
152 103
39 144
128 302
108

694
833●

873●

●562
138●

257●

294
677●

433●
365●

●20

1032
809●

942
1021●

127
988●
720●
366●

671●

695●
866
867●

586
283●
●744　354●

255●

3 miles

5 km

162

Map 11

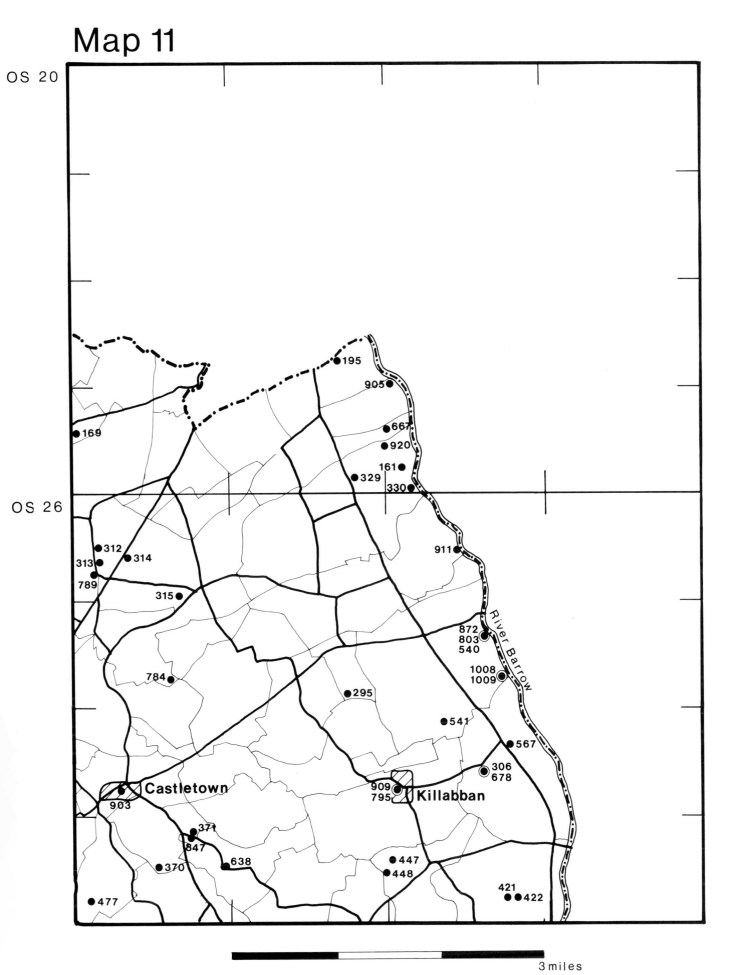

OS 20

OS 26

● 195

● 905

● 169

● 667

● 920

161 ●
● 329
330 ●

● 911

312 ●
● 314
313 ●
789 ●

315 ●

872 ●
803
540

River Barrow

1008 ●
1009

784 ●

● 295

● 541

● 567

306 ●
678

909 ●
795

Castletown

903 ●

Killabban

371 ●
847 ●

370 ●
● 638

● 447
● 448

421 ●
● 422

● 477

3 miles

5 km

163

Map 12

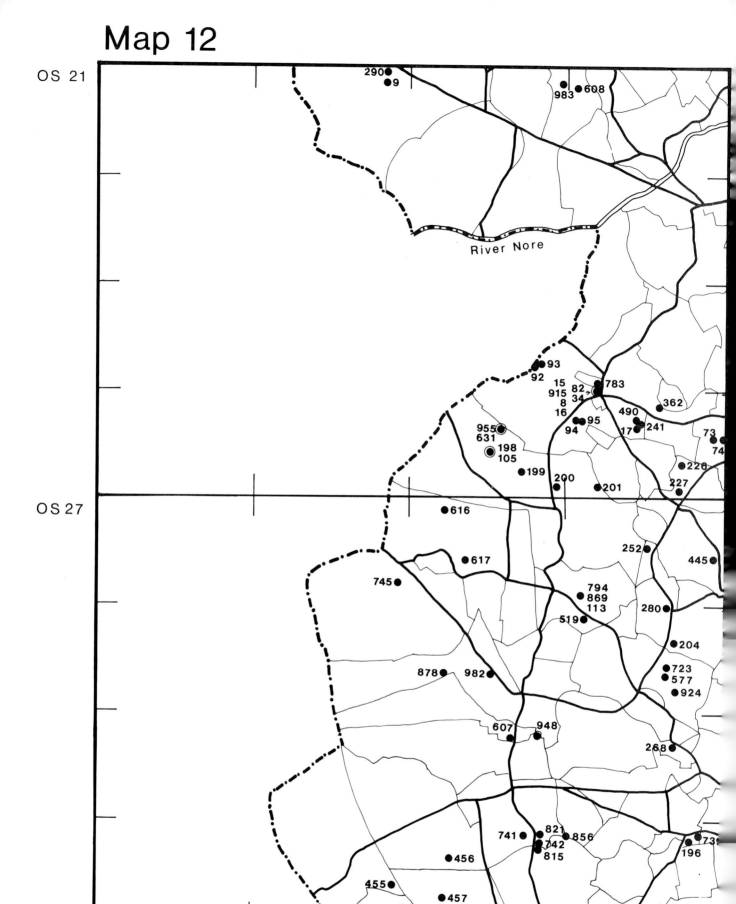

290
●9

983 ●608

River Nore

●93
92

15
915 82> 783
8   34
16

955 ●
631   ●95
94   490 362
198   17 241   73
105   ●226 74

●199 200
201   227

●616

●617   252

745 ●   445●

794
869   280●
113
519
204●

878● 982●   723
577
924

607● 948●

268●

821
741● ●856   739
742   196
815

●456

455● ●457

469   134● 676
135

3 miles

5 km

Map 13

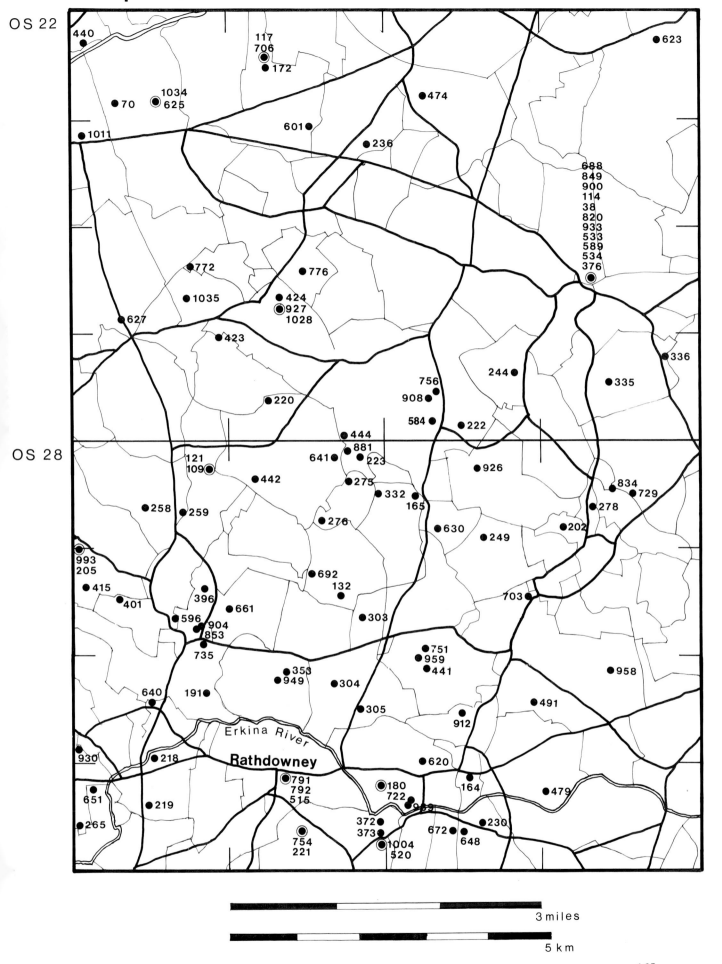

440

117
706
172

623

70   1034
625

474

1011

601

236

688
849
900
114
38
820
933
533
589
534
376

772

776

1035

424
927
1028

627

423

336

220

244

335

756
908

584

222

444

881

121
109

641   223

926

442

275

834
729

258   259

332
165

278

276

630

202

249

993
205

692
132

415

703

401

396

661

596
904
853

751
959
441

958

735

353
949

304

491

640   191

305

912

Erkina River

Rathdowney

930   218

620

651

791
792
515

180
722

164

479

219

939

372
373

672

230

648

265

754
221

1004
520

3 miles

5 km

Map 14

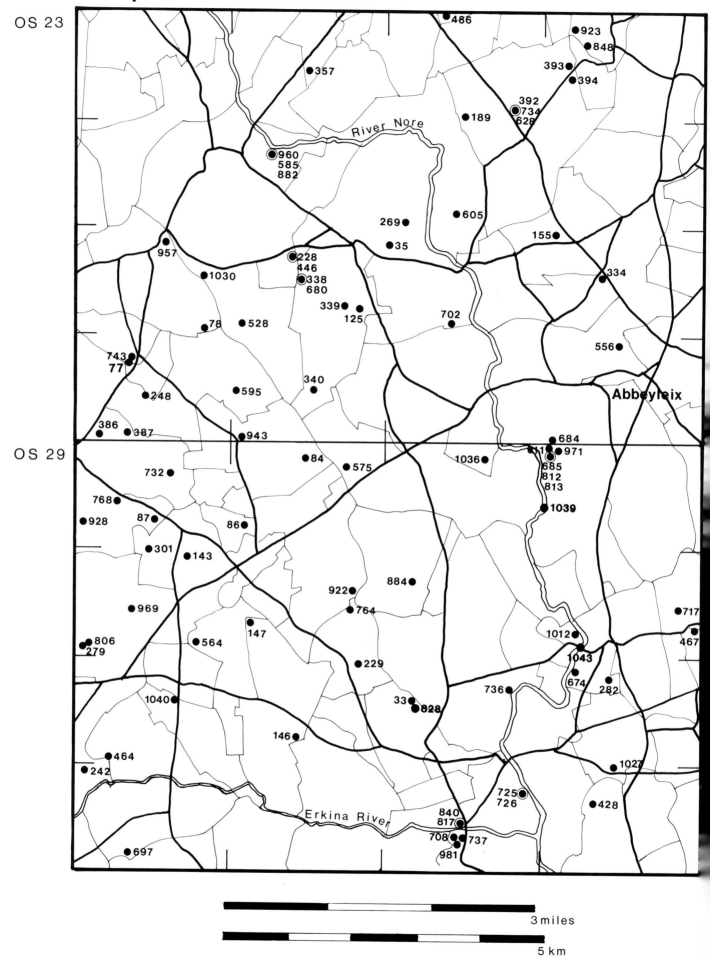

OS 23

OS 29

486
923
848
393
394
357
392
734
628
189
River Nore
960
585
882
605
269
35
155
957
334
228
446
338
680
339
125
702
78
528
556
743
77
340
Abbeyleix
248
595
684
386
387
943
1116
971
84
575
1036
685
812
813
732
1039
768
87
928
86
301
143
969
884
806
279
147
922
764
564
717
1012
229
467
1040
1043
674
282
736
33
828
464
146
242
1027
725
726
428
Erkina River
840
817
708
737
697
981

3 miles

5 km

Map 15

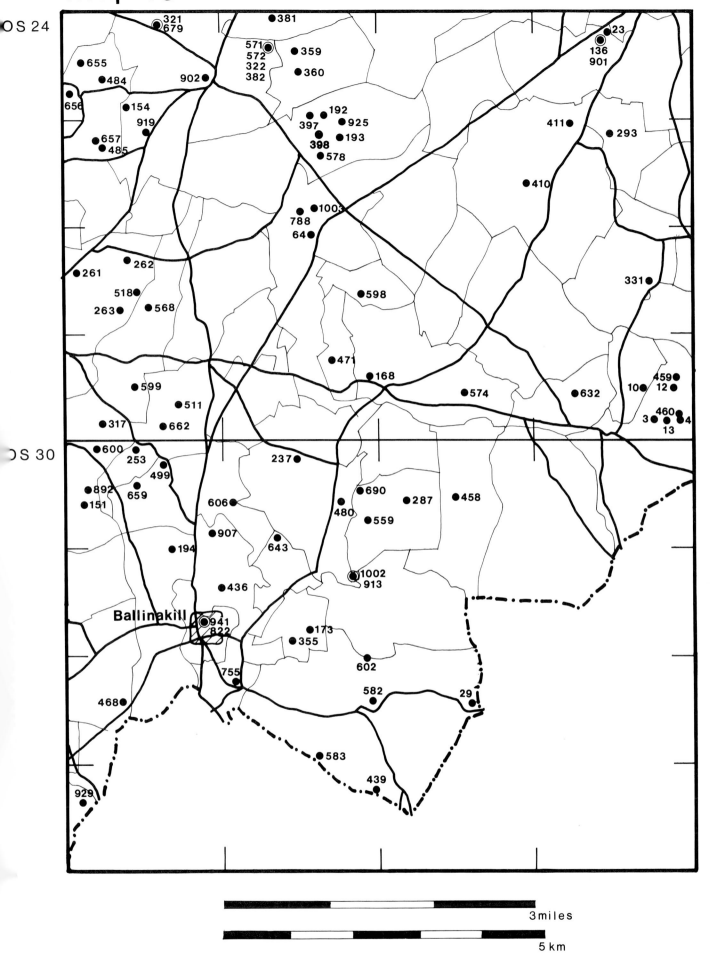

321
679
381
571
572
322
382
359
360
655
484
656
154
919
657
485
192
397
925
398
193
578
23
136
901
411
293
410
1003
788
64
262
261
331
518
263
568
598
471
168
599
574
632
459
12
10
511
460
3
4
13
317
662
600
253
237
499
892
659
690
287
458
151
606
480
559
907
643
194
1002
913
436
Ballinakill
941
822
173
355
755
602
468
582
29
583
439
929

3 miles

5 km

Map 16

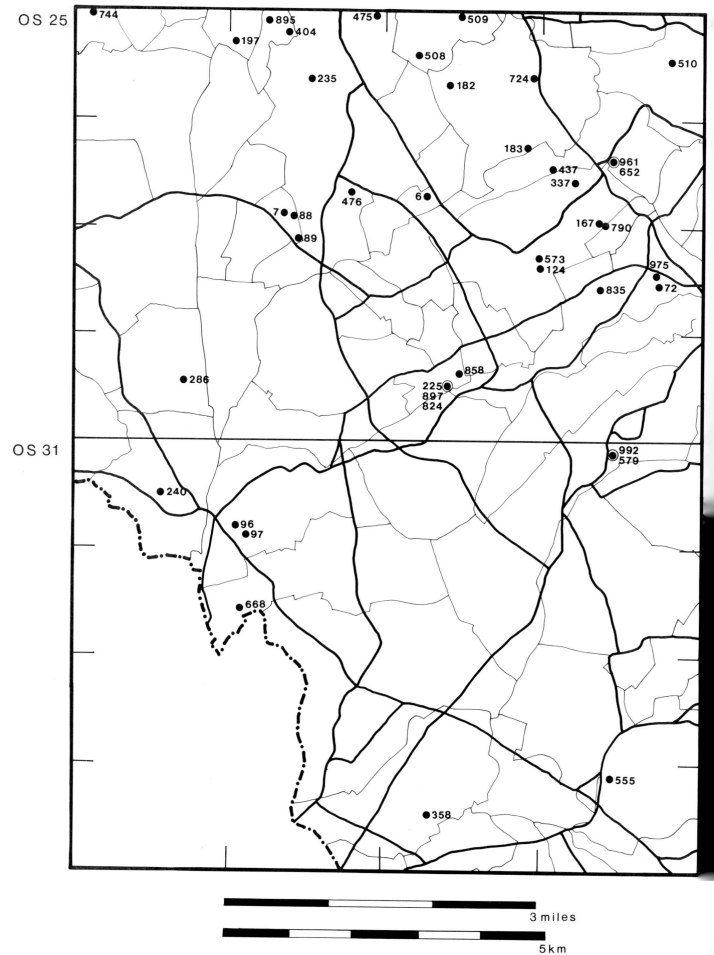

744
895
404
197
475
509
508
235
182
724
510
183
437
961
652
337
476
6
167
790
7 88
89
573
124
975
72
835

286
858
225
897
824
992
579
240
96
97
668
555
358

3 miles

5 km

168

Map 17

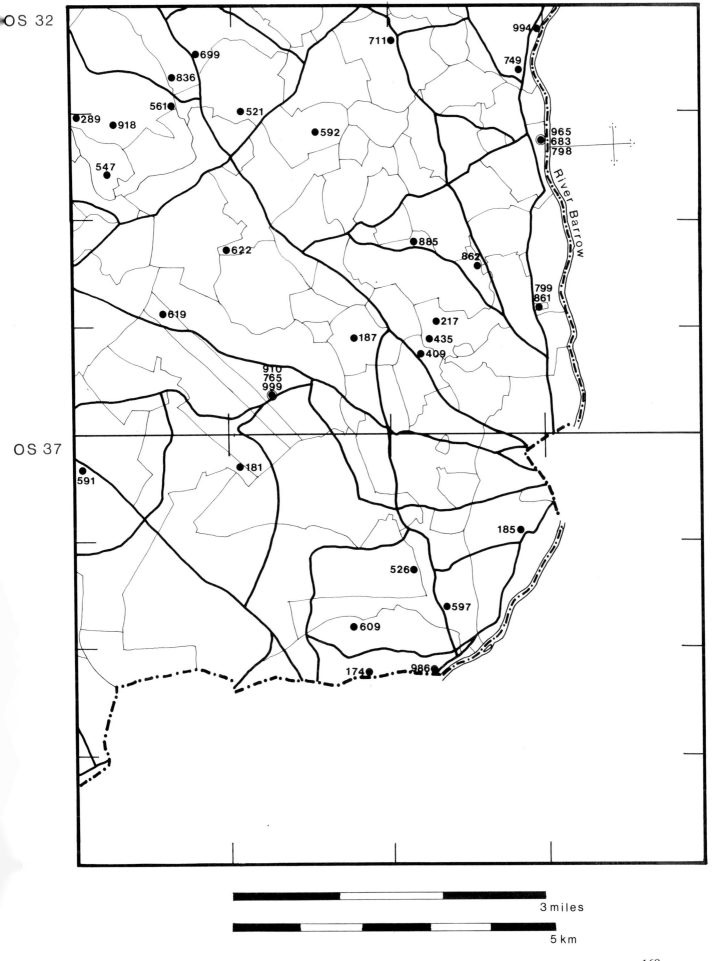

994
749

711

699

836

561

●289 ●918

●521

●592

547

965
683
798

River Barrow

622

●885

862

799
861

619

●217

187

●435
●409

910
765
999

181

591

185

526●

597

●609

174●   986●

3 miles

5 km

Map 18

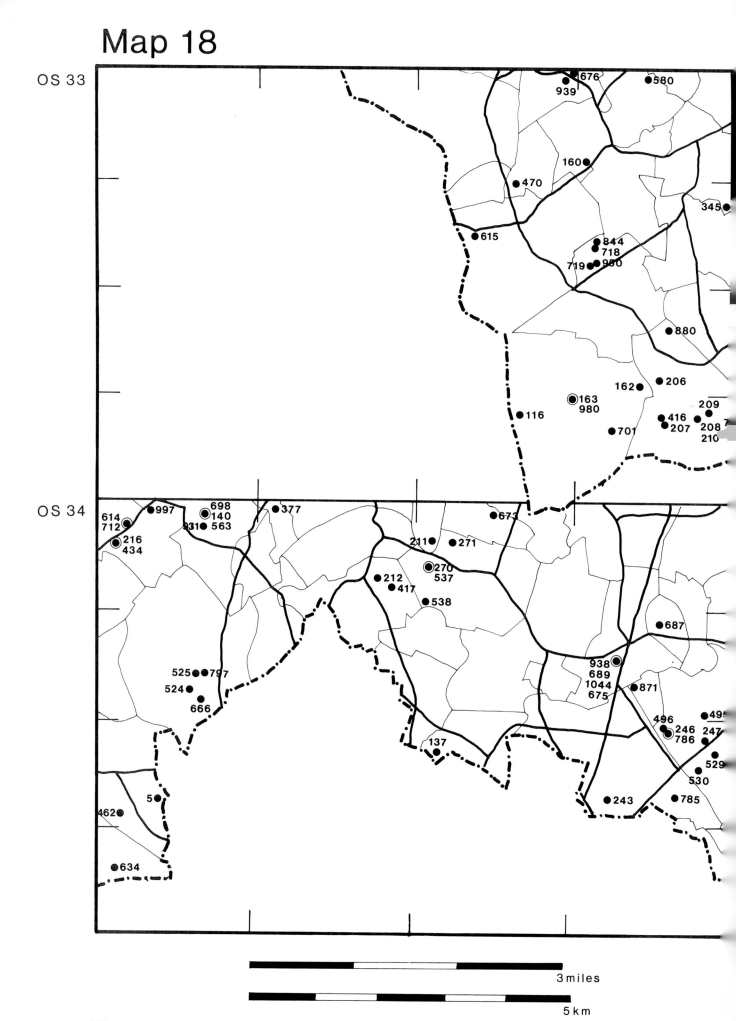

OS 33

OS 34

939 ●676   ●580

●160

●470

●615

●844
●718
719 ●●980

345●

●880

162● ●206

◉163
980

●116

209
●
416 ●●207 ●208
●701   210

614 ◉ ●997   ◉698   ●377
712   140
      ◉216 931●563
      434

673●

211● ●271

◉270
537

212●
●417

●538

●687

938◉
689
1044
675

●871

525●●797
524●
   ●666

137●

496◉
246 247●
786

499●

529●
530●

5●

462●

●634

●243 ●785

3 miles

5 km

170

Map 19

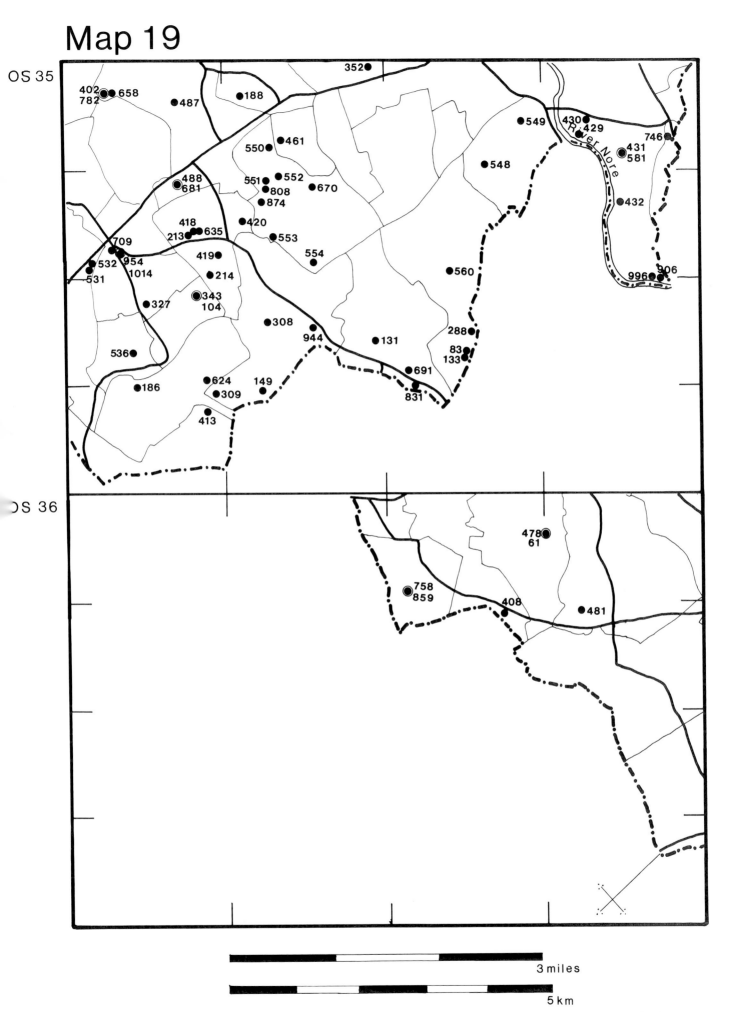

3 miles

5 km

171